Creating the School Family

Bully-Proofing Classrooms Through Emotional Intelligence

By Dr. Becky Bailey

with
Holly Christian, Vicky Hepler and Amy Speidel

800.842.2846
P.O. Box 622407
Oviedo, Florida 32762
ConsciousDiscipline.com

Copyright © 2011 Dr. Becky Bailey, Ph. D.

Published by
Loving Guidance, Inc.
P.O. Box 622407
Oviedo, FL 32762

The author of this book may be contacted through Loving Guidance, Inc.
Phone: 800.842.2846
Fax: 407.366.4293
Online at ConsciousDiscipline.com

All rights reserved. No part of this book may be reproduced in whole or in part without written permission from the publisher, except by reviewers who may quote brief excerpts in connection with a review in a newspaper, magazine, or electronic publication; nor may any part of this book be reproduced, stored in a retrieval system, or transmitted in any form or by any means electronic, mechanical, photocopying, recording, or other, without written permission from the publisher.

ISBN: 978-1-889609-32-4

Cover Design: Brandi Besher
Editor: Julie Ruffo
Line Editor: Sarah Whalen-Kraft
Page Design: Anthony Valdez

Printed in the United States of America

This book is dedicated to you, the wonderful educators who know in your hearts and minds that discipline is not something we **do to** children, but something we **develop within them.** It is also dedicated to my mother, Frances Bailey.

My hope is that someday, awareness of our collective interdependence would make the concept of bullying inconceivable.

Acknowledgements

It has been said by many that it takes a village to raise a child, and for this book, it took much of the planet and nearly nine years! My list of wonderful people to thank is extensive. It starts with the first person who took the time to listen when I would call and say, "Can I read you something?" At this early stage, Linda Harris would listen to my many starts and give excellent feedback. Loving Guidance Associate Vicky Hepler has been writing activities for this book from the beginning. Her patience in all the do-overs is appreciated. In addition to Vicky, Loving Guidance Associate Amy Speidel added insight and organization in all areas, and public school teacher Holly Christian contributed activities for the older grades. These brilliant teachers applied their talents to this book to give back to the many wonderful teachers who put their hearts and souls into their jobs every day.

In the beginning of Conscious Discipline, there were pioneers who were the first in the country to create School Families in their classrooms and schools. My sincere gratitude goes out to Sarah Simpson, Patricia Peaden, Kristen Abel, Roxanne Schreffler and Kim Whitney. Their courage blazed a wonderful path for others. The pictures in this book provide a peek into today's School Families around the globe. Thank you to all the teachers and children for their gracious photographic contributions. Contributions in this book ranging from Lysa Fisher's work with children with autism to Lesa Rice's work with children in Head Start. My hope is that Amy Zolessi from the United States and Lety Valero from Mexico would do the honors of accepting my thanks on behalf of the numerous teacher and student contributions from around the world.

Just as it is important to thank the teachers and students, it is also important to thank the schools themselves for opening their doors to Conscious Discipline. I would like to thank the following elementary schools as a representation of all schools practicing Conscious

Discipline: Fern Creek, Bessey Creek, Porter, Little River, Castle Creek, Adams and The Pine School. There were also countless Head Start programs and early childhood centers who made this book possible. I am hoping that Eton school in Mexico City (Mexico), Pam Beard's preschool in northern Virginia, Belinda Lorch's program in Florida and Farias Early Childhood Center in Texas would graciously accept the honors on behalf of all the Conscious Discipline early childhood programs. Several schools have won national recognition using Conscious Discipline. My wish is that Renee Sutherland and Knox County Head Start, who were honored as one of ten National Head Start Centers for Excellence in the United States, would accept my thanks and represent all schools that have made outstanding achievements using Conscious Discipline.

A big thank you goes to everyone at my office. Without them, none of what I do is possible. My deep gratitude and appreciation goes to the Loving Guidance Associates and the Certified Conscious Discipline Instructors who contributed to this book through their many experiences, anecdotes, inspirations, hard work and encouragements. None of this would be possible without your spirit supporting me.

On a bigger plane I would like to thank my family, extended family and Carol Howe, the mentor who heads my spiritual family. These close connections have shaped and changed my mental models of who I am.

On a more grounded level, my thanks also go to the creative team who brought this book to print: Robert Hess for his creative direction, Brandi Besher for the cover design, Anthony Valdez for the page design, Sarah Whalen-Kraft for line editing, Tracey Tucker for her diligence with the references and Julie Ruffo who is my writing voice editor. Julie, in my mind is my co-writer. Most of the words you read are mine; however, every sentence, paragraph, and chapter organization is massaged by Julie's expertise. We speak in one voice and I am deeply honored to resonate with such a talented person. We make a wonderful team. My hope is that you, the reader, enjoy the fruits of these extraordinary people's labor and find the information within these pages useful in your journey.

Table of Contents

9	Foreword
15	Chapter 1 — **The School Culture: Why traditional models are a disadvantage to our children**
29	Chapter 2 — **The School Family: Using the power of connection to create school reform**
47	Chapter 3 — **The School Family Structures: The foundation of emotionally intelligent classrooms**
59	Chapter 4 — **Friends and Family Board**
77	Chapter 5 — **The Safekeeper**
99	Chapter 6 — **Visual Rules and Routines**
129	Chapter 7 — **Ways to Be Helpful Boards and Books**
145	Chapter 8 — **Beginning the Day the Brain Smart® Way**
165	Chapter 9 — **Safe Place**
199	Chapter 10 — **School Family Rituals**
223	Chapter 11 — **Classroom Jobs**
247	Chapter 12 — **Time Machine**
277	Chapter 13 — **Celebration Center**
301	Chapter 14 — **We Care Center**
321	Chapter 15 — **Class Meetings**
343	Epilogue

Foreword

My name is Becky Bailey. I wrote this book about connection, that wonderful feeling you experience knowing you are a significant part of something larger than yourself. Connection is knowing deep in our souls that each individual matters, we are intricately interconnected and our small place in the ecosystem of humanity is significant. We are needed, we are valued contributors, we are uniquely adored, and we are on this earth for a purpose bigger than we could ever comprehend. My goal with this book is to support educators in creating this experience for themselves, and providing children with an environment in which they, too, can experience the truth of these powerful statements about connection.

Growing up, my family moved around a lot because my dad was in the Secret Service. Moving is challenging for everyone and it certainly shaped my life in interesting ways. I left a lot of friends behind, and as an adult I find myself less willing to let people truly know me. Part of my heart still carries around the scars from losing so many friends. On the other hand, the constant barrage of new schools, cities, sights and sounds have fostered a love of travel in me as an adult. I enjoy challenges like figuring the public transportation system in foreign lands and communicating without the knowledge of native languages.

With my mobile upbringing, the concept of a School Family makes perfect sense to me. I wish I had a grounded sense of connection as my family moved from place to place. I always hoped that when I arrived at a new school, I would have an instant buddy to show me around and eat lunch with on that first day. It would have been nice to put my family picture up on a board along with everyone else's, even if it didn't stay the whole year. Every time I moved on, I hoped those I left behind would wish me well. I hoped they would create a memento to help me remember them and help them remember me for a bit longer.

Few schools did these types of things back then, but even one of them would have made a great difference in my childhood. Now, with Conscious Discipline entering so many schools, new children do have an instant buddy to rely on, a Friends and Family Board on which to join their family photos with others, a wish well board to help friends remember others during times of loss, and a goodbye book full of friends' drawings and well wishes to take with them when they leave the School Family.

I am thankful for my life experiences. They've led me to know scientifically and practically that safety, connection and problem solving are the keys to healthy individuals, families, schools and communities. Certainly, I am glad research supports what my heart knows to be true, but it is my heart that has encouraged me to write this book. I know the power of connecting with your school, connecting with your teacher, and sharing learning experiences with friends because I have been in schools where these experiences are fostered and in those where they are ignored. I have experienced the connection that can provide a springboard for learning, hope and joy, and the disconnection that can catapult a child into helplessness, destructive choices and sabotage. A healthy School Family, like a secure bond with parents, empowers teachers, schools, parents and children to achieve their goals and more. The following stories show how a School Family has fostered one father's growth and a school district's transformation.

> ***My name is Jonathan Doria.*** *I am a father who had the wonderful opportunity of having my child attend Farias Early Childhood Center, a Conscious Discipline school. I remember just a few short years ago nervously enrolling our child into his first school. We had no earthly idea what to expect. We had heard many horror stories about registration and unpleasant encounters between teachers and parents in other schools. All fears were immediately erased when wife Mary, son Chris and I entered the front doors of Farias. We were greeted as if we were royalty! The warm smiles and acknowledgement from the staff gently embraced us and made us feel welcome. We were directed to the cafeteria where a pleasant voice said, "Welcome to the Farias School family!" Needless to say, they had me at "hello."*

> *Instantly, I began thinking of how I could become a bigger part of this School Family. I offered to volunteer my services as a professional photographer to raise funds for the school. I simply fell in love with Farias and Conscious Discipline. I realized how wonderful it would be to work in a school that had such a positive environment, and this prompted me to return to school myself to work toward my Bachelor's degree in Education.*

While I continued working towards my teaching degree, I accumulated enough hours to work as a substitute teacher. This gave me an opportunity to work at schools other than Farias. Time and time again, I was disappointed that I did not feel the same connection or sense of family at other schools. I became increasingly determined to continue the mission of the School Family approach to education.

Who would have imaged that my first experience in my child's School Family would touch and motivate me to earn by bachelors degree and ultimately return to Farias as a full-time teacher. Yet, here I am, currently in my second year as a teacher at Farias. Finally, I have found my niche in life. I am now in the exciting position of utilizing all the School Family components that I was exposed to as a parent. I am creating the same safe, structured and loving School Family environment for my students that Farias provided for my family all those years ago. The power of the School Family changed my son and also changed me in wonderful ways.

My name is Peggy Osborne. *In 2001, Sharon Jackson, the director of the early childhood program in College Station ISD, and I attended a conference titled, "Changing Children, Changing Practice: A New Look at Early Childhood Education." We anxiously awaited the keynote speaker, Dr. Becky Bailey, to begin the session. We were not disappointed; the session spoke to our heart and minds. From that spark, we began the process of teaching Conscious Discipline to a small handful of Head Start Teachers.*

Our teachers were empowered and amazed by the positive impact the School Family culture had on their centers, on the children in their care and in their own lives. In 2003, our trainings expanded to include teaching assistants and family service facilitators. By 2005, we had trained our whole Head Start agency.

Soon, kindergarten and first grade teachers began to notice the social and emotional growth in the children who entered their classrooms from our centers. "Where is that problem solving language coming from?" "What book did you all study?" "Is this training only offered to Head Start personnel?" Teachers brought these requests and comments to our office, and we soon began offering the training to district personnel.

In 2008, the decision was made that Conscious Discipline would become the adopted social/emotional philosophy for all elementary schools in College Station. We are so grateful for our supportive Superintendent Dr. Eddie Coulson, and the other administrators for supporting this district-wide effort! What an exciting journey this has been… and it all started with four-year-olds!

So what do these three journeys have to do with bullying? Everything! We have all experienced the power of authentic connection and interdependence to transform individuals, schools and districts. As a nation, we've tried the quick fixes of bully-free zones, no tolerance and metal detectors, and they simply do not work. In fact, we've seen these efforts do little more than postpone or send the bullying underground (making it harder to detect). The real solution to solving the bully-victim problem lies in our willingness and ability to self-regulate well enough to authentically connect and care for each other.

Healthy development proceeds from dependence, through independence, and into interdependence. Most of us persist in dependence or independence. As we choose to extend our journey into interdependence, our schools and other institutions will naturally follow. It is only through realizing our mutual interdependence that school bullies and global wars will ultimately become impossible. I wish us all well on this journey!

Chapter 1

The School Culture: Why traditional models are a disadvantage to our children.

Recently I joined my extended family in celebrating my aunt's 80th birthday. As we decorated for the party, I was struck by the diversity of opinions, actions and dress of all who had gathered. Some people dressed in their Sunday best, and some commented on their attire. Some started drinking beer at noon, and some commented on their drinking. Some people worked hard, and some commented about who was helping and who was not. Amid all of this diversity, laughter and the ensuing conflicts, we were family. We knew it, we felt it and we loved it.

We are social creatures. We raise and are raised by others, live in family groups, go to school in classes and are embedded in communities. We cooperate, compete and communicate. We not only live socially, we think socially. We are not machines, thinking linearly and logically. Ask your children what they did at school, and if you receive any answers at all, they generally will be social (not academic-related) ones such as: I played with Tyrone, Sarah got in trouble or the teacher picked on me. It is time for education to embrace all that we are! There is no separate cognitive me, social me or physical me. There is just me in relationship with you, and all the rest emerges from that simple truth.

From "Factory" to "Family":
Reestablishing the foundation of community

This basic truth we experience in so many facets of our lives leads us to the conclusion that to create a healthy school culture that prevents bullying from becoming a social norm, we must do three things. We must shift from a traditional "factory" model to a "family" model for creating optimal school climates. We must examine our relationship with power in order to ensure that our family model for the classroom is a healthy family model. And we must strengthen our focus on building the self-regulation skills of children in our care, so safety permeates all classrooms and each child increases his or her potential for success in life.

Historically and in most schools today, classrooms are designed on a factory model of education that has been around since the early 1900s. Take a moment and conjure an image of a factory, what it manufactures, its goals and the overall feel of the working environment. You probably imagined a factory making some type of widget such as T-shirts, silicon chips or refrigerator parts. In this image, you might see obedient workers performing rote, repetitive tasks with little meaning. The factory's goal is to make as many standardized widgets as efficiently as possible, using quality control standards. Management relies on firing or punishing those who do not meet the daily standards and rewarding those who exceed them. The overarching feeling is one of apathy, boredom and fear—fear of not meeting today's quota or set standards.

How many principals, teachers, children and parents are fearful their children will not meet the set standards of today? In the factory model of education, the child is unconsciously seen as a widget. The goal is to pour a standardized curriculum into each widget's head on a specific timeline. Nonconforming child widgets are seen as blocks to production, efficiency and accountability. They are often and repeatedly punished or expelled for their disruption to the system. Some of you, however, gave birth to nonconforming children. Your children are creative, movement-oriented or simply cannot tolerate the boredom of the assembly-line approach to education. They may have differences in their learning styles or attention abilities that make it challenging to move swiftly and easily from grade to grade like the other child widgets. What frustrations have you and your family experienced? Can you see the impact of a factory educational model on your children? Can you see how it is destined to leave some children behind? The children left behind or marginalized for their differences become targets for bullying and/or become bullies themselves.

In our Loving Guidance office, we hire "junior staff"—high school students who are usually children of our regular employees. They have all been bright, contributing members to the company. Recently, one of our employee moms was literally jumping up and down shouting, "He did it. He's graduating! He's graduating from high school. Thank God!" It amazed me that this exceptionally talented young man who works in our office could barely make it through the high school system.

Factory-model schools are designed to produce dropouts. Factories eliminate product failures as early as possible, in the service of efficiency. The goal is to find the deficient widgets, remediate if possible, and if not, get rid of them. Our current and continual drop-out crisis is no surprise. Dr. Richard Foster (2000), an expert on school leadership, believes the biggest task facing schools in the 21st century is to reverse the process of depersonalization that began over a century ago when schools adopted a factory model. In a report called "Locating the Dropout Crisis" (Balfanz & Legters, 2004), researchers at Johns Hopkins University found that one in five high schools in the United States graduate fewer than 60 percent of their students. A student drops out of school every 26 seconds (Carter, 2008). In addition to dropping out of school, children are kicked out. A study conducted at the Yale Child Study Center led by Walter Gilliam in 2005 found that four-year-olds are expelled at more than three times the rate of children in grades K-12.

It is becoming widely accepted that the standardized competitive factory model is not an effective learning model, and so we must begin undoing decades of programming and reinvent our classrooms. We must create a new model for building positive school cultures, one that accepts differences, builds unity and brings all children into the fold as caring, contributing members of the School Family.

From "Family" to "Healthy Family": Changing our relationship with power

As a child, I hated it when my parents argued. I would go into my room and bury my head under the pillow, praying they would stop, get a divorce or solve the problem. It took another decade before I realized they were never going to stop or get a divorce or solve the problem. My dad traveled all the time. He was a Secret Service agent and traveled with the presidents. When he was gone, things went very smoothly between my mom, my brother and myself. My mom became used to making all the decisions, running the house, working and raising us kids. She had all the power in the house, and was comfortable sharing it with my brother and me. We were empowered to make age-appropriate choices for ourselves. If our choices backfired in our faces, Mom was there to comfort us but not to save us from the consequences of those choices.

When Dad was home, it was a different story. He wanted to walk in and be the boss. My mom would step back to some degree, but often she would stand up to him. In those moments, the conflicts were scary. One day, my Dad was complaining that there was no butter pecan ice cream in the freezer, yelling at my mom about it. My mom was yelling back that he was being a jerk. I thought to myself, if he truly wanted ice cream he could just go to the store and buy a gallon. Then it dawned on me that the argument was not about the ice cream; it was about who ruled. They were fighting over power.

Each teacher and administrator holds a set of beliefs based on the power structure experienced within their family of origin. Our family of origin taught us what power is and how to deal with it. We learned how to communicate our wants, needs and feelings passively, aggressively, assertively or passive-aggressively. We learned to resolve problems or sweep them under the rug. Many of us have upgraded our skills set from those received from our family of origin, only to find that we revert to those behaviors in times of stress. We find ourselves disciplining as we were disciplined, and teaching how we were taught unless we consciously choose to change. The School Family model within Conscious Discipline seeks to first raise awareness of our existing relationship to power, and then to transform it into a shared power model that provides an optimal learning environment for children and work environment for adults.

Perhaps no area is the result of adults' dysfunctional relationship with power more evident than the crisis we are facing with bullying in the schools. Two meta-analyses have been published evaluating the outcomes of anti-bullying programs (Merrell, Gueldner, Ross & Isava, 2008; Smith, Pepler & Rigby, 2004); in both of these the effects of all interventions fell almost exclusively in the categories of "small," "negligible" or "none." Our attempts to address the national epidemic of bullying in schools have essentially done nothing to solve the problem. At some point we must say to ourselves, there has got to be a better way. There is, and the answer lies within ourselves and our relationship with power. We are accustomed to relying on unhealthy power models rather than shared power models, especially in the classroom.

All bully-victim dyads, from domestic violence in the home to fighting on the playground, are based on an imbalance of power. Marginalized people tend to lack self-regulation skills; they cognitively perceive others as "out to get them" or blame themselves for their own victimization. They tend to be argumentative and angry (bullies) or passive and anxious (victims). If we create a School Family that is built on inclusion and connection, which excludes and marginalizes no one, the culture itself becomes bully proof. Children's aggressive behaviors become teaching moments that create an opportunity for all to learn a new skill and reinforce the inclusive nature of our shared commitment to one another. As we change our relationship with power, shifting from dominant power to personal power that can be shared with others, schools can become bully-proof zones.

Assessing the Culture of Power from Your Family of Origin

In your family of origin, was power shared among members, with the adults providing leadership? Was there one dominant person who made most of the decisions? Or did you experience constant conflict as your parents bickered about who had the power? For some families, the way of dealing with power is so unstable that chaos results in a never-ending spiral of powerlessness for all members. Our experience and relationship with power will, for the most part, dictate the following set of social and emotional skills:

1. Connection: How safe do you feel in letting people get close to you? If you get close to others, do you fear losing yourself in the relationship? Do you prefer more distance and space at the expense of closeness?

2. Communication: How willing are you to ask for help, state your desires or express your needs? How do you communicate–passively, aggressively, assertively or passive-aggressively?

3. Problem-solving: What set of problem solving skills do you possess, if any? Can you hear both sides of an issue and then negotiate? Do you prefer to deny the problem in hopes it will go away in time? Do you tend to blame others or attempt to be right at all costs? Can you open your mind and brainstorm, or do

you hear attack and judgments instead of solutions? Do you tend to focus on the problem and who was at fault instead of focusing on finding solutions?

4. Feelings: Can you express your feelings? Do you distract yourself from them by eating, shopping, drinking or through other addictions? Do you know the difference between a feeling (I feel sad) and a thought or opinion (I feel like you're growing distant)? Do you know the difference between judgments (What has this country come to!) and feelings (I feel frustrated with airport procedures)?

5. Dealing with loss and change: Do you allow yourself to grieve or do you attempt to get busy and move on? Do you acknowledge your losses or do you tend to minimize or maximize them? Do you get stuck in grief, obsessing on how things should have been?

6. Values: Do you reflect upon your values or blindly accept the values of others as your own? Do you live by your values or are they words lacking action?

7. Autonomy: Are you the boss of you or do you tend to give your power away to others in hopes of pleasing them? Can you self-govern yourself or do you attempt to control others?

Complete the "Culture of Power" assessment on the next page. You may find that your family of origin falls in more than one column or in a combination of several columns. For example, when my family consisted of my mom, my brother and me, we generally experienced shared power with moments of dominant power (when mom was at her wits' end). When Dad was home, the relationships generally shifted to the dominant and conflicted categories.

The Bully-Victim Dyad is Characterized by an Imbalance of Power

Which column, or columns, best describes your family of origin? Put a check in each box that seems like it best applies.

	Competent/Positive	Faltering/Negative	Troubled/Negative	Severely/Negative
Power	Shared Power: Power securely in hands of adults and children. The goal is to facilitate the development of personal power within members.	Dominant Power: One person is dominant, usually based on role. Can be stable if the submissive one accepts that position.	Conflicted Coercive Power: Constant struggle by adults for power. No one accepts a submissive position. Bickering is the norm. ✓	Chaos: Everyone must think/feel the same. Disagreement is a threat. Detachment, disempowerment, isolation. Appears odd to others.
Connection	Fosters interdependence and connection. Relationships focus on caring, contribution, authentic communication.	Relationship does not meet the emotional needs of either. Sadness, anger, each blames other. Unhappy wife, detached husband. No real connection. ✓	Little or no connection because sharing provides the other person with ammunition for attack. Relationship is focused on power and control.	No connection but a malignant "we"-ness where everyone must think and feel the same. Individuality is obliterated.
Communication	Communication is two-way, clear. People feel listened to, understood, can state feelings safely. "I feel, I think" are common. Each person's upset is generally owned, not blamed on others.	Communication is one-way and clear. Defensiveness is common. Difficulty seeing from others' perspectives. Unable to openly, honestly, authentically communicate.	Communication varies from raw domination to hidden use of power. Difficulty knowing what others think/feel. Tendency to defend, barter, use sarcasm instead of communicate. ✓	Communication is hard to follow, non-logical, non-sequenced. Members often appear not to hear each other and/or may seem to have a private language.
Problem Solving	Able to identify problems early. Little blaming. Focus is on solutions. Use problem solving that elicits ideas from all.	Problem solving done by dominant party, who "knows best." Little negotiation. In classrooms, would be rewards/punishment. ✓	Denial, avoidance, blame make problem solving almost impossible. Problems persist due to denial, withdrawal or postponement.	Problems are often disregarded. Severe problems such as mental illness will be brushed aside as nervousness.
Feelings	Mood is positive, expression is encouraged, empathetic responses are usual. Openness is the norm. Acceptance of differences is fostered.	Avoidance or masking of feelings to avoid setting off the underlying conflict. Mood is more polite than authentic. Occasional empathy.	Expressing feelings is dangerous because it generally leads to disapproval. ✓	Feelings are frequently denied. The mood is often despair, hopelessness, cynicism.
Dealing with Loss	Losses are acknowledged and dealt with openly. Rituals are meaningful and authentic, not what "should be done."	Seems to be pain in the family that's not being dealt with. Losses are acknowledged with a need to move on quickly. ✓	Don't deal well with loss or change. Rigid rules. "This is the way we do things." Rituals are obligatory.	Have a difficult time with change. Losses are completely denied, including death. This gives families like this an eerie quality.
Values	View of humanity is that people are mostly good, doing the best they can. Use positive intent as lens. Mistakes are human. Complexity vs. black, white, good and bad.	From the outside, the family looks fine. Blame and guilt are bounced around within and without. The dominant person dictates how to view others.	Values are dictated. The world is black, white, good and bad, regardless of circumstances. Punishment and guilt are needed to avoid chaos. ✓	Values are bizarre and mental illness is likely. They seem to have lost touch with reality.

Which dyad do you relate to most? troubled negative

(Competent/Positive, Faltering/Negative, Troubled/Negative, Severely/Negative)

We can similarly assess a school's cultural climate with the "Culture of Power" chart. If the culture of power within a school is shared, the school will have a positive learning environment. The school climate will promote the competency of both the adults and the children in the school. Teachers will live the skills they want to promote in the children. Gossiping and backstabbing will be minimal. Those resisting curricular changes are supported instead of thought to be sabotaging school reform. Everyone in the culture has a voice. Teachers are seen as having differentiated learning needs, as are the children. Respect for individual differences is seen throughout the building.

If the culture of power is dominant, the culture turns negative and optimal learning begins to falter. In these school cultures, emphasis might be on the social-emotional learning of the students while ignoring the adults' social-emotional needs. (Adults are exempt from the learning and teaching they demand of children regarding respect, responsibility, honesty, etc.) Teacher cliques are common and school reform is difficult because trust, connection and problem solving among adults is not nourished.

If the culture of power is conflicted, coercive power, the school will be troubled. In such schools, jostling for power among all parties consumes most of the school energy. Teachers fight among themselves and with administrators. Children fight with each other and with the teachers. Neither teachers nor students enjoy coming to school, and each day is an exercise in survival for everyone.

In a culture of chaos, chaos reigns and severe dysfunction has consumed everyone. Take a moment now to reflect. What type of school do you work in? Can you see a connection between your family of origin's relationship to power and the way you presently run your class, school, program or agency? Think specifically of how you tend to think or act when you are tired or stressed. Then think how often you are tired and stressed. Our relationship with power impacts the culture of our schools, which dictates the level of learning that is possible. I have been in very successful classrooms where power is shared, faltering classrooms where the teachers attempt to maintain absolute control, troubled classrooms where conflict is always brewing and severely troubled classrooms where chaos reigns.

How do you deal with power in your school or agency? Many schools have a rewards and punishment orientation to power. This would indicate a dominant power relationship. The teacher, by his or her position, holds all the power. She or he will judge what is good behavior and reward it and will also determine what is inappropriate behavior and punish it or deliver consequences. Often schools require teachers to conduct prescriptive social-emotional activities within a dominant-power school culture. The result is lack of authenticity. For example, I have seen many teachers invite their students to discuss and help determine the rules and consequences. The result is a class meeting where the children try to please or guess what the teacher wants them to say. They know it is a rewards and punishment-based system, and truly their say-so in that system is minimal. An authentic, shared power discussion cannot exist in a dominant-power school climate.

Self-Regulation:
The missing link for academic success

A growing body of research indicates that children are not ready to start kindergarten or first grade with the skills they need to be successful. This has nothing to do with letters, numbers, days of the week or colors; it is because they lack the critical ability to self-regulate. Recent research indicates that one of the core problems of bullying in school is lack of self-regulation in individuals (Macklem, 2003).

Healthy self-regulation is related to the capacity to tolerate the sensations of distress that accompany an unmet need. An infant feels hungry. This discomfort turns to distress and the child cries. As an attuned adult responds to the infant's distress thousands of times, this creates positive mental models within the child. Children learn that feelings of discomfort, even distress, will soon pass and they are safe. They trust an adult will come. This process of attuned responsiveness to the inner world of the child begins to insert a tiny moment between impulse and action. The responsive parent has planted the first seed of self-regulation.

An attuned, responsive teacher can help children build their capacity to put additional moments between the impulse and the action. If Darnell wants the specific toy Michella has, he must wait his turn. He must learn to tolerate the frustration of not getting exactly what he wanted exactly when he wanted it. A pause between impulse and action allows him to inhibit grabbing or hitting and learn a new higher order skill, such as saying, "May I have a turn, please?" With the capacity to put a moment between a feeling and an action, children can take time to think, plan and come up with an appropriate response to the current challenge. This skill we call "self-regulation."

Self-regulation is necessary for children to access the developing executive skills in the higher centers of their brains. The executive skills allow us to set goals and achieve them despite obstacles and distractions. They involve controlling our behavior and readying us for any situation we may face (Meltzer, 2007). We know young children become upset when the world does not go their way; they have very immature executive skills. These skills develop slowly, starting at about 6 months and continuing until around 24 years, when colloquially we can say, "Well, they finally got their act together."

When children become upset because the world doesn't go their way, adults are called upon to discipline them. If we believe "discipline" means "to punish," we will punish them for lacking self-regulatory skills instead of teaching them how to self-regulate. When we punish them for lacking the ability to self-regulate, we also prevent them from developing the very skills we want to encourage. Choosing to punish a child's lack of self-regulation rather than encourage a pause between impulse and action (i.e., teach new regulatory skills) ultimately creates adults who:

- Find it hard to set goals and stick to them (e.g., weight loss)
- Cannot control impulses (e.g., road rage, yelling at children)
- Try to control the world instead of manage themselves (e.g., control freaks)
- Know what to do, but find actually doing it very difficult (e.g., "Do what I say, not what I do")
- Blame others for their upset states instead of taking responsibility for changing their own lives (e.g., "Look what you made me do")
- Find it hard to focus their attention and be present in the current moment without worrying about the past or the future (e.g., goes to dinner with Person A while talking on a cell phone to Person B)
- Create a world of addictions (shopping, eating, drinking, working, smoking) to distract or medicate themselves from their lack of self-regulatory skills

Do any of the above examples sound familiar? Some of them certainly fit my life. For the most part, we have all been punished for our inability to self-regulate, so we all experience these difficulties to some degree. Had we instead been "disciplined" by being taught the self-regulatory tools needed to manage our internal thoughts and feelings, we would have been better able to achieve successful outcomes.

Self-regulation is the control of our inner states, and most people acknowledge that our inner states dictate our behavior. If we feel loved, valued and appreciated, our behavior tends to be helpful. When you feel less internally conflicted and more content, generally you let people merge on the freeway and forgive the person with 15 items in the 10 items or less lane at the grocery store. The converse is also true. Life looks different when you feel conflicted, are playing out arguments in your head, feel disgruntled and have the general sensation of being out of sorts. Allowing other drivers to merge is then out of the question, and we count shopping cart items as if we are the cart police.

If we agree that inner states dictate behavior, the question becomes, "Why, as a profession, do educators focus completely on behavior when it comes to discipline?" Traditionally, we reward children who successfully meet our demands; we perceive those who don't as unsuccessful and as ruining the learning opportunities of others—and justly punish them. Thus we essentially repeat the past cycle of punishment that leads to underdeveloped self-regulation. Because inner states dictate behavior, we must shift our attention away from rewarding and punishing behavior and toward teaching children to manage their inner states so they can exhibit successful behaviors.

Shifting from punishing to teaching regulatory skills sounds wonderful on paper; however, if you are like me, no one ever actually taught you how to manage your own inner states. You instead experienced an unbalanced culture of power and punishment. The chart below shows the synergetic interplay of power, self-regulation, executive function and social-emotional development. In this chart, a system of shared power promotes self-regulation, which facilitates access to and development of executive skills that build increased social-emotional competence. Greater social-emotional competence yields a culture with greater shared power. In this way, a cycle of mental health is created.

Most of us were raised in a dominant or conflicted culture of power. This impeded our ability to self-regulate since dominant power requires the less-dominant person to be obedient without question. The person with the least power is responsible for regulating the inner state of the most powerful. "If you had only listened to me,

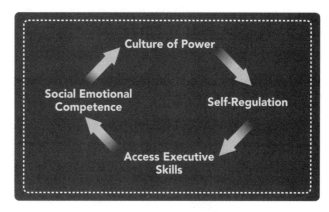

then I wouldn't have to act this way." Both parties lack self-regulation, making it impossible to reach the higher centers of the brain for optimal development of executive skills. Without executive skill development, social-emotional competence is impaired. From a state of impaired social and emotional competence, an increasingly dominant culture of power becomes necessary to maintain order.

Most of us have delayed development of our own executive skills, resulting in compromised self-regulation and social-emotional skills. Yet somehow, we still expect the children in our care to develop these skills healthily. While listening to the Gayle King show on XM radio, I heard a woman call in upset because her daughter's carpool driver was texting and driving at the same time. She instructed her daughter to say to the adult driver, "I feel scared when you text and drive. Please stop." Gayle suggested the mother call the carpool driver and express similar feelings and thoughts. The mother was adamant she could not do this—she would feel embarrassed and too scared. How often do we ask children to do what we ourselves will not?

When we are willing to consciously shift our relationship with power to a shared-power culture of learning, we change the cycle. Only then will we be able to help children learn to self-regulate. We will be able, during conflict moments, to lend our prefrontal lobe executive skills to children in order to scaffold the development of the higher centers of their brains. We will shift our attention to what Lev Vygotsky, a Russian psychologist (1978), suggested is the "child to be." American researchers constantly seek to discover how a child becomes the person he is, focusing on the past and its influence on the present. Vygotsky helps shift our attention to understanding how present interactions with our social world influence who we will become (Gredler & Shields, 2008).

In Conscious Discipline, we influence the person the child will become in two distinct ways. First, the adult must become the person he or she wants the child to be. This means we develop our own self-regulatory skills first, so we can maintain composure and create an emotionally safe environment for learning. Second, the adult must lend the child his or her own executive skills. Lending our executive skills requires us to let go of the desire to punish and instead choose to see discipline issues as the child calling for help. We then provide meaningful assistance by teaching new self-regulatory skills and strengthening their emerging executive development. Such assistance happens directly through conscious social interactions with others and indirectly by immersing them in a School Family that facilitates this lending process.

This approach requires us to raise our emotional intelligence quotient so we can teach and lend skills that might currently be our own weak suits. Conscious Discipline was designed to address this challenge by providing emotionally intelligent classroom structures within the School Family. These structures are the focus of this book, and they are as much for the adult as for the children, assisting both teachers and students to increase their social and emotional learning and self-regulation. They help us break old habits and learn new skills and provide the structure to scaffold our own development and that of our students. They help us manage emotions instead of act them out. They help us see conflict as a teaching tool instead of a sign of disrespect. And they help us model how to be responsible, caring members of a group instead of complaining, gossiping faculty members. Embedded in the School Family are the tools you need to leave the outdated factory model of education, your unhealthy relationship with power and your regulatory issues behind, so you can successfully retrain your mind for increased self-regulation and social-emotional intelligence, and assist the children in your care to do the same. With this transformation, schools, homes and workplaces can become bully-free zones as we ultimately discover that the desire to overpower and manipulate one another is far less powerful than the desire to create healthy relationships.

Chapter 2

The School Family: Using the power of connection to create school reform.

Do you remember going over to a friend's house when you were a child? It could have been just to play or for a sleepover. I distinctly remember the moment at Belinda's slumber party when it was time to go to bed and her mother came in, turned off the lights and said, "You girls be quiet and get some sleep. I don't want to hear a peep out of this room." I thought she would come back later, tuck us in bed, read a story and kiss us on our foreheads like my mom did. I asked Belinda if her mom did that on nights when I wasn't there. She said, "No, why?" Belinda was grossed out by my mom kissing my forehead, and I was dumbfounded to discover that not all families operated like mine. I just assumed if we did it, others did too. Surprisingly enough, Belinda assumed the same.

The School Family does not replace the family unit, but uses the healthy family metaphor as a guideline to create a positive school climate that promotes optimal development of all children, staff and faculty. It builds on the success of the family model for children who already have a balanced family life, and provides a sense of safety and belonging for children who lack the experience of successful relationships at home. A healthy family deals with the sanity and growth of the adults (teachers in school, marriage partners or other caregivers at home) as well as the optimal development of the children. In doing so, not only do all children benefit, but concerns about retaining and recruiting teachers can become a thing of the past.

I propose schools adopt the School Family as the metaphor for creating optimal learning environments for children for the following reasons:

1. It optimizes brain development for physical, social, emotional, spiritual and academic success. The family's goal is for all its members to first survive then thrive, reaching their optimal development. The factory's goal is to produce standardized products. If our mission in schools is to educate citizens to be contributors to a democratic society, then we must produce self-disciplined, intrinsically motivated students who choose to contribute to the welfare of themselves and others. This is the ultimate goal of a family. No other metaphor comes close. At the core of optimal development is self-regulation. At the core of family is survival, which also requires self-regulation to ensure that occurs.

2. It strengthens or provides an invisible set of assets called "family privilege." The healthy family bond provides children with a felt sense of safety, belonging and moral/spiritual values. Some children come to school with this healthy family bond, defined by John Seita and Larry Brendtro (2002) as "Family Privilege," but many do not. Without this sense of safety and belonging, children act out the pain of their unmet needs, and their behaviors become so difficult to manage that learning for all is impeded.

3. It fosters connections within the school so all members feel emotionally safe enough to experience conflict as a learning tool. The School Family creates a healthy connection between all parties in the school (administrators with teachers, teachers with teachers, teachers with parents, children with children, children with teachers, support staff and everyone else). Through this deep sense of belonging, the willingness to change increases and power struggles and resistance to change decreases schoolwide. This context of willingness enables conflict to become an opportunity to learn missing self-regulatory, social and emotional skills instead of creating a constant power struggle.

4. It creates a bully-proof climate based on safety, connection and problem solving rather than reward and punishment. The School Family changes two major forces that impact bullying: "intention" and the "power base." Consciously or not, most of us view misbehavior with negative intent, labeling the child and the behavior "bad." In a School Family, our intent shifts to a positive one where we see misbehavior as the child's way of communicating unmet needs or a lack of skills. This perceptual shift moves the entire school away from relying on external controls (reward and punishment) and toward developing children's internal guidance and problem-solving resources. The School Family also creates a change in the power base, shifting the school from reliance on dominant and conflicted power to an environment of shared power. With this shift, we abandon attempting to control others in favor of positively scaffolding children's learning self-control and self-regulation. Combined, these two shifts create a monumental change in the overall mental health of our schools.

5. It utilizes everyday life, conflicts and celebrations as the social-emotional curriculum. Add-on prescriptive social skills, bullying prevention, character education and emotional intelligence curriculums are unnecessary in the School Family. Instead, life lessons are embedded in the daily classroom management process. The social-emotional curriculum is a living culture in the classroom; the curriculum arises out of the group dynamic as teachers become images of emotional intelligence in action.

6. It integrates social and emotional learning into the teaching of academic standards, making all learning more brain-compatible and meaningful for teachers, parents and children.

7. It brings the joy back into teaching by opening the hearts of teachers, children and parents, so each can make a difference in the lives of the other.

I will discuss each of the above benefits in more detail in the sections that follow. After each point is explained, you will be asked to consider what it means in your life. I strongly encourage you to read slowly and give your mind time to reflect on the questions posed.

1. Optimizing brain development for physical, social, emotional, spiritual and academic success

Optimal brain development has been a hotbed of discussion in education for well over a decade. One of the core findings from all this attention is that interpersonal relationships shape the function and structure of the brain. In my workshops I say, "Connections on the outside literally create connections on the inside." It is critical for us to understand that connections with others on the outside actually do create neural connections inside our brains that shape how we see life and react or respond to it. Humans are social beings, and the social structures we experience have a profound impact on who we are and who we become. Our earliest relationships with parents, siblings, family members, friends and teachers shape five critical functions.

- **Early relationships shape how we handle stress in life and how much stress is too much before we blow.** Every teacher knows a child who goes off-line with the slightest provocation. As soon as the world does not go his way, his ability to control his impulses and process information goes out the window, along with the ability to teach him. A child's ability to self-regulate is largely determined by the quality of the early social relationships in his family. What is your initial reaction when the world does not go your way?

- **Early relationships shape the way we perceive our world.** Is the glass half full or half empty? We each have a different perception of our world. Some children, for example, perceive others' actions as intentionally mean. For these children, an accidental bump leads to a chronic, unrelenting war against the offender. We create our perception of the world from the blueprint that our family system provides. Are you more likely to seek solutions or discuss the problem, searching for the guilty party?

- **Early relationships shape how we organize our memories into mental models to anticipate the future.** Our early social experiences create unconscious mental models. Almost every teacher has reached out to greet a child only to have her recoil in fright instead of delight. The brain can be called an "anticipation machine." It constantly scans the environment trying to predict what will happen next. Our early family relationships bias us toward such things as fright or delight, trust or distrust, and optimism or pessimism. Check your mental models: How much time do you focus on what you think other people might say or feel, trying to anticipate their reactions in hope of controlling the situation instead of controlling yourself? Do you carry around any of the following beliefs (mental models)?

If you want something done, do it	_____
The only person you can really trust is	_____
Asking for help is a sign of	_____
Big boys don't	_____

- **Early relationships shape our capacity for interpersonal communication.** Some children are able to pick up on the nonverbal facial cues of others, while others miss this important part of communication entirely, and some children seem to understand the impact of their actions on others, while others don't. The ability to read others' emotions, see the world through others' eyes and empathize is developed through our early relationships. We feel hopeful, heard and understood when our nonverbal, verbal and energetic (inner state) communications are aligned. When we mismatch our intent and our words, our communication is impeded and conflict ensues. Our family dynamics can help us on the road to emotional intelligence or become a roadblock to its development. Have you ever heard yourself angrily yelling, "I was just trying to be helpful!" to a loved one or in a harsh tone blurt out, "Yes, I love you, now go play" to your children?

- **Early relationships shape our ability to focus and sustain attention.** Emotional regulation is essential for developing attention. If you can imagine your attentional system as a headlight attached to your forehead, emotional regulation aims the light and steadily points it toward what we value and hold dear. We attend to what is important, and our emotions determine what that might be. If our emotions are regulated and stable, then so is the light of our attention. If our emotions are all over the place, so is our attention. I remember my craziness around menopause. As my emotions roved all over the place, so did my ability to focus and sustain attention. Ask yourself, "What do I attend to? Am I demonstrating the values I profess to hold?"

If a child's family provides the above abilities, then a School Family has the potential to strengthen them. If a child has been traumatized, lacks healthy relationships or lacks family privilege in the early years, then a School Family has the potential to build them from scratch. The School Family model is the only model I know that has a chance of creating an environment that offers every child an even start on the road to success. Research is clear that relationships form the brain circuits responsible for the creation of meaning, the regulation of bodily states, the modulation of emotion, the ability to focus and sustain attention, the organization of memories, and ultimately, the capacity for interpersonal communication. With traditional discipline models, we have been sacrificing all this in the name of attempting to force an unmotivated child to behave and learn. We wrote their names on the board, turned their cards from green to red and offered rewards from the treasure box without ever addressing the core issues behind the behavior. It is time to reorganize our classrooms and school environments in ways that reflect the most up-to-date brain information, so all children have the best possible chance for lifelong success.

2. Providing an invisible set of assets called "family privilege"

I grew up with what John Seita and Larry Brendtro (2002) call "family privilege," an invisible set of assets that were generated from a functional original bond with my family. This healthy family bond provides a felt sense of safety, belonging and moral/spiritual values. It creates the mental and emotional space for a child to "be a child."

Because of my family privilege, I felt safe enough, loved enough and capable enough to explore every corner of my physical and mental world. Family privilege afforded me the luxury of imagining I was Davy Crockett, a rock star, a princess and an inventor. I could make up any story, direct the play and change roles at any time. I didn't have to parent my parents or parent myself. I didn't have to worry about where my next meal would come from, whether my mother was coming back or who was going to keep me safe. I didn't have to stay on alert for violence or chaos. I was free to create with my toys, expand my mind with possibilities and lie in the grass, creating dragons in the clouds. I experienced a loving bond with my family that guaranteed my survival, affording me the growth that stems from a felt sense of safety, a sense of belonging and optimal learning experiences. Family privilege provided my brain, body and spirit the potential to develop in optimal ways.

Many of us can't imagine what life would be like without family privilege. We assume that, like the air we breathe, it is available to almost everyone. Sadly, it is not. An increasing number of children are growing up without stability, where fear and chaos replace the felt sense of safety provided by a connected family bond. A lack of family privilege robs children of delightful, explorative learning opportunities and derails the attachment bond, forming what Seita and Brendtro (2002) have shown to be a deficient or warped life blueprint.

I was at an elementary school in Orlando, Florida one afternoon. A second-grade boy, whom I'll call "Mark," had just tried to hang himself with his belt because recess was canceled due to a school assembly. The teachers who called me couldn't believe what had happened. Most were experiencing a mixture of disbelief and blame, saying things like, "I can't believe he's that upset over missing recess! He's so dramatic." As I spoke with Mark, the contrast between my family privilege and his lack of family privilege became acutely apparent. At the moment, Mark was homeless and staying at the local shelter. I asked him if there was any place to play at the shelter. He sat quietly, with his head down. I asked if maybe there was a courtyard area. He said, "That's where the men do their business." I asked if there was a television or game room. Mark said, "That's where the drugs are." I asked if there was a kid's playroom he could stay in. He said, "There are 15 kids in there, and they steal from and beat up little kids like me." I then asked, "What is the hardest part about being at the homeless shelter?" With my family privilege assumptions, I was thinking Mark's answer might be no clean clothes causing embarrassment at school or the fear of not knowing where he might stay from day to day. He said, "We don't get anything to eat on Saturdays. The church people bring food on Sundays." There was no family privilege for Mark, no cloud dragons for him to explore in the sky, just real dragons that threatened his very existence, altered his brain to organize around fear instead of love and derailed any blueprint for a successful life.

The number of children lacking family privilege is growing in all demographics. Stressed adults lack the ability to form the bonds necessary for their children to develop optimally. Hurried lifestyles, poor quality child care, work pressures, divorces, addictions, disabilities, poverty, criminality and depression are interfering with parenting, putting family privilege at risk in all sectors of society.

Some of you may assume this book is essential for all at-risk children, and you are right. However, as long as any of our children are at risk, then every child lives in an at-risk community. This book and the School Family program are for all children. When homes fail to provide family privilege, it then becomes the responsibility of schools, communities and churches to fill in the gap. Deficient school climates derail optimal development regardless of socioeconomic status. Violence results when children on the edge encounter negative school climates. The combination of children on the edge and negative school climates is explosive, as we have seen from gang-ridden inner cities to the bully-ridden suburb of Columbine. If children do not experience family privilege from some source, we can almost guarantee they will commit violence against themselves (chronic self-sabotage, cutting, anorexia, suicide) or violence against others. Schools can become an oasis for resiliency or a battleground of resistance for children who are lacking family privilege. We know that the optimal learning state consists of high challenge and low stress. As we continue to raise our educational standards, we do create high challenge. However, when we put already stressed children and teachers in an environment of high challenge, we create additional stress, dysfunction and a propensity for violence.

The School Family is our key to building a positive school climate. It lowers the stress of all its members–children, teachers and administrators–allowing high challenge to be just that: challenging. It strengthens family privilege for those lucky enough to have experienced it, and provides family privilege resiliency for those who haven't. The School Family teaches and models respectful relationships based on helpfulness and contribution. It shows children how conflict can be used as a growth opportunity instead of a justification to inflict more pain. The School Family models what a healthy family looks like, feels like and sounds like. Regardless of the amount of dysfunction they have previously experienced, every child in the School Family will experience a blueprint for healthy communication and a healthy family structure. That alone is worth its weight in gold for future generations because it becomes a built-in parent education program for the children and staff who work with them. Without this approach, the school will simply compound the derailment of brain development that is occurring at home, ensuring violence and academic failures for at-risk children. It is my deep belief that if we are going to have safe middle and high schools, then our early childhood programs and elementary schools must be built on a School Family philosophy.

3. Fostering connections within the school so all members feel emotionally safe enough to experience conflict as a learning tool

The motivation for our behavior comes from being in a relationship. We know this from our own life experience. Imagine you and your significant other are watching TV on the couch. You get up to go to the bathroom. Your partner says, "While you're up, will you bring me a snack?" When everything is going well in your relationship, you are likely to be cooperative. Your response might be, "Sure, what would you like?" Now, imagine your relationship is on the rocks and you're wondering why you're with this person in the first place. Your response is probably a bit resistant. In your head or out loud, you say, "You've got legs, get it yourself!" The same pattern of behavior holds true for our children. Connection promotes cooperation and willingness, while disconnected children are oppositional.

Connection has become popular in recent years, due in large part to the number of self-help books that promote relationships as a source of well-being. Often, we think of connection in terms of harmony, warm support and pleasant feelings. This certainly is one aspect of connection, but it does not include the critical component of conflict. In Conscious Discipline, connection is a very specific term. It refers to the unified sense of relating to one another in such a way that we feel safe enough emotionally to experience conflict and use it as a learning tool. As Maureen Walker (2004) states, "Connection provides safety from contempt and humiliation; however, it does not promise comfort. It often is a portal to increased conflict, because safety in relationships allows differences to surface." The way we handle the differences that arise between us is crucial. If we can respond to conflict in a way that increases our sense of worth, enhances clarity and strengthens the desire for connection, then we have facilitated growth. If we find ourselves reacting to conflict in detrimental ways (avoiding, manipulating, "happying up," abusing), the connection is weakened and individual differences devalued. Weak connections have huge side effects, with disrespect for self and others at the core. When we lack positive regard, we generate more conflict. With more conflict comes more disconnection, and chronic disconnection is the root of all misbehavior.

In school, misbehavior often looks like underachieving, acting out, bullying or defiance. In adult life, misbehavior often falls under the broad category of addiction. The specific connections developed through Conscious Discipline and the School Family unhook this cycle of disconnect by creating a safe environment for conflict to be explored and utilized as a way of teaching life skills. The structures suggested in this book provide a means to becoming more present and connected with your class. They encourage each class member—including you—to be authentic, compassionate and respectful. They also help you to respectfully negotiate conflict in a way that strengthens the School Family.

4. Creating a bully-proof climate based on safety, connection and problem solving rather than reward and punishment

The most potent single cause of bullying is a negative peer group climate (Brendtro, Ness, & Mitchell, 2001). Every classroom and every school has a school climate that is integrally linked to the school's motivation system. A "reward and punishment" motivational system generally relies on externally applied, tangible consequences. These systems include treasure boxes, stickers, marks on the board, token systems, apples falling from a tree, and traffic lights that change colors. In these systems, we impose artificial external consequences for meeting or not meeting the class rules. The external consequence sets the behavioral expectations.

Reward and punishment systems are based on the teacher judging the child's behavior to be good or bad, then delivering loot for good behavior and losses for bad behavior. This creates a competitive culture of "haves" and "have-nots." To get attention in this system, you must be exceptional good or exceptionally bad. The remaining children are basically invisible. Think back to your school days. Were you the good, the bad or the invisible child? How did that feel to you?

This segregated system of good kids and bad kids also creates a segregated value system. The "bad" children are treated with one set of skills and values, while the good kids are treated with another set. We unconsciously set up a mental model that says if we can define a child as "bad" (e.g., weird or different), then we can justify treating him or her poorly. It is okay to publicly humiliate bad kids by putting their names on the board, moving their clips, and so on. It's okay to call them names, either actually or implied: "What's the matter with you? Don't you understand the rules?" (i.e., "Are you too stupid to understand the rules?"). It's okay to exclude them by sending them to time out or forcing them to miss recess. And in many states, it is okay to physically paddle them. Reward and punishment unconsciously encourages adults to model bullying behavior. One day I overheard my nephew being verbally aggressive with his friends. I asked what was going on. Out of his mouth popped words modeled on my own behavior, "I asked nicely twice, and then I had to start yelling." Ouch! That one hurt, but it was a very powerful lesson for me. I had been unconsciously modeling, "Do what I say when I say it, and you will be treated with respect and dignity. If not, bullying is a reasonable tool for me to use against you."

If you choose, you can leave the reward-punishment system behind and build a classroom with an internal focus on reflection, relationships and problem solving instead. Internal motivation systems rely on our natural desire to be in relationship with others. By developing a sense of community rather than a segregated system of "haves" and "have-nots," you cease to model bullying, help bring disconnected children into the fold, and use natural consequences rather than artificial ones as feedback for lasting behavioral change.

Conscious Discipline is relationship-based, and utilizes the School Family for its motivation system. Students' motivation to behave comes from the internal pleasure they have when they help others, feel cared for and experience the joy of thriving in a culture that offers safety and positive regard. It also comes from the natural internal angst they feel when they treat others poorly or do not contribute their part to the whole. Children in a School Family are motivated by the 4-C's: caring, connection, contribution and conflict resolution.

If a child in a reward and punishment classroom shoves another student in line, he might lose points, miss recess or lose a trip to the treasure box. In a relationship and problem-solving classroom, the child would experience the impact of his behavior on others. The teacher would coach the victim to say, "I don't like it when you shove me. Please walk slowly behind me in line." If the child has a relationship with the student he shoved, he may feel a twinge of angst for his hurtful actions. This hint of internal discomfort generates a willingness to see and do things differently. The result is a willingness to learn new skills. The "shover" might be coached, "You wanted him to walk faster. You may not shove. When you want him to go faster, say, 'Please move up closer to the others. We're too far back in line.'"

When we coach children to resolve conflicts respectfully, we enhance and activate the higher centers of their brains. Their focus is placed internally on problem solving and learning new skills. However, this coaching will not succeed unless it is embedded in a culture of caring. Without first developing the safety and connection of a School Family, the child coached to say, "I don't like it when you shove me," might say it reluctantly or with attitude. The child who pushed might simply respond, "So, get a life." The safety and connection components are key to the success of your problem solving. The three work together because willingness is embedded in relationships. The following chart shows the relationship between conflict and resolution with power and intention. The greater the shared power and positive intent within the school, the greater the willingness and the more likely misbehavior and conflict will be resolved. Conversely, the greater the dominant power and negative intent are in a school, the less likely you will have the healthy relationships that lead to willingness to change behavior and the cooperation necessary to resolve problems for the common good.

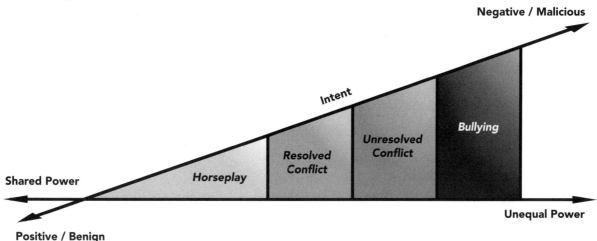

Adapted from Bullying in American Schools: A Social-Ecological Perspective on Prevention and Intervention Book by Dorothy L. Espelage, Susan M. Swearer; 2004.

You might think, "Whoa, wait a minute! I've been teaching long enough to know that some children don't care about the internal angst they create in themselves and others!" My response to this is twofold: 1) I have been teaching long enough to know that those children don't care because they don't feel they've been cared for; and 2) consequences are not effective for children who do not care. The traditional system of reward and punishment constantly removes or alienates children who already feel alienated. When a child does not care what privileges he loses or what opportunities he gains, consequences become completely ineffective. Conscious Discipline uses a different system, providing an environment where these alienated, consequence-proof students feel safe and connected enough to care again. Research conducted by Hoffman, Hutchinson and Reiss (2009) concludes that as a teacher's reliance on rewards and punishment increases, so does negativity in the school climate. It shows that shifting to the safety, connection and problem-solving approach of Conscious Discipline reduces discipline referrals and simultaneously improves the school climate.

5. Using everyday life, conflicts and celebrations as the social-emotional curriculum

In many of my workshops, I ask parent participants, "What do you want included in your child's education?" I give them the following list from which to choose:

- Gaining knowledge
- Learning responsibility
- Being drug-free
- Being nonviolent
- Caring

As one would expect, every parent votes for all of them. They certainly want their children to gain knowledge, but it seems equally important to them that they learn responsibility, grow up drug-free and nonviolent, and ultimately become caring individuals. Then I tell them that the curriculum is too crowded. Teachers don't have time to address all five issues and meet the accountability standards of statewide testing. "So," I ask, "which ones do you want to eliminate from the curriculum?" They always insist none!

What if there was a way to achieve all these dimensions of education without placing additional curriculum demands on teachers? What if we could have our cake and eat it, too? By creating a school family that combines social-emotional learning and classroom management into one seamless curriculum, the needs of the whole child can be met without additional lessons such as character education programs, social skills training or violence prevention interventions.

40   *Creating the School Family*

Often called the "missing piece" in school improvement efforts, the field of social and emotional learning (SEL) reflects a growing recognition that a child's success in school and life can be advanced with the aid of healthy social and emotional development. SEL is the process through which children and adults acquire the knowledge, attitudes, and skills to:

- Recognize and manage their emotions
- Set and achieve positive goals
- Demonstrate caring and concern for others
- Establish and maintain positive relationships
- Make responsible decisions
- Handle interpersonal situations effectively

These critical competencies involve skills that enable children to calm themselves when angry, initiate friendships and resolve conflicts respectfully, make ethical and safe choices, and contribute constructively to their community (Payton et al., 2008; Elias et al., 1997; Zins & Elias, 2006). *The Positive Impact of Social and Emotional Learning from Kindergarten to Eighth-Grade Students* technical report summarizes results from three large-scale reviews of research on the impact of SEL programs on elementary and middle-school students (Payton et al., 2008). Collectively, the three reviews included 317 studies and involved 324,303 children. The results showed that SEL programs improved students' social-emotional skills, attitudes about self and others, connections to school, positive social behavior and academic performance. They also reduced students' conduct problems and emotional distress. In addition, social-emotional learning improved students' academic performance by 11 to 17 percentile points across the three reviews, indicating that SEL programs offer students a practical educational benefit.

Research conducted on the use of Conscious Discipline mimics and surpasses these findings. A reduction of aggressive acts in an early childhood class (Figures 1 and 2) can be seen in classes and schools utilizing Conscious Discipline.

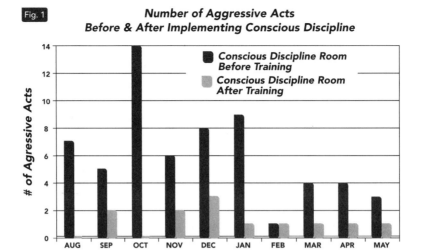

Fig. 1 **Number of Aggressive Acts Before & After Implementing Conscious Discipline**

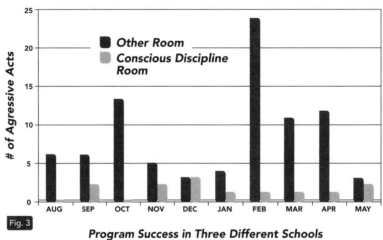

Fig. 2 **Number of Aggressive Acts in Conscious Discipline Room Compared to Traditional Room During the Same Year**

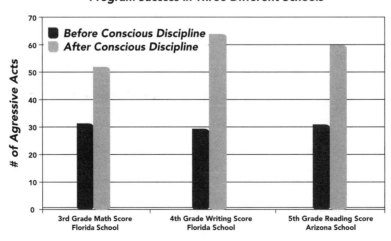

Fig. 3 **Program Success in Three Different Schools**

Refer to ConsciousDiscipline.com/Research for more in-depth explanation and additional research.

An increase in standardized test scores can also be seen in a sample of schools that began implementing Conscious Discipline schoolwide (Figure 3). Fern Creek Elementary*, one of the sample schools in Figure 3, raised their state-assessed school grade from a "D" to an "A" by implementing Conscious Discipline, and remained an "A" school for three consecutive years. This high-risk, high-poverty school also increased individual standardized test scores and decreased aggressive acts with the use of Conscious Discipline.

The question becomes, "Where do we get extra time in the day to address all this essential social and emotional learning?" The answer is this: We get it by conducting ourselves in such a way that our actions become a model of social-emotional learning. We learn to perceive conflict differently so we can respond differently. We change our relationship with power. We become conscious, mindful teachers. We utilize Conscious Discipline and the School Family to increase our own emotional intelligence, so that the day-to-day workings of our classroom become our SEL program for the children in our care.

6. Integrating social and emotional learning into the teaching of academic standards

Contrary to popular notions, the brain is not a sponge; it is a sieve. That which a child deems unimportant goes down the proverbial drain. Conscious Discipline is an eclectic program drawing from multidisciplinary fields and various theories. The social-constructivist work of Lev Vygotsky is one such contribution. The major theme of Vygotsky's theoretical framework is that social interaction plays a fundamental role in the development of cognition. Vygotsky (1978) states: "Every function in the child's cultural development appears twice: first, on the social level, and later, on the individual level; first, between people (interpsychological) and then inside the child (intrapsychological). This applies equally to attention, to memory, and to the formation of concepts. All the higher functions originate as actual relationships between individuals." In short, relationships dictate all learning.

Writing becomes meaningful in the School Family as children compose "We Care" notes for those who are sick or discouraged. Reading takes on new depth of meaning as children explore "routine" books that show how to be successful during the day and class-made books that recall interactions they experienced with each other. Math rises in importance as

---

* You can view a short trailer for a documentary about their tremendous accomplishments by visiting www.ConsciousDiscipline.com and clicking on "The Fern Creek Story." You may also request a copy of the full-length documentary at ferncreekdocumentary@lovingguidance.com

each person counts the number of helpful acts done during the day. Social studies become a living, breathing entity in a democratic classroom as children tackle problem solving in class meetings. Science gains meaning from the study of one's own brain in terms of how brain states impact learning, making friends and self-control. As we integrate SEL opportunities into the achievement of academic standards, learning becomes not just more intrinsically meaningful, it actually becomes truly learned, so that retaining and transferring the information is possible. We are no longer teaching to the test, we are teaching to the children.

7. Bringing the joy back into teaching

Many teachers have been working for over a decade to change their academic curriculum from an efficient factory to one based on the science of learning. Many classrooms now include cooperative learning strategies, multiple intelligence lesson planning, differentiated learning, scaffolding, critical thinking and reflection. The push for standardized testing has frustrated some of these efforts, but progress is being made. There is an emerging awareness of the importance of SEL, yet classroom management systems tend to remain in an autocratic, factory production mode.

It is not uncommon to see schools striving for best practices in reading, math and pedagogy, while still relying on a management system based on external motivation and prescriptive character education programs. In most U.S. elementary schools, marks on the board for bad behavior and treasure boxes for good behavior remain the mainstay. Teachers try to control their classrooms while attempting to empower students at the same time. This is a task that simply cannot be accomplished. Most careers now require a complex, creative combination of emotional, social, practical and academic intelligences, not the factory standards of patience, perseverance and repetition. Yet the factory model of education is still alive and well. These constant, opposing struggles are eating away at the teaching profession, with the result of teachers losing heart.

As a teacher for 30-plus years, I can relate to these feelings. We came into the profession to make a difference, to light up the children's faces, to see them discover the beauty of reading, writing, singing and getting along. We did not come to be boot-camp sergeants, stuffing irrelevant information into resistant minds, spending more time policing than teaching. We came to teach for the joy of teaching. The good news is that the most current science-based learning models present us with the information and opportunity to do just that! When we align a developmentally appropriate curriculum with classroom management that fosters self-regulation, we align our brains with our hearts and learning comes naturally. Creating a School Family fosters this alignment, helping us to feel we are doing the right thing for ourselves, our schools, our children and their families.

Let's Get Started

Shifting your motivation system from rewards to relationships, from factory to family is not an easy process. It is, however, a very rewarding journey. The first step in building the School Family is to literally change your mind. The process begins with accepting a new way of thinking about classroom design and management. Decide for yourself: Am I committed to the factory model, whether unconsciously or consciously? What was my original relationship with power? Am I willing to change my view of power? Am I ready to expand my thinking to include a model that encompasses all styles of learning, and integrates the social, emotional, physical, cognitive and moral development of all children? Am I willing to explore using a family metaphor and begin creating a School Family?

If you feel drawn to this new paradigm, start this very instant. Call your classroom a School Family. Post a "Welcome to our School Family" sign on your door. When you welcome your parents and students at the beginning of the year, say, "Welcome to our School Family." Name or have your students name your School Family. Maybe you are "The 5th Grade School Family" or "The Buddy Bear School Family." You no longer teach in a school classroom, you teach to your School Family. You can begin to change today.

Begin creating your School Family from the inside out. That inner tug of willingness to change is all that's required to begin this journey. The next chapter presents an overview of the emotionally intelligent classroom structures that will support you in creating your School Family. I will then discuss each structure in detail in the chapters that follow. Although it might seem a bit scary as you embark on this new adventure, remember, fear is simply excitement without oxygen. When you feel the tightening sensation of fear or discomfort, take a deep breath, let it be and keep going. It is an honor to be on this fascinating journey with you. You can do it! Let's get started!

Chapter 3

The School Family Structures: The foundation of emotionally intelligent classrooms

Mrs. Bowen brought her son Evan to school on a Thursday after he had been absent with the flu all week. Evan could have ridden the bus, but Mrs. Bowen felt an urgency to talk with his teacher. As she entered the classroom, she motioned to Ms. Kerrington to meet with her in private. The mood of the conversation was similar to when two parents sneak a private moment to discuss birthday arrangements for a child. Mrs. Bowen began, "I don't know exactly what you are doing at school, but Evan has assured me all week that when he returned, the children would sing him a song and he would have notes written by his friends welcoming him back. I just wanted to check with you to make sure this is still happening, and it wasn't just something you did on special occasions. He has been both sick and excited to return to school all week. He also said his class was wishing him well every morning. If this didn't happen or isn't true, please don't tell him. He was so confident his class really cared about him that his ability to handle being sick was the best I have seen."

The teacher assured Mrs. Bowen that Evan was exactly right, and that all those things did and would happen. Then she told her, "Not only did we wish Evan well each morning, we included you as well. It's tough being a single mom; I know because I'm one too. We put your name on our Wish-Well Board next to Evan's so we were thinking of both of you." Ms. Kerrington then took her to the Wish-Well Board where the names of both mother and son appeared. Mrs. Bowen's eyes welled up and she left the room, simply saying, "Bless you."

I see stories like these play out all across the country as parents are taken aback by the tremendous and unexpected impact a classroom built on safety and connection can have on their children and themselves. The Wish-Well Board discussed in this example is one of several structures encouraged in a Conscious Discipline classroom. This personal story is one of many that demonstrate the power of simple acts to bring deeper meaning to education and the potential for classroom structures to bridge the gap between home and school.

Just as a home belongs to everyone in the family, so does the School Family belong to all its members. What is one of the first things you do when you start a new job? You create your space. You do little things to make the classroom feel like your home away from home, like taping pictures of loved ones to the side of a filing cabinet. Once the classroom feels like it's "ours," then we move on to more professional concerns.

If we want children to feel valued, positive and accepted, then the classroom environment must also encourage them to see their classroom as a home away from home. The message we want to send to children is that they are part of the learning process and they have ownership in creating a caring learning environment. For children to excel, we must design a classroom environment that meets their social, emotional and academic needs and sends the message that they can influence how those needs are met.

Environmental Support for Self-regulation and Social Emotional Learning

In designing our classrooms for learning, we seek to create spaces and provide materials that will enable students to be academically successful. If we are going to study insects, we will plan for success with books, visuals, activities and materials. We must plan the same way for the social and emotional domains of learning. In addition, we must also be prepared for the unexpected. We cannot plan for a child's extended absence because of illness, the death of a family member or pet, a divorce, or simply a child's elation about learning to ride a bike. We must design our classroom environment so it can handle events when they arise as a natural part of life, including:

- Sadness over sick pets and parents, and even the deaths of those we love
- Shock of having a parent incarcerated or loved ones removed from the home
- Excitement of celebrating soccer games won, teeth lost, new skateboard tricks achieved, perfect scores on math quizzes, a new job for mom, etc.

- Hurt, embarrassment and frustration from name calling, pushing, shoving and other hurtful acts
- Disappointment over life events such as forgetting permission slips or not seeing Dad, who promised to visit but didn't show up
- Frustrations and built-up anger toward a world that is generally not going your way
- Fear of and humiliation from failing to meet the academic standards expected in the classroom
- Joy and elation from events like field trips, the Super Bowl, local concerts or television shows
- Guilt caused by lying, stealing and cheating
- Concerns over personal health issues, friendships, approval and belonging

Every teacher and administrator would agree that classrooms harbor a constant flux of emotions because of our social nature. These emotions generate different states within us. Some states, such as joy and excitement, can facilitate learning. Others, such as anxiety and fear, can shut down the higher centers of the brain, making the achievement of academic goals impossible. If we are going to maximize learning opportunities, we must create environments where children are able to process their emotions and transform their inner states. They must be enveloped by a responsive school culture that acknowledges their inner lives as well as their external behaviors and accomplishments. In general terms, our goal is to create classroom environments that do the following:

1. Provide children and adults with the opportunity to see themselves as part of a School Family that is an extension of the home family.
   Friends and Family Board: Chapter 4
   School Family rituals: Chapter 10

2. Provide systems whereby children can celebrate the successes, achievements and events they deem important.
   School Family rituals: Chapter 10
   Celebration Center: Chapter 13

3. Provide children and adults with an abundance of images showing expected behavior.
   Visual rules and routines: Chapter 6
   Ways to be helpful: Chapter 7

4. Provide children and adults an opportunity to change negative inner states into positive, optimistic states that are conducive to optimal learning.
   Brain Smart Start: Chapter 8
   Safe Place: Chapter 9

5. Provide adults and children a system in which hurtful interactions can be utilized to teach life social skills.
   Time Machine: Chapter 12
   Class meetings: Chapter 15

6. Provide children the opportunity to support and care for one another.
   Ways to be helpful: Chapter 7
   School Family rituals: Chapter 10
   We Care Center: Chapter 14

7. Provide children with the opportunity to contribute to and be responsible for the safe, smooth running of the classroom.
   Safekeeper: Chapter 5
   Visual rules and routines: Chapter 6
   Job Board: Chapter 11
   Class meetings: Chapter 15

Emotionally Intelligent Classroom Structures

The structures and chapters listed above are central components of Conscious Discipline that meet the self-regulatory and social-emotional needs of all members of your school. Each of the structures provides unique opportunities to meet the needs of all children. Some structures will resonate with you immediately; some will ask you to step outside your comfort zone. I explain each in detail, with one chapter per structure. Below is a brief overview of each structure and its role in creating your School Family.

Friends and Family Board

The Friends and Family Board establishes the School Family, names it and identifies its members. It also links the home family with the School Family. This link helps children manage the process of being away from those they love, and provides a place for them to find comfort in knowing their loved ones support them. This structure is the hub of the "Getting to know you" activities most teachers already have in place for the start of the school year. It consists of a board or book displaying the children and staff's family photos.

The Safekeeper

The Safekeeper ritual represents the foundation of Conscious Discipline: a total commitment to physical, emotional and social safety. This ritual begins each day with a focus on safety, the most cherished and important factor for a successful day of learning. It states the conscious job description of teachers: "My job is to keep you safe." The job description for the students is, "Your job is to help keep it safe." This ritual and mindset is essential to the social and academic success of your classroom because the brain functions optimally when a person feels safe.

Visual Rules and Routines

The purpose of visual routines is to provide children with images of what they can do to be successful members of a classroom. They specifically outline the expected behavior, provide a classroom structure that creates consistency and predictability, and allows teachers to shift from dominant power to shared power. This predictability and consistency is essential to creating a felt sense of safety in the school and classroom. It helps children learn to govern themselves by using visuals that they internalize. Visual rules help children make wise choices, as well as help teach adults how to offer children two positive choices instead of a positive choice (clean up) and a negative choice (miss recess).

Ways to Be Helpful Board

The purpose of the Ways to Be Helpful Board is twofold: 1) It provides visual images of ways children can help each other in order to develop the skill of helpfulness; and 2) It honors the ways children are helpful to each other. It is not a bulletin board stating teacher expectations. Helpfulness already exists in every classroom, but historically, we have not attended to it. Our focus tends to be on the inappropriate events that occur, not the helpful ones. The Ways to be Helpful Board supports your commitment to focus your attention and the children's attention on helpful acts. The creation and constant additions to this board teach children how to be successful in their class job description to "help keep the classroom safe."

Brain Smart Start

Conscious Discipline advocates beginning the day with the Brain Smart Start in order to ease the transition from home to school and create an optimal learning state within both teacher and child. It consists of four activities: uniting, disengaging the stress response, connecting and committing. These four types of activities prepare children for a day of learning while teaching them useful skills they will need during times of distress. Learning takes place in situations with high challenge and low stress. The Brain Smart Start helps each child and every teacher start the day with low stress and alert attention.

Safe Place

The Safe Place provides a learning center in the classroom where children can go to change their inner state from upset to peaceful and composed. The Safe Place will be the hub from which your lessons in anger management and self-regulation will emerge. The Safe Place plays a major role in teaching children how to regulate their own inner states in order to maximize their learning and contribution to the School Family.

School Family Rituals

Rituals provide a way for children to offer their goodness to each other and are the glue that binds your School Family together. Rituals such as "wishing well" provide a healthy way to express concern for others, while ones like the "absent child" ritual let children know their presence at school matters and their absence is noticed. It also provides, like all the rituals, a way to integrate meaningful daily writing and reading into the life of the classroom as children create "welcome back" notes.

Job Board

The Job Board manages the jobs that each child in the classroom will perform. These jobs provide all children with the opportunity to be significant contributors to others through meaningful classroom responsibilities. In your School Family, jobs cease to be badges of specialness awarded to a handful of children and instead become a foundation for good citizenship that is experienced by every child.

Time Machine

The Time Machine utilizes hurtful interpersonal interactions as a teaching tool for learning helpful, assertive communication skills. Through the Time Machine, students are asked if they are willing to go back in time to re-do a hurtful exchange using new language. The teacher coaches the specific language the child will need to get his or her needs met in an acceptable way. The Time Machine is the center of your bully-prevention program because it empowers both victims and bullies to communicate in helpful ways.

Celebration Center

The purpose of the Celebration Center is to celebrate life events, individual achievements and contributions to the School Family. Celebrations could include such things as losing a tooth, learning to ride a bicycle, welcoming a new sibling into a family, observing great-grandmother's birthday, learning to read, earning 100 percent on a spelling test or helping friends through a difficult time. This center is a way for children to honor children. It is not a place where rewards are given for good behavior, and it ultimately replaces a felt need to give rewards to children.

We Care Center

The We Care Center provides children a symbolic way to express empathy and affection for others. The symbolic form will vary from offering an item such as a teddy bear, to written materials such as note cards, to I Love You rituals, to music and movement activities. When members of our home families are sick or having a hard time, we might send a card, email or call them on the phone. The same is true in the Conscious Discipline classroom. In the School Family, children are encouraged to share their support and concern for one another in whatever way they are developmentally capable of doing.

Class Meetings

The purpose of class meetings is to provide a forum and create a climate in which children feel safe enough to celebrate, connect and solve problems. It is the hub of the classroom democratic process and acts, to some degree, as the governing body. As children engage in the self-governing process, they learn and develop the executive skills needed for goal achievement throughout life. As we scaffold these skills, we stimulate the children's prefrontal lobes and strengthen the CEOs of their brains for greater self-control.

How to TEACH Values through Conscious Discipline

This book uses the acronym "TEACH" to organize the process for creating a classroom that lives its highest values and aligns itself with the school, program and district's mission statements. "To teach" means "to demonstrate." With our school culture, we must model the social-emotional skills and values we want our children to learn. If we, as adults, insist on bickering, gossiping or being condescending to those who disagree with us, then that is the character program we teach. If we build our classrooms around humiliating or shunning children who misbehave and "catching children being good" with the intent of manipulating their behavior, then that is the character program we teach. When we scream at children to be quiet, we teach that "losing it" is an acceptable way to get your needs met. If we choose to take a deep breath and respond assertively to a difficult situation, we teach that skill as well.

The behaviors we demonstrate with other adults and with the children in our care are the social skills we are teaching them. We often think that teaching is about "telling," not "demonstrating." When we are able to demonstrate through living our values, only then will we establish true character education and social-emotional learning in our schools. This is the reason we are using TEACH as the acronym around which to organize this book. The hope is that with the help of TEACH, we can create classrooms that demonstrate our highest values. The meaning of the acronym is as follows: T= Teaching Moments, E= Environmental Structures, A= Activities, C= Commitment, H= Helpful Resources.

T = Teaching Moments

The most powerful learning takes place in the moment of need. We create the School Family by seizing moments of joy to celebrate, moments of conflict to resolve, moments of helpfulness to honor and moments with friends to support. In academic terms, if students are excited about a space shuttle launch, a grasshopper someone found at recess or an upcoming presidential election, you would capitalize on that interest. You would create a space shuttle area in the classroom, read an "All about grasshoppers" book or hold mock debates about presidential platforms. These activities would fuel limitless opportunities for meaningful math, science, social studies and language arts experiences. Similarly, we will teach social-emotional skills as the opportunity arises. Visitors to the classroom, absent children, sick grandparents, name-calling and the joy of learning a new skateboard trick provide opportunities to teach meaningfully and in context. You will use each of these moments as teaching opportunities that bring life lessons into everyday classroom situations. The "Teaching Moments" section of each chapter focuses attention on potential teaching opportunities available and how you can transform these moments into life skills.

E = Environmental Structures

Each skill in Conscious Discipline is concretely represented in the classroom through one or more classroom structures. These structures are the heart of this book. They exist as the resources for your social-emotional curriculum. Just as you would provide resources like a magnifying glass or a microscope when teaching science, we also need materials to support our ability to live our values in the emotional arena. These structures are also essential to help you do the following:

- Remember to use your unique teaching moments.
- Demonstrate ways to use teaching moments for both you and your students.
- Provide an avenue for children to begin recognizing their own teaching moments.
- Prompt children to learn the skills necessary and to feel increased responsibility for living the values the school espouses.
- Integrate classroom management into your existing curriculum for a seamless approach to teaching the whole child.
- Bring joy and welcome life into the classroom for both you and the children.
- Create an environment that maximizes learning for all children.

A = Activities

Conscious Discipline is not a prescriptive program where you are given specific lessons in a linear fashion. For some teachers, this may feel uncomfortable at first. It sometimes seems easier to follow a curriculum that says "I will do this today" and to have a linear unfolding of activities that achieve stated objectives within a stated time frame. Conscious Discipline is different in that it teaches within the context of life (and research indicates learning in context is the most effective way to teach). The curriculum for Conscious Discipline is generated from the unique interpersonal interactions in your classroom, making it impossible to foretell what is needed on any given day. Instead of linear instructions, Conscious Discipline provides sample activities to jump-start your own creative teaching process. The activities in this section are designed for the specific age groups listed; however, I encourage you to read them all. An activity in a different age group may spark an idea you could use for your age group with a little creative tweaking. Use these activities, the information contained throughout this book and your own personal experience as the foundation for creating brilliant learning activities in your classroom.

= Commitment

There is a weight-loss saying that asks, "What diet works for you?" and the answer is, "The one you do." The same is true with Conscious Discipline. You will not see results without first taking action. You must build your School Family through action, not just by reading this book. To help you take action, each chapter will ask you to make a commitment. This commitment is yours to make in any way you choose.

Your commitment, in some chapters, may be to consciously choose to do nothing at this time. The point is to become conscious of your choice. It is empowering to know that you are in charge of whether you choose to change or you choose to leave things as they are for a while. If you choose not to take action, then by consciously focusing your brain on your choice, you are training yourself to take back your power. You may notice that you shift away from a victim approach or a need to make excuses for your inaction. We need to accept that it is equally okay to decide to move forward or to say, "My plate is full at this time."

Pay attention to your response to the commitments in this book. You may find yourself wanting to skip the section. This might indicate that you are afraid of your own power. You may find yourself making commitments you do not keep, which could indicate a desire to sabotage yourself. Or you may find yourself struggling over which commitment to make, which might indicate a need to be perfect. Your response to the commitments could, if you allow it, bring into your awareness a deeper understanding of how your thinking supports you or inhibits your success.

= Helpful resources

Each chapter will include helpful resources to support your journey. These resources will include literature, music and other items that will support the social-emotional learning discussed earlier in the chapter. Some of these items are available on our website: www.ConsciousDiscipline.com, but most can be purchased through your local bookseller or found on the Internet.

> **Teacher Tip:**
>
> The structures described in chapters 4-15 of this book work together to create a School Family. As you read, you will note that each chapter works fluidly in conjunction with the others, but is also designed to stand alone. The most effective way to use this book is the way that works best for you. You can read it cover to cover, or skip around to the structures you are curious about. Begin by implementing the structures you feel most drawn to, or begin with the ones you feel would be most helpful to your classroom. The key to success is to choose a chapter and commit to implementing the structure described within it.

The remaining chapters in this book detail the environmental structures of Conscious Discipline that will embed social and emotional awareness within your classroom management system in order to make true self-discipline possible. We start each new school year with getting to know our children and their families. This process is not just about learning their names, favorites foods and what they did over the summer. It is a year-long process that allows us to know them well enough to see the world from their perspective and offer guidance that best suits their individual development. As we begin the process of getting to know one another, we also have the opportunity to define our School Family. So, we will start with a simple, yet powerful structure called the Friends and Family Board.

Chapter 4

Friends and Family Board

Jerod was a fourth-grade boy labeled with high-functioning autism. Imagine yourself with weak focal vision and poor perception of three-dimensionality. Your hearing cannot filter extraneous noise. Your tactile system is so sensitized that it feels the air moving across your skin. When you enter school, you enter a space where someone may touch you, where lights and sounds assault you, and where you may be asked to do things your muscle tone and balance don't support (like sit up straight or walk slowly). Jerod faced many such challenges every day.

Jerod moved to a school in Arizona that was using Conscious Discipline. Fortunately, his teacher recognized his varied and constant upset behavior as a form of communication instead of insubordination or disrespect. His teacher was slightly knowledgeable about autism, but not enough to understand what Jerod needed to stay mentally organized. At the beginning of the year, she had created a School Family, so her classroom was a culture of compassion. She knew her class would open their hearts to Jerod and do what they could to include him and help him be successful. Even with the School Family's support, however, nothing seemed to help Jerod manage his overwhelmed feelings.

One night at an open house, the teacher took pictures of all the families that came, explaining they would be starting a Friends and Family Board at school. The Friends and Family Board would be a place in the classroom where children could post pictures of their loved ones. She began the project at the open house, but children could bring in additional pictures from home. The next day at school, Jerod, in a disorganized state of upset, saw his family's picture on her desk. He picked it up, put it to his chest and rocked gently. This soothed him and he was able to organize himself enough to function in the classroom. From that moment on, each time Jerod felt overwhelmed, he would get his family photo, hold it to his chest and rock gently in order to manage his sensory confusion.

How many of us carry pictures of those we love in our purse, wallet or phone? The wallpaper for my phone is a photo of my dog, Murphy. I see his cute little face beaming with unconditional love, and my heart melts. How many of us, when we organize our class or on the first day of a new job, find some small place for a picture of our family? I can't tell you how many classrooms I have visited where teachers don't have a space of their own, yet they find a place for a family picture on a file cabinet or in a hidden nook. It makes sense that if seeing images of our own family is important to us, we would provide the same opportunity for the children. When they enter a new classroom, whether at age two or ten, they need a place to display pictures of their family. They also need to be able to visit those photos and share them with their friends, just as we do. More than likely, they will be satisfied just knowing a picture is there; like our family's picture on the filing cabinet, we may not look at it daily, but the fact it's there is comforting.

Friends and Family vs. Don't Talk to Strangers!

Over the years, we've become obsessed with security. As a result, we've put in place a whole host of policies and procedures. One of those was the "Don't Talk to Strangers" approach for children. Security expert Bruce Schneier, in his book *Beyond Fear* (2003), stated, "I think 'don't talk to strangers' is just about the worst possible advice you can give a child. Most people are friendly and helpful, and if a child is in distress, asking the help of a stranger is probably the best possible thing he can do." This advice would have helped Brennan Hawkins, the 11-year-old boy who was lost in the Utah wilderness for four days. The parents said Brennan had seen people with horses and an ATV searching for him, but avoided them because of what he had been taught. "He stayed off the trail, he avoided strangers," Jody Hawkins said. "His biggest fear, he told me, was that someone would steal him." The National Center for Missing and Exploited Children (1991, 2005, 2010) never supported the "don't talk to strangers" message, mainly because their experience shows that most abducted children are taken by someone familiar to them. Most young children, when questioned, will describe a "stranger" as someone who is ugly or mean. They don't perceive "nice-looking" or friendly people as strangers. If someone talks to a child or is around a child more than once, that person loses his or her "stranger" status. Here is what we have learned from the "stranger danger" approach:

- Children don't get it
- Adults don't practice it
- It does not protect children
- It effectively eliminates a key source of help if a child is in trouble

So what does this have to do with the Friends and Family Board? We want to let children know that we get help from and give help to our friends and family. We focus on what we want children to do, not what we don't want to happen. We want to show them who actively supports their success in school, with pictures of the principal, the janitor, cafeteria people, and the speech pathologist on our Friends and Family Board. Rather than have children wondering, "Is this person a stranger?" we want them to see photos of all the people who support them—visual proof that the home family and the School Family are working together to help them be all they can be. As children grow in age, their circle of support grows with them. These messages are valued and concretely demonstrated by the Friends and Family Board.

The Power of Unity: The Extended Family Philosophy

In Conscious Discipline, the power of unity is demonstrated and experienced daily through the entity called the School Family. It symbolizes the fundamental principle that we are all in this together, from families to schools to communities to nations, and finally to our global community. Once we start to view a school as an extended family, we change the school culture and how we treat one another. Social bonding motivates children to live in harmony with the standards of the group. Look at the growth of the Internet in terms of such social networking sites such as MySpace and Facebook. Declaring our friends, posting them and staying connected is a need of all people of all ages. Filling this is exactly what the Friends and Family Board accomplishes in our classrooms.

Strong connections have been shown to prevent a wide variety of high-risk behaviors, including precocious sexuality, drug abuse and violence. Urie Bronfenbrenner (1979) put it simply: "Each child should have at least one person who is irrationally crazy about him or her." Archbishop Desmond Tutu (2002) said, "We must surmount the 'us and them' syndrome and learn to treat each person as part of our family." Native peoples throughout history have known the power of the tribe. Throughout time there have always been biological parents who are unable to fulfill their parenting ambitions. Today, there are large numbers of families whose parenting skills and resources are insufficient to meet the needs of their children. Schools and communities (both secular and spiritual) cannot afford to ignore their tribal responsibilities. There are no "throwaway" children. We cannot suspend and expel the children that challenge our own social and emotional intelligence. Every family has members that challenge the social order—weird Uncle Bob or cousin Pam, the drama queen. We must dig deep within ourselves to connect, understand and support all our family members. With each child who is marginalized, a new societal enemy is created. The Friends and Family Board helps connect all children to the School Family, and connects the School Family to the home family. There are no outsiders in our "tribe."

The Friends and Family Board is the classroom structure that represents one of our highest goals as educators, which is to support and strengthen children and families. The board is a visual that says, "We are partners in the educational process," for children, families and teachers. It sends children the message, "The people on this board are your home family who care deeply for you, and we are your School Family who also care deeply about you and your success." We want children to visually know that anytime they need reassurance, there is someone "irrationally crazy" about them.

Power of Unity: We are all in this together
Skill: Encouragement through noticing
Structure: Friends and Family Board
Value: Partnering with homes

The teaching moments with the Friends and Family Board are instantaneous, spontaneous and ever-present. The following stories and strategies demonstrate these moments.

In a small preschool class, several months after 9/11, a little girl and a teacher simultaneously began to tear up. It might have appeared that this was a random coincidence, but four-year-old Tyler knew what he was seeing. The little girl's father and the teacher's son had both been deployed to Afghanistan recently, and Tyler understood that they were missing their loved ones. Tyler walked over to his classmate and his teacher, grabbed both their hands, and said, "When I am missing my mommy, I go over to the Friends and Family Board and let her smile love at me." This moment of intuitive compassion from Tyler was a huge, comforting gesture for the little girl and the teacher. As the three of them walked to the Friends and Family Board, the School Family and the home family became true partners.

Mrs. Wells, a third-grade teacher, decided to put her Friends and Family Board on the wall by her Safe Place to provide children an opportunity to view their loved ones as a support for regaining composure. Madeline had just lost her mother in a tragic horseback-riding accident; her mother, an avid and talented rider, was thrown from a spooked horse. When Madeline returned to school, the Safe Place became her haven whenever sadness overwhelmed her. Madeline shared with her School Family that, as she is going through the day, sometimes things happen that make her think of her mom. She then goes to the Safe Place and looks at the picture of her family. She said, "Just knowing I could feel sad and be with my family when I need to helps me get through the day."

Mrs. Peck, a teacher of three-year-olds, makes home visits at the start of each school year. She takes her own Friends and Family Book with her to share with the families. She shows page after page of her family, her two children, their dog Ringo and the cat Droopy. As she shared with one family, the nervous mom relaxed and three-year-old Daquan pointed to the photos. A connection between the home family and the School Family had begun. After sharing her book with the new families, Mrs. Peck leaves a blank page with them so they can put pictures of their family on it and bring it to school. As the pages trickle in, Mrs. Peck binds them into a book that she "reads" during circle time. "Here is a picture of a little boy who has a mommy with brown hair, a

cat and . . ." It takes only seconds before someone giggles with delight and shouts, "It's me!" This is one of the most-read books in the class.

Teachers highlight these wonderful moments when the School Family becomes an extension of the home family through the encouragement skill of "noticing." Noticing is simply stating what you see without judging whether you believe the behavior or event is good or bad. Noticing is honoring and celebrating something as opposed to "catching children being good." Generally, the intention behind catching them being good is to have acceptable behavior repeated. Noticing, however, has the intention of honoring. It is about being present with children and truly seeing all their beauty. It does not use the moment as a tool to create more like it—it simply acknowledges it. It taps into the power of mindfulness and the gift of presence. In the above stories, the teacher might "notice" these events by saying:

"Tyler, you noticed your friend and your teacher were feeling sad. You saw the looks on their faces and tears in their eyes, so you helped them move over to the Friends and Family Board. That was caring."

"Madeline, you came to be with your family picture in the Safe Place. Sometimes just seeing them all together again helps your heart. You are taking care of yourself."

"You read our class Friends and Family Book. Your eyes looked at each picture like this (demonstrate with your eyes how they were tracking). Your finger pointed to many photos and you knew almost everyone's name. You care about your School Family."

For many teachers, the above skill of noticing is awkward at first. We tend to feel a strong urge at the end to say, "Good job" or "Thank you." We are so used to judgments that it is difficult just to notice. For those who find this almost impossible, end your sentence with "Good for you," "You did it" or "That was helpful (caring, kind, etc.)." You can read more about the skill of noticing in the *Conscious Discipline* book. (Bailey, 2000)

Finally, another important teaching moment is when new people enter the School Family. This could be the speech pathologist who comes once a week, the music teacher, a new student, or Juliana's aunt from Argentina who visits the classroom. Each of these provides an opportunity to put another picture on the Friends and Family Board. As children watch their Friends and Family Board grow, we plant the seed that we all belong to and are a part of something larger than ourselves.

E = Environmental Structure: The Friends and Family Board or Book

The brain is asking three important questions at all times: "Am I safe?" "Am I loved?" "What can I learn from this?" In order for children and teachers to focus their attention on question number three, the first two questions must be answered "yes." By having pictures of their family and friends present within the room, children are more likely to begin the slow process of answering the first two questions in the affirmative.

Purpose: The Friends and Family Board (or Book) is designed to help students get to know one another and to generate pictures of loved ones in order to link the home family and the School Family. Children begin to understand, very concretely, that they belong to something bigger than their family, their School Family, their community and their nation. They belong to the family of humanity, and they have more in common with others than they have differences.

How to set up the Friends and Family Board: Select a display space for this yearlong project. If wall space is not available, use a photo album or scrapbook. At Eton School in Mexico City, one teacher has each child bring in a framed picture of his or her family, then displays them on a countertop (similar to how they might be displayed at home). If you are an administrator, make a Friends and Family Board for your staff and faculty. These are often located in lounge areas, but I have seen them displayed in a hallway, where both children and their parents hover around it.

How to introduce the Friends and Family Board: The following ideas are for all ages and will help you introduce this structure to your students. The "Activities" section that follows contains age-specific ideas for your Friends and Family structure. Use these activities to spark your creative genius to customize and create new Friends and Family ideas of your own.

Chapter 4: Friends and Family Board

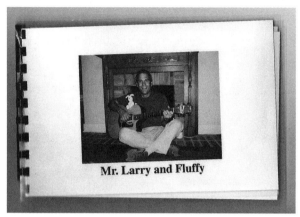

Create a photo album of your family and your life that you feel comfortable sharing with your students. One of the foundational aspects of Conscious Discipline is a willingness to give to others the actions and intent you hope to receive. You might also think of this as, "Don't ask others to do what you are not willing to do yourself." If you want children and families to be open and share with you, the best way to accomplish that is to be open and share with them. Communicate with them, and they are more likely to communicate with you. You may choose to share your album with students individually, at a morning meeting, at circle time or on home visits.

Start the year by taking pictures of children during home visits, open house or the first day of school. Post these photos on the Friends and Family Board or in a Friends and Family Book. Alternately, you might ask parents to send in pictures for the Friends and Family Board or ask them to create a family page for your School Family Friends and Family Book.

If money or access to a camera is an issue, be creative. If this structure resonates with you, then you will find a way to collect pictures. At Fern Creek Elementary School, 20 percent of the children are homeless, yet each year the teachers manage to obtain pictures of every family. One year, they arranged for a bus to pick up families from the homeless shelter and bring them to school for dinner and a children's music concert. Many pictures were taken at that time, and the Friends and Family Boards grew.

Let the children know by your example that the Friends and Family Board is a living entity in the classroom. The board grows as you and your students take trips, gain new siblings, move into new apartments, acquire new pets, visit cousins, and meet the principal in the school. Each visitor to the classroom becomes a new member of the family.

Many curriculum programs start off the year with an "all about me" theme or some form of getting to know one another. In the higher grades, this is replaced with social studies and science lessons, as children explore and discover family structures of animals and other cultures. The Friends and Family Board can be a jumping-off place for all these areas of study. By starting with what is already meaningful to children, you can create a natural bridge to other relevant curricula.

General Activities
All Ages

Family Show and Tell

Gather children and show them a picture of your family. Tell the children you want to introduce the School Family to your home family, then say, "Now let's meet everyone's home family." Let the children take turns showing their family pictures. Explain that you will display all the photos on the Friends and Family Board.

Shubert's New Friend

I wrote a series of books for children that demonstrate real-life emotional intelligence. In this book, a new friend is entering the classroom. The class prepares for the arrival by creating a greeting and taking a picture to put on the Friends and Family Board. The new friend looks different, and teasing and laughing follow. Help children learn to accept differences and welcome all people in the School Family. Discuss the importance of putting new students on your Friends and Family Board. Complete the corresponding Shubert worksheet, available for download at www.ConsciousDiscipline.com.

Puzzle People

Purchase puzzle-shaped people that fit together from www.reallygoodstuff.com, Oriental Trading Company or a similar source. Before giving each child a puzzle piece to decorate, glue his/her photo to the "head." Make sure you have a puzzle piece

Chapter 4: Friends and Family Board

for yourself as well. Gather children in the circle area and have them put the puzzle together. After it is assembled, explain to them that the School Family is like a puzzle. All the pieces fit together to complete the picture, just like we all fit together to create our School Family.

> **General Activities Younger (3-8 years)**

Placemat Collages

Have students bring in pictures of their family (or take photos as the parents drop them off). Assemble the pictures into a collage and laminate. The laminated collage becomes a placemat to use when the children have snacks or lunch. This is also a great activity to do at home for small children with families that live far away; it gives young children a chance to connect with grandparents, aunts, uncles and others they may not see on a regular basis.

Who Is This?

Ask parents to make a Friends and Family page for the class book including pictures that are meaningful for their child. During circle time or small-group time, share the pages and see if other classmates can guess who the page is about.

The People in Our School

It can be helpful to keep a magnetic board that holds photo magnets of the school staff. Remove magnetic photos as needed to assist students in recognizing staff members. For example, if a child is taking attendance to the office, you would remove the attendance clerk's photo and hand it to the child, saying, "This is Mrs. Justice. Please give the folder to her when you get to the office." If it is music day, place the music teacher's photo on the Morning Message Board or your Daily Routine Chart. When it's time to go to music, pass the music teacher's picture around the circle and say, "Mr. Bud is the Safekeeper during music."

> **General Activities Older (9-12 years)**

The Friends and Family Board becomes very personal with older children. Many times it is the "friends" portion that really hooks older students on the structure because they like to see themselves with their friends. When students arrive at school in the first few days of the term, take several pictures of children by themselves and with their friends. Make two copies of the single-student pictures, one to post on the Friends and Family Board and others to use with activities like the ones that follow.

Tell Me More

As students add pictures of their friends and family, have them write a family name with a few family traits. The traits could be something that is important to the family, the people included in the family, or things that represent the family. For example, "Smith": S̲miling, m̲ake good friends, i̲maginative, t̲houghtful, h̲appy."

Personal "Friends and Family" Files

Space is often limited in our classrooms. Many times we use file folders to make word walls, conversion charts and so on. Use one panel of a file folder to make a personal Friends and Family File. The students can use pictures from home or field trips to fill the file throughout the year. This type of file can also be placed on the computer, creating a School Family "Ourspace."

Defining Us

Have students brainstorm the definition of a home family and School Family. Combine these ideas into a class definition of a School Family to post in your classroom.

Who Am I?

Tape a picture from the Friends and Family Board onto each student's back. (Each student will have another student's image taped to them.) The students then move around the room, asking yes and no questions to see if they can guess who the friend is "on their back." Allow only a few minutes to ask questions, then ask them to write the name of the person taped to their back.

A variation of this activity is to choose one student to leave the room (the guesser), and then choose a picture from the Friends and Family Board (secret student). The guesser returns to the classroom and asks questions to the group to identify the secret student. You can include a time limit or a question limit for each student's turn, to move the game along more quickly.

Class-Made Books Younger (3-8 years)

Our School Family

Title this book "The (School Family name) School Family." Place a photo with the text "(child's name) is in our School Family!" on each page. The last page of this book will be a group photo with the text, "We are a family! The (School Family name) School Family." For example: "We are a family! The Buddy Bear School Family!"

My School Family

Use the song "My School Family" from the music CD *It Starts in the Heart* to create a class book. Your first page will be a group photo with the text, "This is my School Family." The other pages will include photos of children waving to a friend, shaking hands with a friend, giving a pinky hug to a friend, and giving a high five to a friend (to follow along with the words to the song). You will need eight photos of waving, six photos of shaking hands, four photos of pinky hugs and two photos of high fives. Show each child in one of the photos in addition to the group photo. Once the children are familiar with the song, they will read and sing it over and over again.

We Have a Friend

Draw a gingerbread man on a sheet of paper and photocopy it, with the following text printed underneath: "We have a friend who you all know and (name) is her/his name. Hello (name)!" Glue a photograph of each child's face onto the gingerbread person's head. Ask children to fill in their names and decorate the page by coloring in clothing, accessories and scenery. Laminate the pages, if possible, and assemble into a book.

Use this book as part of your Brain Smart Start to greet each child (see chapter 8). Read it every day for the first few weeks of school so the children get to know who is in their School Family. After they know the book well, take turns sending it home so each child can introduce the School Family to the home family. When a child is absent, change the last line when you read it aloud to "We wish you well (name). We will see you soon!" If someone leaves your School Family, change the last line to, "We wish you well (name). You're always in our hearts!"

Class-Made Books Older (9-12 years)

My Life in a Bag

Give each child a paper lunch bag. Have them place in the bag two things that are true about themselves and one that is not true. They can use pictures, sentence strips or actual objects (baseball, sewing kits, etc.). Have students present their bags to the rest of the class, and see if the others can guess what isn't true in each bag. Then, based on their bags, have students write a three-paragraph essay about themselves. "My name is _____ and I love to _____. I love it because_____." The last paragraph would be, "One thing I don't like/do is _____." Turn these essays into a class book titled "Betcha Didn't Know!"

Our School Family Name

(See Chapter 8) Have the students decide on a name for their School Family, for example, "Mrs. Abel's All Stars" or "The Eagles." Then create an acrostic with the name. Each letter will represent a value the class has or holds in high regard. For example, the name "Eagles" might be represented this way: Everyone together, always kind, good readers, loving classmates, eager learners, safety first. Use the name and acrostic to create a School Family flag or poster for the classroom door.

School Family Songs and Chants

The Friends and Family Board is the hub of the School Family, and the first step to defining your class as a School Family. As you become a family together, it is important for the class to create a School Family song or chant. All students can be involved in the conversation about how they would like their School Family to be and how they wish to define themselves.

It is helpful to provide younger children with chants and songs with prewritten words that reflect what you and your students want in the classroom. Older children can brainstorm their own class song or chant based on what they value. Do they want members who talk behind each other's backs or who speak directly to them? Do they want special groups of kids who are cool while others are left out, or do they want one team where everyone has each other's back?

Below are some songs and chants that can be used in younger classrooms, or as a starting point for intermediate students to create songs about what is important to them in their School Family. There is also a "Friendship Chant" on the music CD *It Starts in the Heart*. Young students can use this as their song, while older students can listen to it, then create their own chant using the instrumental version (also included on the CD).

My School Family
Tune: "You Are My Sunshine":
>You are my family, my School Family.
>I hope you know, friends, that I like you.
>It's great whenever we are together,
>When we're apart, I'll keep you in my heart.

We Are a School Family
Tune: "Mary Had a Little Lamb":
>We are a School Family, you and me, you and me.
>We are a School Family, we'll give a shout HURRAH!

Echo Chant:
>I don't know what you've been told (children echo)
>(Your School Family Name) are good as gold (children echo)
>We're a family that has heart (children echo)
>Each of us will do our part (children echo)
>(Say together): 1-2-3-4 We Care!
>1-2-3-4 We Care!

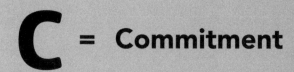

I am willing to see the world from the eyes of a child by constantly linking the home family with the School Family. I will creatively make this link concrete for my students by having a Friends and Family Board or Book.

Signature _____   Date _____

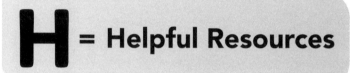

Music

All Ages

***It Starts in the Heart* by Jack Hartmann and Dr. Becky Bailey**
Songs: "My School Family," "I Wish You Well" (English and Spanish) "Friendship Chant," "Welcome," "People to People"

***I Love You Rituals, Vol. 2* by Dr. Becky Bailey**
Songs: "We Wish You Well," "Wonderful Woman," "I Like to Be with You"

***Brain Boogie Boosters* by The Learning Station and Dr. Becky Bailey**
Songs: "Greetings," "Friends Connect," "Team of Two"

***We Are Family* by Sister Sledge**
Song: "We Are Family"

Barney's Favorites, Vol. 1
Songs: "My Family's Just Right for Me," "I Love You"

World Playground **by Putumayo Kids**
Songs: All

Literature Younger (3-8 years)

***The Relatives Came* by Cynthia Rylant.** The relatives come to visit from Virginia and everyone has a wonderful time.

***The Keeping Quilt* by Patricia Polacco.** A homemade quilt ties together the lives of four generations of an immigrant Jewish family, remaining a symbol of their enduring love and faith.

***A Rainbow of Friends: A Book to Celebrate Diversity* by P. K. Hallinan.** Wonderful for exploring and accepting diversity.

***We All Sing with the Same Voice* by J. Philip Miller and Sheppard M. Greene.** This book comes with a music CD and is a great song to sign. You can look up the signs at www.aslpro.com

***The Family Book* by Todd Parr.** This book represents a variety of families, some big and some small, some with only one parent and some with two moms or dads, some quiet and some noisy, but all alike in some ways and special no matter what.

***The Two of Them* by Aliki.** Describes the relationship of a grandfather and his granddaughter from her birth to his death.

***Julius, the Baby of the World* by Kevin Henkes.** Lilly is convinced that the arrival of her new baby brother is the worst thing that has happened in their house, until Cousin Garland comes to visit.

Literature Older (9-12 years)

***The Other Side* by Jacqueline Woodson.** Two girls, one white and one black, gradually get to know each other as they sit on the fence that divides their town and hope someday there won't be a fence to sit on, just a field in which to play.

***The Five Chinese Brothers* by Claire Bish and Kurt Wese.** Shows how diverse families and the skills within them can be, and relates the idea that families stick together.

***You and Me Together: Moms, Dads and Kids Around the World* by Barbara Kerley.**

Represents diverse families from around the world, including maps showing where they live.

***The Moon by Night: The Austin Family Chronicles* by Madeleine L'Engle.** Explores the confusion and complexities of moving, faith and first love, all within the framework of a supportive family.

***Amelia's Road* by Linda Altman.** Tired of moving around so much, Amelia, the daughter of migrant farmworkers, dreams of a stable home.

Additional Aids

www.Orientaltrading.com* and *www.reallygoodstuff.com have project materials for creating a class photo or quilt, and large puzzle pieces that children can decorate and fit together into one large class puzzle.

www.Lessonplanspage.com is a site for free lesson plans on a wide selection of topics (most notably here, Social Studies), and a range of ages from preschool to high school.

www.Putumayo.com has a large selection of world music on CDs for children.

Chapter 5

The Safekeeper

Over a hundred children were evacuated from a preschool a few miles from the Pentagon on September 11, 2001. The smoke from the explosion at the Pentagon filled the school, threatening the children. The school was closed on September 12 and reopened again on the 13th. As the children entered the room that day, they said goodbye to their parents, who were still in shock, as was most of the country. One father said, "Thank God for your Safekeeper ritual. Our child had us put family pictures in a box last night to help remind us we were still safe." He hugged the teacher tightly and headed out the door. The children continued their morning routine. They placed their backpacks and other belongings into their assigned cubbies. Hanging in each child's cubbie was a ribbon necklace with a heart dangling from it, with the child's photograph inside the heart. The children removed their necklaces carefully and placed them around their necks.

Mrs. Beard started her day, like she always did, with her Safekeeper ritual. Carrying her treasure box ceremonially to circle time, she began by reviewing her job description for the day. She said, "My job is to keep you _____." The children hollered, "SAFE!" in response. Then making eye contact, smiling and pointing around the circle to as many children as possible, she called out, "And your job is _____." In unison they responded, "To help keep it safe." Mrs. Beard pulled out her treasure box, handling it like a precious family heirloom. "I have 20 beautiful treasures to keep safe. I'm going to keep Gianna safe, Jonathan safe, Carlie safe." On a typical day, the children would remove their necklaces and place them in the treasure box. This day, Mrs. Beard noticed children were clasping their Safekeeper necklaces and hesitant to put them in the box. One boy spoke up bravely and asked, "Can we keep our Safekeeper necklaces on today?" They collectively decided that is what they would do.

The above story shows our universal need to feel safe and the power of feeling safe. The felt sense of safety that so many Americans have been privileged to experience was assaulted on 9/11. Fortunately, these three-, four- and five-year-old children had a healthy coping strategy to help them pull through.

Whether we are conscious of it or not, we often consider that our job, when disciplining children, is to MAKE them behave properly. It is our job to control the children, to control our class, and to demonstrate that control to our advisers and others. If we fail to control the children, we are failures as teachers. Likewise, if, as parents, we fail to MAKE our children behave, we deem ourselves equally inadequate. But when we try to make a child behave, we give ourselves an impossible task. Take a moment to reflect: How successful have you ever been at making others do something? How often have you made a smoker quit smoking, a drinker quit drinking or an eight-month-old baby eat peas? When we attempt to MAKE or GET others to change, we end up relying on threatening, coercive or manipulative strategies. Generally, these are the same strategies the child is using. We end up in a power struggle with them, modeling the exact skills we are trying to eliminate. Conscious Discipline asks us to adopt a new, mindful job description for both the children and ourselves.

For younger children:
My job is to keep you safe.
Your job is to help keep it safe.

For older students:
My job is to keep you safe enough
to learn and be successful at school.

Your job is to help others feel safe enough
and supported enough to be successful at school.

In short, we seek to start the day and start the school year by focusing (or refocusing) ourselves and our students on safety and helpfulness instead of power and control. One of the many things I learned from 9/11 is the power of the perception of safety. In everyday life, relating behaviors in terms of whether they are safe or not is more effective than focusing on good or bad and right or wrong. Right and wrong, good and bad can change from household to household and from culture to culture. However, a felt sense of safety is universal, sacred and honored. It is a need we can all relate to. It is not just for preschool classrooms; as we experienced after 9/11, it is for all of us.

Mr. Giovanni, a fifth-grade teacher, has a basket by his classroom door. Beside the basket are Popsicle sticks the students have decorated with their best graffiti art. Each morning, students put their personal sticks in the basket as they enter the room. He uses this procedure to take attendance and for his Safekeeper ritual. After announcements, he holds up the basket and says, "I promise to keep you safe enough to learn and be successful today. As members of our School Family, you have agreed to help keep it safe. Take a moment right now to think about what you will do today to help others."

Of course, saying we will keep our children safe and being able to consciously do so requires effort. Historically, we have considered safety in schools only in terms of physical needs, such as covering electrical outlets, screening for weapons and conducting fire drills. We have only recently begun to look at safety in terms of the social, emotional and psychological needs of the children and each other. Most of us, raised on judgment and external rewards, believe on some level that to be safe we must get everyone to like us, approve of us or agree with our opinions. We can, however, choose to pass on a different set of governing beliefs to the children in our care. We now recognize that classroom safety ultimately requires the following from us:

- A willingness to take 100 percent responsibility for our own upset instead of blaming others for "making" us act or feel in certain ways.
  Instead of saying: "Look how you made her feel!"
  We could say: "See her face. Her face is saying, 'Ouch! Touch me gently'"

- A willingness to accept each moment as it is now instead of demanding it should be different.
  Instead of saying: "What should you be doing right now?"
  We could say: "It's time for math, open your book to page 12."

- A willingness to understand that our perception of an event dictates our emotional state and our actions.
  Instead of perceiving: "He is just a mean bully who hits for no reason!"
  We could perceive: "He has no idea how to make friends and needs my help to achieve that goal."

- A willingness to focus on what you want instead of what you don't want.
  Instead of saying: "Stop tugging on her hair! Do you want to lose recess?"
  We could say: "When you want your friend's attention, touch her gently on the arm like this and say her name."

- A willingness to understand that the only person we can MAKE change is ourself.
  Instead of thinking: "What would MAKE my child finish her homework?"
  We could think: "How can I help my child be successful at completing her homework?"

- A willingness to be conscious of our intent and mindful of our actions as we interact with each other and ourselves.
  Instead of thinking: "He will pay for this. I am doing this for his own good!"
  We could think: "My upset is not about the child at all. I feel tired and run down and need to take a moment so I can help my child, not hurt him."

- A willingness to expand our minds enough so that we grasp the notion that we literally are all connected to one another.
  Instead of saying: "Leave him alone. You focus on your own self. He doesn't need your help!"
  We could say: "You offered your friend some help with her work so she could be successful. That was helpful. I am going to show you how to help her without you doing all her work."

The Power of Being Brain Smart: Understanding the Impact of Stress on Learning

Conscious Discipline is based on a simple brain-state model that demonstrates what happens within our brains when we feel threatened or stressed. In stressful situations, the higher centers of the brain shut down, and blood flow is redirected to the survival systems. This shift of blood flow is conducive not for learning but for fighting (defiance) or fleeing (withdrawing). Many children come to school with their survival systems up and running. For those children, we must help them feel safe enough to let down their guard in order to access the higher centers of their brains for learning. Other children find the academics or social issues at school threatening. These students also need our help to feel safe enough and connected enough to risk making mistakes on their road to success. The remaining children arrive at school ready to learn, and they need only our encouragement to stay on track.

In general terms, children come to school in one of three states, and the state they arrive in depends on how their day begins with their family or during the ride to school. Each brain state can be represented by one of three questions:

- **Some children come to school asking, "Am I safe?"** These are the difficult children. They have armored themselves with defense systems meant to protect them from a world they perceive is full of threats, betrayal and loss. They may come in fighting, pushing, defiant, oppositional or shut down. These children bring their symbolic weapons (defiance) to class because they believe they need these skills to stay safe throughout the day.

- **Some children come to school asking, "Am I loved?"** and spend the day seeking attention or approval. Their energy is not focused on math or other subjects. Instead, they arrive with a need to be seen, and spend their learning energy on attempts to get the teacher or other children to focus on them.

- **Some children come to school asking, "What can I learn?"** These children come with a brain that is integrated and ready to optimize the day at school.

Faculty and staff also arrive at school in one of these three states, asking some form of the same three questions. On some days, one question is more prevalent than another. So, how do we meet the social and emotional needs of both children and teachers? We do it by creating classrooms based on safety, connection and problem solving. We shift from a simple "rules and consequences" paradigm to a whole-child approach to classroom management.

The brain functions optimally when a person feels safe and adequately challenged, thus we begin creating the School Family by focusing on safety. Once safety is established, connection and engagement are possible. Think of this in your own life. As adults, when we are feeling unsafe, we retreat from the world. We seek out our "safety people" to reassure us and help us process our anxiety. If we are without safety people, we generally retreat into some form of addiction. We may choose overworking, binge eating, obsessive cleaning, excessive drinking, grueling workouts or other ways to temporarily refocus our anxiety. We reduce our engagement with life, hunker down in our addictions, and learning and problem solving take a back seat until we return to stable ground. Once we feel safe enough to risk engaging, we then move back into the world and are willing to learn new ideas or solve problems as needed. The same is true for children; however, children generally have not developed addictive coping strategies, so their behavior becomes a cry for help. Our goal is to create a felt sense of safety by hearing the cry for help, decoding the message and meeting the underlying need, so the children's development can continue and learning can succeed.

A school built on safety and connection provides a climate where problem solving can flourish. In a School Family, a child who pushes another child to be first at the water fountain feels safe and connected enough to learn to say, "I'm super thirsty, may I get a sip?" The child who was pushed is more willing to learn to respond with, "No, please wait until I'm done." Without a safe, connected School Family, the above is not possible because the willingness factor is missing. The child is more likely to respond to your coaching with, "I'm not asking him anything! I was here first!" And on the slim chance you could entice the pushed child to say, "Please wait 'til I'm done," the words would likely fall on deaf ears or earn bullying on the playground later. A safe classroom paves the way for a connected classroom. Connection is the key to willingness, and willingness is the gateway to all learning and problem solving.

Power of being brain smart: The brain functions optimally when we feel safe
Skill: Languages of safety
Structure: Safekeeper ritual
Value: Equality

T = Teaching Moments

The classroom or school offers many opportunities to create a felt sense of safety for students, families and staff. The major teaching moments can be classified into three areas: Modeling active calming, starting your year and using the language of safety.

Modeling Active Calming

The most powerful teaching moments always are the result of your ability to model the skills you want your children to demonstrate. For you to model safety, you must be vigilant in self-regulating your own emotional states. In Conscious Discipline, I call this "active calming" and begin teaching it with the simple phrase, "Be a S.T.A.R." "Be a S.T.A.R." for children means they are to Smile, Take a deep breath And Relax. The type of deep belly breathing fostered by being a S.T.A.R. shuts down the stress response. For adults, active calming involves more than the simple act of deep belly breathing. Adults must create a truly coherent moment where our energetic state, nonverbal expressions and words are in alignment. Children know when we are faking it. They sense when our words don't match our tone of voice, nonverbal body position and facial expression. Everyone has had the experience of saying, "You seem upset," only to hear the person bark back, "I'm fine!" This misalignment is frustrating for adults and extremely confusing for children. When our mind, body, tone and words do not align, children don't know what or who to trust. If we are going to provide safety for children, we must be able to truly calm ourselves and access a peaceful, contented inner state to meet the challenge at hand.

To actively compose yourself, Conscious Discipline offers a three-step process:

1. Be a S.T.A.R.: Take three deep breaths before you begin to speak.
2. Affirm to yourself, "I'm safe. Keep breathing. I can handle this."
3. Wish well: Open your heart to the moment. Let go of your belief that this is about you, be willing to recognize the child is calling for help and wish the child well.

There will be times when you forget all of the above and find yourself blaming others for your upset, demanding things go your way and trying to stop behavior (instead of using it to teach). As soon as you recover, forgive yourself. Let go of those moments. Regain composure, say "Oops," share your processes with the children, and move on. Sharing your process out loud turns it into a teaching moment by refocusing on the behavior you want to see from both the children and yourself. Take ownership of your actions, and share what happened internally. Through modeling, this will help the children recognize their own internal processes and take responsibility for their own actions. It might sound something like this: "I was just yelling at you to sit down and be quiet. I felt frustrated that you were not listening to me. I forgot to be a S.T.A.R. and blamed you for my upset. I am in charge of me, and I am back on track now. Put your hands on your shoulders and take a deep breath with me. As you inhale, raise your elbows up. As you breathe out, lower your elbows down slowly. Now, let's start over."

Starting Your Year

How you start your year sets the tone of your classroom. You could start off in a very traditional manner in which you cover the rules or create them together with the students. Then you generate the consequences to those rules. The focus rests on what will happen to you if you break the rules. Conscious Discipline asks you to start off the year by living and replicating the democratic process. You start by clearly defining what a felt sense of safety would be like for all students. What would safety look like, sound like and feel like? From this foundation in safety, the class creates principles to live by. You will visually represent the principles in the classroom as a constant reminder of your commitments. The rest of the year, your goal is to model and teach the concrete behaviors that empower class members to live those principles. In this manner, the focus rests on learning how to help one another succeed, rather than on what happens when you fail.

Imagine two classrooms. Classroom A uses the traditional job description of teachers that silently states, "It is my job to make you behave." Classroom B starts off with the Conscious Discipline job description that openly states, "It is my job to keep you safe. And it is your job to help keep it safe." Classroom A starts off the year based on a prescribed system of rules and consequences, and Classroom B begins with a focus on safety and helpfulness. The two scenarios are laid out below. As you read, think about the possible long-term ramifications of these beginnings.

Classroom A: The Traditional Start

Mrs. Bartlet began her year in kindergarten just as she had for the past 22 years. She had the children sit on the circle rug to begin introducing them to the class discipline system.

"Welcome, boys and girls, to kindergarten. I am your teacher, Mrs. Bartlet. We are going to have a wonderful year together. You are big boys and girls now, and will learn many things in school. To help you learn and have good days at school, we have an apple tree. The apple tree is filled with apples. Your name is on one of the apples. To have a good day, you will need to listen to Mrs. Bartlet and do what I say. If you follow the rules, your apple will stay on the tree. If you do not follow the class rules, your apple will fall. If it falls to a lower branch, you will not be able to do some fun things. If it falls on the floor I will have to call your parents. How many of you want to keep your apple high on the tree and listen to Mrs. Bartlet?" Some hands are raised, some children point to themselves and others just sit and stare off into space. As the day continues, she explains the rules such as, "Listen when others speak" and "Use gentle hands."

When Juliet came home from kindergarten that day, the first thing she said to her mother was, "My apple is on the tree!" Followed by, "Jason's apple is on the floor." Her mother didn't have a clue what she was talking about, so she responded with what most moms of young children do in that situation. She nodded and replied, "Umm-hmm, honey."

Classroom B: The Conscious Discipline Start

Mr. Slawson gathers his kindergarten children on the circle-time rug. Each child is sitting on a different-colored square. He begins by saying, "Welcome to kindergarten. My job is to keep you safe at school. Your job is going to be to help me keep it safe. You will help me keep the classroom safe by being kind and helpful to each other. Each morning we will remind ourselves of this very important job by doing our Safekeeper ritual. You each have a Popsicle stick with your picture and a star on the top. I have a treasure box. All of you are my treasures for this whole year, and you are all a part of our School Family. Every morning I will ask you if you're willing to do your job to help keep our School Family safe. If you're willing to help me, you will put your stick in the treasure box. When I shut the box and hold it to my heart, that means I will do my job."

Logan came home from his first day of school and said to his mom, "My teacher is going to keep me safe and I can help him. Today I helped by pushing in my chair."

The start of your school year will set the stage either to divide the class into "good" and "bad" kids or to foster a classroom where children are seen as whole and equal. Taken to a higher level, one model supports the United States Constitution's affirmation of every person's rights and equality, and the other actually undermines its potential. In classroom A, we teach cognitively concrete children to divide the world into two categories, the good guys and the bad guys. The good guys have their apples on the tree and the bad guys have their apples on the floor. In kindergarten, apples and the teacher's judgment define the categories. We don't realize it, but we are training the children to categorize people as either valuable or unworthy. Later, these people will be cognitively known as "better thans" and "less thans." By high school, we have effectively trained children to separate out their own "better thans," whether they be the slender, pretty people, people of a certain race, peers with expensive "stuff," and more. The "less than" category will also be filled with certain people, and thanks to the apple tree approach, we have taught children that it's okay to deprive the "less thans" of certain privileges. You can structure a class that is divided or one based on safety, equality and helpfulness.

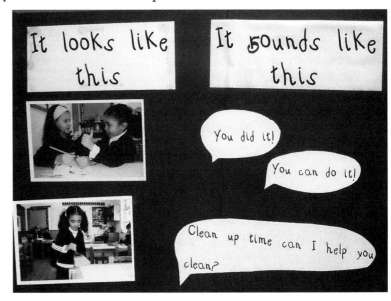

Start your year based on safety and helpfulness. Brainstorm with the children what safety would look like, sound like and feel like. The brain learns best through contrast, so give students contrasting examples. Have one student grab something from another. Ask the class to reflect, "Is this behavior safe? Is this behavior helpful?" Then replay the scene with the student saying, "May I look at your pencil?" instead of grabbing it. Now, ask the class to reflect on this scene. Ask your students, "What type of classroom do you want, one that encourages grabbing things or asking for a turn?"

Creating the Language of Safety: Commands and Verbal Reminders

In our classrooms, we have a choice to rely on the language of fear and separateness or the language of safety and helpfulness. In Conscious Discipline, the language is one of safety and helpfulness. When we say, "Our job is to keep the children safe," we must back that up with our words and actions. When we say, "The child's job is to help keep it safe," we must coach the child to develop the skills necessary for being helpful. There are many opportunities to use the language of safety and helpfulness throughout the day, but the main place we can use this language is in our commands.

Most classrooms rely on the language of fear. This language can be as obvious as, "Do you want to go to the office? Keep up that behavior and that is exactly what will happen!" We might hear, "If you want time on the computer today, you'd better sit still and get your work done." Or we might use subtle fear statements such as, "I like the way Antonia is sitting," which implies, "If you please me, I will like you. If you don't please me, I won't." In a similar vein, we use the language of separateness instead of unity. Often we hear, "Do your own work," "Keep your hands to yourself," and "Mind your own business." Certainly, we want children to use their own skills to complete their work, we want them to learn how to interact with others without hurting them, and we want them to be conscious of their own thoughts, feelings and actions; however, the above language does not achieve those goals. It simply separates without providing an alternative, positive skill. Using the language of fear and separateness sets you up as judge, jury and punisher, teaching children to do the same.

The language of safety, on the other hand, relies on unity and helpfulness as a frame of reference. The following demonstrates the contrast between using the language of fear or the language of safety:

Language of fear and separation	Language of safety and unity
If you don't put time into your homework, your grades will drop.	Your homework tonight will take at least 45 minutes to complete. Think about when you will do it. What materials will you need? Where will you do it? Turn to your partner and share your answers.
If you want to have time on the computer, you'd better get started on this work.	What would help you get started on your class work? Do you need to discuss some of the questions? Do you need help from a friend?
Keep your eyes on your own paper.	If you have questions or need help, raise your hand.
Walking feet, walking feet, walking feet!	Walk in the classroom just like this (demonstrate), so you are safe and so is everyone else.
Stand up, push your chair in and line up.	Stand up, push your chair in so everyone can walk safely, and line up.

E = Environmental Structure: Safekeeper Box & Ritual

The environmental structure for the Safekeeper is the Safekeeper box and representative figurines for each child.

Purpose: The Safekeeper box is a container that holds the individual class members' commitment to safety and helpfulness. It holds, in symbolic form, that which is precious and sacred to the success of all.

How to set up your Safekeeper ritual: For young children, the Safekeeper box could be designed to look like a treasure chest. Older children can come up with a container they can relate to. One third-grade classroom decided to use a toy replica of a combination safe. They decided that if the point was to "keep each other safe," then an actual safe would be the best symbol to use. Whatever container you or your class decides upon, it only needs to be large enough to hold each student's representative figurine or picture. The only criterion for the box is that it is worthy of holding valued treasures: your students.

You will also need symbolic representations of each child to put in the box. Children can create their own Safekeeper piece or you can supply them for the class. You or your students will want to agree on a type of representative figure, and then create your own unique pieces. Below are some ideas.

- **Photos:** Take a picture of each child in the class. Cut the photo in a circle and glue it in the middle of a star shape. Children can decorate the star. If you have access to a die-cut machine, you can punch out stars, circles or your class mascot.

- **Clothespin people:** Purchase wooden clothespins and stands from a craft store. First, make arms by wrapping a chenille wire (5" length) around the part of the clothespin that indents. Cut a small piece of cloth (4"x1½") with a slit in the middle so it can go over the top of the clothespin to make the shirt. Tie yarn around the middle. Take pictures of the children and print out their faces about one-inch tall. Cut out the faces and glue them to the top part of the clothespins. Place the clothespin in the stand.

- **Stand-ups:** Make full-body stand-ups of each child by taking a photo (fun poses make for interesting displays). Cut out the picture along the outline of each child and laminate. Use large binder clips (from an office supply store), and attach each photo to a binder clip "stand."

> **Teacher Tip:**
>
> - Place a copy of your Safekeeper song or chant in the Safekeeper box for the substitute to use when you are absent.
>
> - Make a book showing what it looks like when your School Family does this ritual. Students can "check out" the book to take home to their family. This also supports the students as they explain the ritual to substitute teachers, and allows the substitute to see exactly what the ritual entails.
>
> - After the first week, assign a student the job of placing the figurines or photos on display for the next day as part of your dismissal routine.
>
> - As the year progresses, add additional commitments to the process, such as "I will keep it safe at school today by pushing in my chair" or "I will keep it safe at school by being a S.T.A.R. when I'm angry and going to the Safe Place." Vary these a little to keep it from becoming an automatic and unconscious process.

The Safekeeper box and the representative figurines become the foundation for the Safekeeper ritual. Use this ritual to start the day by focusing both you and your students on what is most cherished and most important for a successful day of learning—safety. The Safekeeper ritual can be done in many ways. The ultimate goal is for the students and the teacher to consciously place their representative figurine into the Safekeeper box while making a commitment to help keep the classroom a safe place to learn. Many classrooms combine this process with attendance taking, and thus accomplish two goals with one procedure. The key to the process is to consciously commit. In the Activities section below, you will read different ways teachers have introduced and conducted this very important ritual.

At the end of each day, you will need to remove the symbolic figures from your Safekeeper box and display them for the students to access the next morning. This task can be assigned to a student by including it as a classroom job on your School Family Job Board. (See Chapter 11)

How to introduce your Safekeeper ritual: At the beginning of the year each student will select the symbolic representation of him or herself to place in the box every day. If you use an abstract representation, ask students to share why they choose their particular item.

At the Conscious Discipline Institute, we set out small objects such as animals, cars, trucks and superheroes as symbolic selections for attendees. On the first day, each attendee selects an object or animal that best represents him or her at that specific time in life. Sometime during the first day, participants take a moment to share with one another why they chose the figurine they did. The year my mother died, I selected a golf club because she loved golf. The next year I selected a fish because I had recently gone scuba diving on the Great Barrier Reef in Australia. Young children benefit from more realistic images because these images are more meaningful to them. Teachers of young children often attach a photo of each child's face to a wooden craft stick or attach a photo of their whole body to a binder clip.

Once children have chosen their figures, begin a discussion about safety and commitments as described earlier in this chapter. Teach the job description "My job is to keep it safe. Your job is to help keep it safe," and talk about what being safe looks like, feels like and sounds like. Introduce your Safekeeper ritual, and conduct one or more of the activities below to support children's understanding of this structure.

A = Activities

General Activities — All Ages

The Safekeeper Ritual

At the start of the day, during a group meeting, your Brain Smart Start or a specific moment designed for it, conduct the Safekeeper ritual with your class. You may want the children to be responsible for bringing their figurines with them, or you may bring all the pieces and the Safekeeper box with you.

Begin the ritual with a chant or song. There is a "Safekeeper" song on the *Kindness Counts* CD. Some teachers create their own chants and poems. Older children will be able to compose their own class chant, rap or song, and the motions to go with it.

Younger (3-8 years)
Welcome to our School Family.
Guess who I am?
I'm the Safekeeper, I am, I am.
My job is to keep you safe.
Your job is to help keep it that way.
Oh _____, oh _____,
We're going to have a great day.
(written by Sara Simpson)

Or

I'm the Safekeeper, that is me.
My job is safety, you will see.
You have a job that's important, too.
Be safe with your friends, they'll be safe with you.

We sing our "School Family" song.

We put our safe selves in the Treasure Box.

Older (9-12 years)
Tune: "We Will Rock You" by Queen
We are a School Family.
You will keep it safe here.
Our job is to help you.

As you sing your song or directly afterward, invite each child to place his or her representative figurine in the box. End the ritual by ceremoniously closing the box and setting it in a safe place.

Commitment Posters

After introducing the concept of the Safekeeper, discuss the importance of making and maintaining commitments. Talk about how each person in the School Family helps promote and protect the principle of safety in the classroom. Guide the discussion so students are able to see the many ways that safety is upheld, both physically and emotionally. On a large poster, write down the statements children generate in the discussion. As you write, begin each statement with the phrase, "I am willing to _____." Ask students to think about what they can commit to as part of the safety team. As each student feels ready, have him or her sign the class commitment poster. If students choose, they can also add a specific way in which they plan to support safety. Display the poster in your room so that students are reminded daily of the importance of being on the class safety team.

Venn Diagrams

Divide the children in your class into three to six groups, depending on the size of the class. Have each group look at a different aspect of safety. One group will record the "look" of safety, another the "sound" of safety and the last will find words to describe the "feel" of safety. Once you have the lists, add them to a Venn diagram. Do the same with the aspects of helpfulness.

Another Venn diagram that is great to do with safety is to focus on activities that are safe at school, those not safe at school and those in the middle: For older students, things that are safe at school might be including others in our School Family, taking care of younger students and choosing to take a break when feeling upset. School activities that are not safe would be gossiping, forming cliques, modeling behaviors that are not "leadership" behaviors, and so on. Some "in the middle" activities include choosing not to play with someone sometimes or choosing to "pass" on an activity.

Taking It Global

Discuss the relationship between unsafe classrooms and community violence. Ask questions such as:

> If our classroom is not safe, what kinds of things might you see?
> If our neighborhood is not safe, what kinds of things might you see?
> If our country is not safe, what kinds of things might you see?
> If our world is not safe, what kinds of things might you see?

Shubert Rants and Raves

Shubert wants life to go his way and rants and raves when he can't make that happen. Mrs. Bookbinder, his teacher, remains the Safekeeper as she gently supports Shubert while he calms and learns he is strong enough to manage the upsets in his life. After reading the book, discuss the different ways Mrs. Bookbinder keeps the classroom safe, the ways the rest of the class help keep it safe and how Shubert will choose differently next time so he can help keep it safe. Ask your class, "What can I do as the Safekeeper to help you feel safe?" Complete the corresponding Shubert worksheet, available for download at www.ConsciousDiscipline.com.

Class-Made Books — All Ages

You Are Safe

In addition to the Safekeeper ritual, it is important for children to experience the power of being held in safety throughout the day. Create a class book titled "You Are Safe in Your School Family" that reinforces the message of safety. Take a photograph of each child. Give younger children a sheet of paper to decorate that says, "(Child's name) is a treasure to our School Family. We will help keep him/her safe." Ask older students to print "My job is to help our School Family feel safe, sound safe, and look safe" on their page, and write about ways they will help keep the classroom safe. Attach each child's photograph to his/her page and bind them together into a book. The book can be kept next to the Safekeeper box or in your book center.

Choose Wisely

Create a book titled "Choosing Wisely" that depicts the choices children can make to stay safe. As a class, brainstorm common situations where we can choose between safe and unsafe. Include both physical and emotional scenarios. Write two choices, "safe" and "unsafe," for each situation on separate sheets of paper. For example, "It is unsafe to leave the class without telling the teacher." "It is safe to check with the teacher before leaving the room." Let children add their own illustrations. Bind the pages into a book, with the two choices facing inward toward each other.

My Teacher Keeps Me Safe

Just as children are held accountable for helping the classroom run safely, the teacher is responsible to the children to create a safe school culture. In order to do this she/he must know what is expected from the children's point of view. Create a book titled "My Teacher Is the Safekeeper" where children have the opportunity to fill in sentence starters like "I want my teacher to keep me safe by _____. I feel scared at school sometimes when _____."

Music & Movement — All Ages

Safekeeper Song

Play the "Safekeeper" song on the *Kindness Counts* CD by Dr. Becky Bailey and Mr. Al and conduct the movements as described in the song. Point to girls when it says, "She's a Safekeeper," to boys when it says, "He's a Safekeeper," and have children hug themselves when it says the word, "safe."

C = Commitment

I am willing to consciously accept my new job description as the Safekeeper in the classroom. I profoundly acknowledge that the safety of the children is directly related to my being able to maintain a peaceful, composed inner state. With this information I dedicate myself to practice active calming.

Signature _____   Date _____

H = Helpful Resources

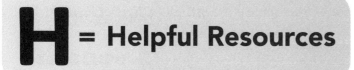

Music

***Kindness Counts* by Dr. Becky Bailey and Mr. Al**
Songs: "Safekeeper," "Love Is a Circle," "We All Count," "Encouraging Words"

***It Starts in the Heart* by Jack Hartmann and Dr. Becky Bailey**
Songs: "I Wish You Well," (English and Spanish) "Friendship Chant," "All Together" (English and Spanish)

***I Love You Rituals, Volume 1* by Dr. Becky Bailey and Mar Harman**
Song: "Georgie Porgie"

***I Love You Rituals, Volume 2* by Dr. Becky Bailey**
Songs: "We Wish You Well," "I'm a Helpful Person," "Three Nice Mice"

***Brain Boogie Boosters* by The Learning Station and Dr. Becky Bailey**
Songs: "Watch Me Listen," "Peace Like a River," "It's a Marvelous Day"

Literature — Younger

***Don't Fidget a Feather* by Erica Silverman.** Duck and Gander challenge each other to a "freeze-in-place" contest, but must decide whether personal safety is more important than winning the competition.

***I Know a Lady* by Charlotte Zolotow.** Sally describes a loving and lovable old lady in her neighborhood and shares why the children gather at her place, where they experience acceptance and safety.

***Mr. George Baker* by Amy Hest.** Harry sits on the porch with Mr. George Baker, an African American who is 100 years old but can still dance and play the drums; they are waiting for the school bus that will take them both to the class where they are learning to read.

***They Didn't Use Their Heads* by Jo Ann Stover.** In a lighthearted fashion, this book points out how our actions and choices have negative and positive effects, and that consequences will follow suit.

Literature — Older

***What to Do When You Worry Too Much: A Kid's Guide to Overcoming Anxiety* by Dawn Huebner.** This interactive self-help book is designed to guide 6-to 12-year-olds and their parents or teachers through the cognitive-behavioral techniques used to treat generalized anxiety.

***Trouble Talk* by Trudy Ludwig.** Maya gets help from a school counselor when the new student she has tried to befriend upsets her by spreading rumors, saying hurtful things and sharing information that is not hers to share.

***Stand Tall, Molly Lou Melon* by Patty Lovell.** Even when a classmate is hurtful and makes fun of her at school, Molly remembers what her grandmother told her and she feels good about herself.

***Friendship Rules* by Peggy Moss.** Alexandra tells one of her best friend's most important secrets in an effort to be accepted by a cool new girl at school, then realizes what she's lost and seeks to rebuild her friendship.

Teacher Tip:

Knowing what safety looks like, feels like and sounds like is the key to success.

Chapter 6

Visual Rules and Routines

Years ago I had the privilege to work with the Native American Pueblo of Acoma in New Mexico. Through a series of unbelievable synchronistic events while on vacation, I was offered a job by the tribe. Although honored to be one of the few white people hired by the Tribal Council, I was completely ignorant of our cultural differences and felt unqualified to run their Parent Child Development programs. Most important, I had a wonderful paying job on the East Coast, lived in a community with supportive friends and had a very settled relationship with my significant other. I was not going to move two thousand miles from all this to live in the middle of nowhere. Yet somehow, overlooking an ancient valley with Acoma City on the right and the Enchanted Mesa on the left, I knew this move was part of my destiny. As much as I fought it, on a deep level I knew I would take the job and leave a very good life behind.

During the first six months of the job, I felt completely overwhelmed. Everything was new including the language, the values and the cultural practices. I knew nothing about the Acoma people, except the stereotypes and bias I had learned in school and through the media. I thought for weeks that their outdoor adobe ovens were doghouses. I kept wondering why they loved dogs so much and where these dogs were hiding because I never saw them. Needless to say, my learning curve was huge and my anxiety was high. My brain kept looking for meaningful patterns and all I could find were doghouses without dogs.

As time went on, I felt more secure and confident. Eventually, the daily routines provided my brain with necessary patterns that reduced my anxiety enough to extrapolate some cultural nuances of behavior. Through this, new learning occurred, and I became less unconsciously offensive to those I served and more successful in my new endeavor. As I look back, I can see events from the tribe's perspective. From their view, I could easily have been perceived as disrespectful, hyperactive and a slow learner as I struggled to make sense of their culture that was so different from my own. How many children who come to school, unable to pick up the patterns of school life, are also seen in a negative light as they struggle to make sense of a school culture that is different from their home culture?

My story parallels what happens to children when they enter school. It shows how the brain needs predictable routines in order to process new learning. The brain is a pattern-seeking and a pattern-making device. Our perceptual system is bombarded daily with billions upon billions of bits of information. Paying attention to all this information simultaneously could literally drive us crazy. Instead, our brain allows what is familiar (the pattern) to become background, so new information (learning) can be processed in the foreground.

Ninety-nine percent of all learning is nonconscious (Jensen, 2005). Our conscious and nonconscious processing systems work together for optimal learning. The shifting of information from novelty (right hemisphere) to routine (left hemisphere) is the cornerstone of learning (Goldberg, 2002). When you first learn to drive, everything requires a conscious thought and action. Now, however, you can probably drive home at night without ever remembering that you turned on the headlights. The same is true for children. When children first enter school, everything is novel. As days pass predictably and consistently, most children will eventually be able to function without much conscious effort to figure out where to put their backpacks or how new worksheets will be distributed. This leaves the higher centers of their brains free to take in new information.

Routines, also called procedures, are essential to building the School Family. They form the skeleton that supports the School Family and provides the structure for its success. They provide us with a felt sense of safety and the opportunity to access the higher centers of our brain. An essential part of our job as the Safekeeper is to structure classrooms with predictability and consistency. It is our job to understand the complexity of our classrooms, break down the day into regular routines and actively teach these routines to our students. It is important to shift from trying to control children to structuring the learning environment. That shift can begin when we understand the differences between rules and routines.

Rules Versus Routines

There is a difference between rules and routines. A rule seeks to regulate behavior or stop misbehavior. Rules are enforced. A broken rule delivers a specific consequence, which is meant to eliminate the behavior. A routine, however, is simply the way you expect something to be done. It is a procedure that, when followed, brings order and predictability to the classroom. Routines are taught. By confusing rules and routines, we create inconsistency in the classroom and the school. Often teachers have a set of rules that look like the following:

Older:
- Follow directions
- Complete work on time
- Respect fellow classmates
- Raise your hand and wait to be called on
- Stay on task
- Respect other people's property
- Always do your best

Younger:
- Be kind
- Keep your hands and feet to yourself
- Have listening ears
- Show mutual respect

How would you like your local police officers to use rules like these to govern your community? Imagine being fined for not doing your best as a parent or for not being respectful to your neighbor when you called him a dingbat for allowing his dog to poop in your yard. My guess is that you would object. Yet these are exactly the types of "rules" we use to govern our classrooms.

Many of the rules stated above are really malleable guidelines, and as such, they cannot be consistently enforced. For example, take the rule that states, "Raise your hand and wait to be called on." Teachers sometimes ignore this rule when a child who rarely speaks offers an answer, or when someone says something brilliant. In these cases, the rule is easily overlooked. On the other hand, the rule is stringently enforced when the person speaking out is Rodney, who always interrupts. Imagine that in this same class you are repeatedly told to keep your hands and feet to yourself. Then the teacher instructs everyone to stand up and hold hands with a friend. These kinds of inconsistencies and mixed messages create anxiety. A child's brain will be on high alert, vigilantly using great energy trying to find predictability and stay safe in such an environment. The children will, like me in Acoma, be looking for the dogs who live in all those "doghouses."

Effective teachers know the difference between rules and routines, and have routines for everything from sharpening pencils to throwing away trash. They take time to teach the routines to the children. This is best done through the MAP method.

M = <u>M</u>odel your procedures and expectations
A = <u>A</u>dd visuals
P = <u>P</u>ractice, practice, practice

If a child refuses to follow the routines she/he teaches, the teacher must assume that additional information or a different way of presenting the information is needed. Teaching a routine is no different from teaching long division. If a child fails to understand long division, we don't put his name on the board, cancel his recess time or have him turn a card from green to red. We simply try to relay the information in a different way. The same holds true for routines. The child might need more modeling, more concrete specific visuals or more practice. If, after all this, he still is unwilling to follow the day's routines, then it is a relationship issue. Disconnected children are disruptive. You would then begin to work on repairing your relationship with the child and reconnecting the child with his or her School Family.

Adding Visuals: The Antidote to Chaos

During the Conscious Discipline Institute one summer in Orlando, Florida, I asked participants to think of the times in their day at school or at home when chaos reigns. Chaos is an urgent call for visual routines. Many participants pointed to similar transition times such as going to the restroom, walking down the halls and eating in the cafeteria. Pepa, the principal from Eton Toddler School in Mexico City, Mexico, chose to tackle her fire drills. Although she had gone over the fire-drill procedure with the young children and they had discussed and practiced the process, as soon as the siren sounded, tears and fears erupted like a volcano. What she had forgotten, and what many of us forget, is that children need to see their routines in pictures. Providing images for children is similar to a gymnast rehearsing her balance beam routine in her head before actually doing it. Visual images provide rehearsals for students. They allow students to rehearse a routine over and over again at any given time. Armed with this new information, Pepa created a Fire Drill Book for the children. The classroom teachers read the book often, the children "read" the book's pictures, and they take it home for the parents to read as well. When it came time for the next fire drill, the children were ready. Like Olympic gymnasts, the toddlers rose to the occasion, managed their anxiety with predictability and mastered the loud noise of the alarm.

Take a moment now to think about where you have chaos in your day. This indicates where you need to create a routine and break it down visually. The visual could be a single picture that applies to a difficulty one child is experiencing, or a series of pictures representing each step in a process for the whole class. The picture here is taped to James's desk. At the end of each day, James is to look in his desk to see if it looks like the picture. If not, he has a visual of the organization that is needed.

Your visual routines could also be offered to the children or parents in book form. These books can be read to and read by the whole class, and housed in the class library. The children can check them out to read to their parents at home. You may also wish to provide books for parents so they can help their child's success. Meghan had trouble managing her morning routine and preparing her materials for class. Her teacher created a book to help her remember what to do and in what order. The predictability created a felt sense of safety while scaffolding Meghan's emerging organizational skills for future success. Other children in the classroom also benefited from referencing the book.

Visual Rules with Two Positive Choices

As discussed earlier, rules are to be enforced. Most teachers think of consequences as something negative the adult must create and deliver to the children. In truth, consequences are always happening; we just aren't always conscious of them. Every thought, feeling and action has a consequence. The consequence of being polite to others is generally increased cooperation. The consequence of being rude to others is generally decreased cooperation. The consequence of eating more fruits and vegetables is generally a smaller waistline. The consequence of eating more cakes and candies is generally a larger waistline. The consequence of holding a grudge is generally mood depression, while the consequence of wishing well is generally mood elevation. Consequences can be negative or positive and do not need to be imposed. The power behind consequences lies in our awareness of them. In order to change a behavior, we must be conscious of our actions and their consequences, whether those consequences are natural or imposed. Young children are still developing awareness of their behavior and of the consequences of their actions. Visual representations of the rules are essential for children to understand what they must do to follow the rule and accept its consequences.

For children in early childhood and elementary school, it is most helpful to post two pictures of what children can

104   *Creating the School Family*

do, and one picture of what is unacceptable behavior, for each rule you follow. For example, you would create pictures that illustrate, "You may raise your hand to speak," "You may wait for a turn to speak" and "You may not talk at the same time."

The consequence of forgetting a rule is to choose again. For example, Mattie is talking while others are talking. The teacher points to the visual rule on the wall and says, "Mattie, you may not talk while others are talking. Look up here at your choices about what is helpful in our School Family, and make another choice." The teacher points to the pictures and reads, "You may raise your hand or wait for a turn to speak. Which is better for you?" The goal is to constantly point out and paint a picture of the behavior you expect from the child. When a child loses sight of what to do, our job is to bring their cognitive resources back to that point of focus.

This approach is a huge shift from current practices. Generally, the first consequence of misbehavior is some type of warning, followed by the loss of some privilege. We don't encourage children to choose again and we use fear of punishment to motivate a different behavior choice. Rules, even ones written in positive language, are created energetically from what we don't want. If we build a classroom foundation based on behaviors we don't want to see, we will be trying to stop unwanted behaviors instead of teaching and encouraging socially acceptable ones. This lays the groundwork for a class structure built on fear, manipulation, coercion and discouragement. By shifting to an intense focus on the behaviors we want to see and offering opportunities to choose again, we can inspire and encourage youngsters to be successful. Using visual rules that depict two positive choices and a negative choice, offers the opportunity to choose again rather than punishment. Using rules in this manner:

- Treats misbehavior as an opportunity to learn rather than seeing it as a call to punish the "guilty" party.
- Provides the teacher with a quick visual reference for offering two positive choices without having to come up with them on the spot.
- Transforms misbehavior into a choice to learn and practice prosocial skills.
- Empowers teachers to focus on what they want, and models this behavior for children.
- Teaches children to create positive mental images of their own goals and expectations.
- Encourages children to turn poor choices into wise decisions. Sends the powerful message, "You are inherently good. You made a poor choice this time, and you have the power to choose better next time."

Some of you may be thinking, "Well, what if I teach the routines, add all the pictures and use visual rules, and they still don't choose to cooperate?" Whether you choose to make the switch I'm suggesting or continue what you're doing now, some children will be defiant because willingness is not created through routines and rules, with or without visuals. Willingness comes from the safety and connection you have created in your School Family. It comes from the health of each and every relationship in the school. Your most important role is to help the children, adults and parents be more successful at achieving the set expectations. Visual rules and routines will help, even though some children may still be less willing to cooperate. Start teaching your routines, MAP out their success, and offer visual rules to help children choose again. Additional connecting strategies discussed in other chapters will help children who have issues about willingness to cooperate.

Lending Your Prefrontal Lobes to Students

Darius had the messiest desk in the history of fourth grade. He lost papers all the time, and it took him longer than anyone else to locate his work materials, homework or coat (he had lost three coats already this year). His teacher, Mr. Henderson, constantly reminded Darius to clean up, nagged him to stay organized, and kept him in from recess to clean up his desk and gather his materials together. Finally, Mr. Henderson decided there must be a better way. Although Darius was the worst, others in the class also had organizational

---

STEP 1: *Ask Yourself, "What materials do I need?" (check those that apply below)*

- Wastebasket for trash
- Paper clips
- 3-ring notebook
- Others (write out)
- File folders to put papers in
- Stapler
- Class organizer

STEP 2: *Say to Yourself, "I'm going to follow the routine below until I am finished."*

- Empty out desk
- Sort everything into two piles: "Save" and "Don't Save"
- Throw the "Don't Save" pile in the wastebasket
- Sort remaining items into two piles: "School Materials" and "Take Home"
- Place the "Take Home" pile in your backpack
- Sort "School Materials" by subject and "Other"
- Organize each subject pile based on teacher instructions
- If you forget the teacher instructions, ask a friend
- Decide what to do with the "Other" pile (if you need help, ask a friend)
- Put all "School Materials" neatly back in your desk
- Ask your friends, "Anybody need some help?"

STEP 3: *Say to Yourself, "I did it. Good for me! Now I can find things more easily next time."*

---

106 *Creating the School Family*

troubles. Mr. Henderson decided that Friday afternoons would be desk-cleaning time. Those who had clean desks could start on their homework for the weekend or work on a class project while the others cleaned up their desks. The whole class brainstormed the steps they would need to follow for the cleanup, generating the preceding checklist, and a group of students took pictures of the major steps as they were done. Now, every Friday Darius and others who need it have a checklist to help them with the desk-cleaning routine.

The teacher provided structure for Darius and his classmates. He did it in such a way that the whole class had input, could participate and would feel they had a stake in their success. A simple checklist and digital pictures posted in the classroom (or placed in books or on a student's desk) literally create images of your expectations in children's brains. These mental images, complete with self-talk cues like, "What materials do I need?" or, "I did it," become part of the children's internal CEO. Through the visual routine, the teacher provides essential scaffolding for the children's emerging organizational skills.

As we discussed earlier in this book, the CEO of the brain is housed in the prefrontal lobes of the cortex, located just behind your forehead (see Chapter 2). Essentially, this is the boss of your brain. Just like the CEO in a company, the prefrontal lobes help us set and achieve goals. The set of skills that help us achieve goal-directed behavior is called "executive skills." Executive skills help us get organized, resist impulses, stay focused, use time wisely, plan ahead, get started and follow through on tasks, stay in control of our emotions, learn from mistakes, solve problems and be resourceful when needing help. Can you imagine how different your life would be if each of these skills were optimally developed? I know my life would change drastically. First and foremost, I would lose 30 pounds through changes in exercise and eating. I would be able to find the files or information I was looking for with ease. I would have finished writing this book five years ago. I would also be a nicer person when the world does not go my way. If you are like me, some of the executive skills listed above are strong suits and some are weak suits. Many of us don't even recognize our weak suits, and yet we expect most of these skills to be operating for the children in our classrooms, regardless of their age. It's time for a reality check and a new approach because research shows that executive skills take about 24 years to fully mature, and their optimal development requires they be properly supported throughout those 24 years.

Many of you have had times with your children when you're ready to pull your hair out. You have bright, highly intelligent children who can't remember to write down their homework, take the math book home or finish the assignment before bedtime. If they do manage to perform the above miracles, they leave the completed work at home and subsequently receive no credit at school. Executive skills are critical for life success, take a long time to mature and require our assistance for their development. In the beginning of this book, we discussed how vital it is to "lend" children our executive skills in a way that scaffolds the development of their own skills. This creates a huge dilemma for most of us as we recognize, for example, our own procrastination tendencies while striving to teach our children how to initiate tasks and follow through. As you begin to implement visual routines, you will find they are a large part of the solution to this dilemma. Take and post pictures of the steps needed for success in any endeavor, and they become external prefrontal lobes to help children successfully complete the tasks at hand. If your own executive skills are your weak suit, visual routines are imperative as you attempt to lend your prefrontal lobes to your children so they can grow up with executive strengths, even in areas where you experience weakness.

The Power of Free Will

In Conscious Discipline, the skill of making choices develops as we rely increasingly on the power of free will. This power states the only person you can make change is yourself. Free will asks us to become conscious of how much energy we expend attempting to control our classrooms instead of structuring them for success. It asks us to be aware of how much time we spend trying to control what others think, feel and act instead of focusing on what we are thinking, feeling or doing. Free will asks us to shift from "other" control ("Look what you made me do/don't make me have to call your parents") to self-control ("I'm going to call your parents so we can work together to help you").

Routines and rules provide tangible boundaries in the classroom so each School Family member knows what is and isn't acceptable. There are also equally important psychological boundaries that tell us what is and isn't our business. It's our business to know what we think of ourselves and others, but it is not our business to control what others think of us. It's our business to know what we are feeling and how to manage our feelings. It is not our business to tell children what they should feel ("Look how you made her feel, you should be ashamed of yourself"). It is our business to know what we think but not to tell children what they think ("You think just because you got away with that behavior last year, you can do it again this year"). And it's our business to know what we want, not to tell children what they want ("You want to make this worse; keep talking and I'll be happy to give you exactly what you want").

Healthy psychological boundaries within ourselves help us create healthy external boundaries in our classrooms. Unless we consciously use our free will, we will unconsciously confuse rules with routines, attempt to control others instead of structure environments, and create inconsistent and unpredictable classrooms. We must let go of the notion that it is our job to make others change, and take 100 percent responsibility for what we choose to think, feel and do. This is the core of free will.

It is our job to keep the classroom as safe as possible. A safe classroom allows individual differences to emerge, moving the classroom beyond conformity to the power of free will. When control by the teacher is replaced with the shared power embedded in the deliberate structure of rules and routines (as described in this chapter), controlling others is transformed into personal choice and healthy internal and external boundaries.

Power of free will: The only person you can make change is yourself
Skill: Choices
Structure: Visual routines and rules
Value: Responsibility

At Fern Creek Elementary School, there are shared bathrooms in the halls for the upper-grade children: one shared boys' bathroom and one shared girls' bathroom. The rest of the building has bathrooms attached to individual classes. One year it became obvious that the boys' shared bathroom was constantly littered with paper towels and in a state of overall mess by the end of the day. Since the faculty had been using Conscious Discipline for several years they immediately took pictures of what the bathroom ought to look like when you leave the area and posted them on the outside door. When children leave the area with paper towels lying on the sink or floor, a teacher prompts them, "Look at this picture. Now look into the bathroom. Do they

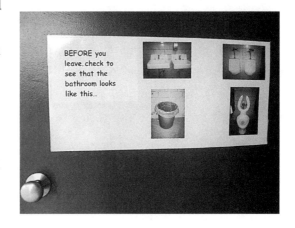

look the same? What could you do to make the bathroom look like this?" The children who left the paper towels on the floor provided a teaching moment for the passing teacher, who then directed the children to use the posted visuals as a reference for expected behavior.

At an early childhood program called "Project Enlightenment" in Raleigh, North Carolina, a young preschooler asked the teacher if he could play with the ball. She immediately referred him to the pictures of the daily schedule and helped him "read" and use his deductive reasoning skills to figure out when playing with the ball is acceptable. She capitalized on a natural teaching moment, helping him find the answer for himself through using the daily visual schedule.

A young mother came to me exhausted. She shared how her 14-month-old baby has trouble going to sleep at night. I asked her to describe his bedtime routine. She said it varies and depends on who is with him. Bingo! Another teaching moment for both mother and child! We designed a six-step routine, starting with bathtime and ending with a kissing ritual that would occur every night. Her job was to post the pictures in his bedroom, to ask everyone putting the child to bed to follow the pictures and to create consistency for her child. It turned out that she needed help to finish the picture-taking task, which created another teaching moment. After some pondering, we solicited the help of her tech-oriented, 12-year-old niece to make the picture book. I am pleased to report both mom and baby are sleeping better.

It is not enough to post visual routines or rules in the classroom or home. You must also use them as you would a dictionary to find a word. Visual rules and routines are references that must be utilized. The more a child uses the visual cues, the more they become internalized images in the brain that govern future behaviors.

Routines and rules are the foundation for creating a safe, organized classroom where optimal learning can occur. Without them, chaos reigns. The three foundational structures for this chapter are Visual Daily Schedules, Visual Routines and Visual Rules. In all cases, the purpose is to let the pictures do the talking. Pictures are more effective at getting the message across because young children's brains encode messages visually. Pictures don't get tired of conveying the same information over and over again. Pictures don't eat up teaching time or require individual attention. Pictures are steadfast, reliable, ever-present and help children become self-sufficient in governing their behavior.

Purpose: To create a felt sense of safety by providing predictability through visuals. A smoothly running classroom requires a Visual Daily Schedule to show children the progression of your entire day, Visual Routines for smaller patterns like handwashing and transition procedures within the day, and Visual Rules to clearly set expectations.

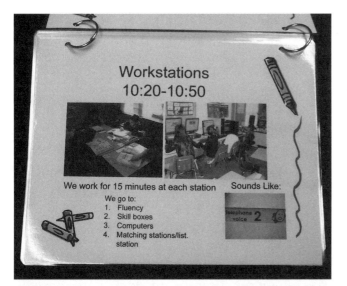

How to set up a Visual Daily Schedule: Your Daily Schedule displays the day's major activity blocks to build predictability and time awareness for your students. This chart will be age-appropriate and occupy a prominent place in the classroom so children and teachers can refer to it frequently. Take photographs, collect clip art or have children make drawings to represent each block of time in your day. In younger

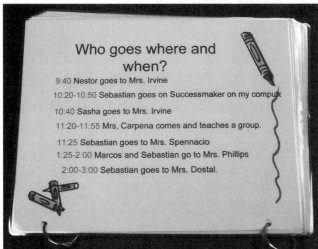

Chapter 6: Visual Rules and Routines

classrooms, photographs of the actual area are more helpful than clip art since young children are concrete thinkers; they are better able to match a photo to the actual space than to a representation of similar space.

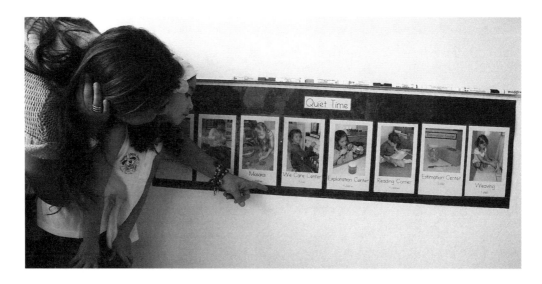

You will also need a way to signify time. Young children have a limited concept of time, so instead of showing the time for each activity (30 minutes, 1 hour), display each portion of the day with a representative size. For example, a 12x18 sheet of construction paper would represent one hour, half of the sheet is 30 minutes, one-sixth of the paper is 10 minutes, and so on. Place the corresponding picture on the appropriate block of time. Children may not understand the difference between 10 minutes and 60 minutes, but they can see the difference in the size of the paper. Sixty minutes is a much bigger paper, and therefore a much longer time. Older students will benefit from attaching small cardboard clocks with moveable hands to indicate the time for each activity; they can then match the time on the display clock with the functional clock in the room.

Finally, you will need some sort of indicator that shows where you are in your day. In younger classrooms, you could use a shape that attaches to the board with Velcro, a clothespin that clips or some other item. For example, if your pre-K School Family name is "The Buddy Bears," you might use a cutout of a bear attached to a piece of Velcro. You would then move the bear from activity to activity as the day progresses. In older classrooms, you might assign a class job that is responsible for marking the transitions.

The ultimate goal is for students to establish internal patterns for their daily schedules. As they continually refer to the pictured steps, the image of what is expected becomes visually reinforced. Students will learn that lunch follows math. If they forget what comes next, they know where to look for the answer rather than involving you or a classmate. Children with autism or Asperger's syndrome need additional visual help and will benefit from individual schedules posted for them to check as needed.

How to introduce the Visual Daily Schedule: In younger classrooms, introduce the Daily Schedule on the very first day as children gather in the circle. Point to the picture that shows the morning circle.

"Look, boys and girls, this says 'Circle time,' and shows children sitting in a circle. After we are done here, the next picture shows children working at tables and says, 'Small group time.' These cards tell us what we are doing and what will come next. The clothespin with a star on it shows what activity we are doing now."

It is best to keep this introduction brief. The key is to refer often to your Visual Daily Schedule during the day so children see that it provides information about the day. For example, when Joey says, "When is snack? I'm hungry," this is your teaching moment. Say, "Look, the star clip is here. It shows we are doing small groups. Next is story time, and then snack time. When the star is here, it will be snack time."

In older classrooms, children are more accustomed to seeing a Daily Schedule; however, it is still necessary and helpful to refer to it often, especially in the first weeks of school.

How to set up Visual Routines: Each activity within the daily schedule also has a procedure children are expected to follow. Clearing desks in preparation for the next activity, washing hands for snacks and lining up for the bathroom all have steps we might assume children have previously learned or will automatically pick up along the way. If they have not automatically learned these, however, you will know because these times will feel chaotic. That chaos, whether coming from one child, a few children or the whole class, is a call for additional assistance in the form of visual routines.

Begin by making a list of the routines your class utilizes. Step back and look at the big picture of how your class functions. How do you signal a transition? Which procedures do children ask the most questions about? What are common sources of frustration or friction? Most often, a trouble spot in your day is an indication that a clear routine is lacking. The following list identifies common areas where children benefit from a visual routine. Mark the routines for which you commit to creating a visual routine to aid your students.

Visual Routine Commitments

- Arrival
- Dismissal
- Signals to shift focus back to the teacher
- Restroom issues
- How to get help
- Lining up and walking in the halls
- Rest time
- Fire drills
- Lock-down procedures
- Snack time
- Lunch and cafeteria procedures
- What to do when you have finished your work and you're waiting for others
- Transition between subject areas
- Daily schedule transitions (small group to large group, outside to inside, etc.)
- Cleaning up

Once you have a list of needed routines, the next step is to illustrate the most common and most troublesome ones. You can accomplish this by photographing children or by collecting clip-art images to create a series of "step-by-step" illustrations. Steps for washing hands might include photos of a child turning on the water, squirting soap, rubbing hands together under the water, turning the water off, drying hands with a paper towel, using the towel to wipe excess water off the counter, and throwing the towel away. These step-by-step    visuals are helpful for all children, but are vital for children with processing difficulties and those with ADD or ADHD. A visual review right before doing a task gives them a clear understanding of what to do and a guide that helps them follow through and stay on task. Children can help with the photos by taking the pictures and being "models" in the depictions. The more you invite them to join in the process, the more likely they are to use the pictures as a guide.

Now that you have developed your routines, post them throughout the classroom and other places children frequent. The "washing hands" routine goes above the sink, and the "clean up the center" routine is posted in each center. By providing a road map of your expectations, children are able to build predictable patterns that aid their compliance. Ultimately, students will know where to look for help (the chart) and how to carry out the steps (the picture reference). If children seem distracted or unclear about what to do next, help them figure it out by referring them to the pictured steps, saying, "Check the chart. What comes next?" A sampling of common routines is listed in the Activities section of this chapter.

How to introduce Visual Routines: Visual Routines are helpful in any setting, but they are the lifeblood of a smoothly running early childhood classroom. In younger classrooms, you will introduce individual routines like the hand-washing routine as the need arises. The first time a student walks to the sink to wash her hands, point to the routine cards posted above it and encourage the whole class to follow along. As Suzie washes her hands, verbally describe what she is doing and point to the appropriate card with each step. Review the process, then end with encouragement: "You did it!" Use a similar introduction in older classrooms, clearly stating the steps you expect them to follow.

How to set up Visual Rule Cards: Rules are best when you show two acceptable choices and one clearly marked "no" choice. Choices for lining up might include a photo showing children lined up straight with their arms at their sides, a photo showing children lined up casually in their own space and a "no" photo of children pushing in line. The Visual Rule Card Set available from www.ConsciousDiscipline.com includes cards for ten rules. Each rule has two examples of what "to do" on one example of what "not to do." There is a set of large cards and a set of small cards for each rule. You can purchase the cards from Loving Guidance or create your own cards that mimic this style.

When students follow the "two 'yes' choices, one 'no' choice" formula, visual rules foster an additional level of consciousness for children. They provide a picture of the unacceptable behavior, allowing children to see themselves in the act of misbehaving, and become aware that their choice is not acceptable. It also gives them a visual of what they can choose to do to return to their job description of "being helpful" in the School Family.

Unlike traditional lists of rules that tend to be posted in one spot of the classroom (and only referenced when there is a violation), you will post your visual rules throughout the classroom. Post your visual rules where common misbehavior is likely. These areas include lining up, cleaning up, staying on your cot during rest time or speaking out of turn. These are the times when temptation is greatest and impulse control is probably lowest. You may also wish to bind your rules into books for your class library.

How to introduce Visual Rules: In younger classrooms, introduce your Visual Rule Cards (either purchased from www.ConsciousDiscipline.com or self-created) on day one or day two. For three- and four-year-olds, choose the five expectations most important to you. Mount the three large images for each rule on same-color construction paper, laminate them and post them in the appropriate places. Use a smaller set to create a book, "Ways to be Helpful in (Ms. Smith's) School Family," and put it in your library. Read one or two rules per day until you have introduced all five rules. Take time to role-play and discuss each rule over the course of the first week. Follow this same formula for pre-K and kindergarten classrooms, but use all ten rules in the Visual Rule Card set (or those you made), and teach two to three rules per day.

In older classrooms, visual rules evolve from class discussions about the qualities we want in our classroom. The rule- and expectation-creating process is discussed in the context of the Safekeeper in Chapter 5 and Class Meetings in Chapter 15. Keeping the classroom safe, learning to be helpful and setting visual rules are closely linked. Start with a group-learning exercise like a lesson based on the book, *I Dream of a World*, which was written by children. Ask the students how they dream of their classroom. Many answers will fall along the lines of "respectful," "safe" and "fun," as opposed to "getting rewards like candy every day." If you do encounter "candy reward" answers, simply make a comment like, "I love candy too, but if I ate it all the time, I might get a stomachache and that's never fun. How about if we say, 'We'll celebrate each other's success,' instead?" When you have a list of ways you want the classroom to be, begin creating the agreements and setting the expectations that will produce the desired kind of classroom.

Enlisting your students in setting rules and expectations in older classrooms fosters a sense of ownership and thus increases compliance. Ask students, "What expectations do you have for this school year?" Compile their answers into a list. As the lesson continues, add or delete from the list based on student answers. Then explain that you also have expectations. Next, take photographs to illustrate the expectations you set as a group, and then post them in appropriate places.

General Activities — All Ages

Routine for the Transition to Large Group

Transitioning from individual work to group activities requires a shift from independent skills like self-motivation and increased attention span to group participation skills like patience, taking turns and compromise. Begin the transition with a movement and/or sound that invites participation. As children join with each other, they automatically shift to a more collective mindset. Incorporate the steps of your transition into the chant, movement or song.

> Clap, clap, clap with me. One and two and three. (Repeat as children join in)
> March your feet. Find your seat. (Repeat until children find their seats.)
> Cross your legs and keep the beat.
> We each have a part. Now we're ready to start.

Or

> Follow the beat with your marching feet.
> Go to the door. Find your spot on the floor.
> Put your finger to your lips and shhh.

Two other songs that can be used to aid transitions are "Watch Me Listen" and "Skip Count" on the *Brain Boogie Boosters* CD from www.ConsciousDiscipline.com. Another wonderful song is "Come Join the Circle" by Paulette Meier on her CD by the same name. Once you determine your transition routine, it is vital not to change it until the children have mastered it and the transition proceeds smoothly. If you choose, you can then introduce other songs as the year and the students' comfort level progress.

Routine for the Transition from Large Group to Small Group or Individual Activity

Students are more likely to transition successfully if they make a choice about where to go before beginning the switch. When you provide structure by letting students know where they are going next and how they will get there, you help them organize their brains so they are better able to comply. The degree of personal choice you offer students will depend on their age and ability. When selecting their next activity, students can choose by picking a card or you can assign them to a small group. Very young or uncertain children will need an assertive command (one choice) and visuals about where to go. Young children and those having a hard time deciding will benefit from your offering them two choices. Older children can choose from several options by themselves.

Once students know where they are going, you can instruct them how to get there or provide choices about how they will get there.

"Now, hop (side step, tiptoe, etc.) to your space."
"How would you like to get there? You may tiptoe or shuffle."

Direct students to talk to themselves. Have them visualize where they are going and how they are going to get there safely before they start moving. Provide examples of self-talk for them: "Am I in the right spot, with the right people? What materials do I need?"

Transition to Next Small Group

When conducting activities in groups that rotate to several areas throughout the classroom, a countdown provides the information needed to be successful. Post photos depicting these three steps at each area or in a central location you can refer to as students are counting down. You will use the same formula and phrases for every rotation throughout the year.

1. On the count of one, help put the materials away
2. On the count of two, stand up and push in your chair
3. On the count of three, walk to the next small group area and begin

Hygiene Routines

Record all the steps children are expected to follow for various hygiene routines and then supply pictures for each step. Post the images in the corresponding areas. Review these with the entire group at the beginning of the year and after any lengthy school breaks. Make personal routine books and do individual reviews with children as needed to help them be successful. Hygiene routines include a bathroom routine, handwashing routine, and a getting a tissue routine. A sample bathroom routine might include text and images for the following steps:

1. Walk to the bathroom
2. Knock to make sure no one is in there
3. Close the door
4. Use the bathroom
5. Wipe your bottom with the toilet paper
6. Flush the toilet
7. Wash your hands using the soap
8. Dry your hands using the paper towel
9. Put the paper towel in the trash can
10. Check to make sure the bathroom is clean
11. Turn off the light
12. Walk to your seat

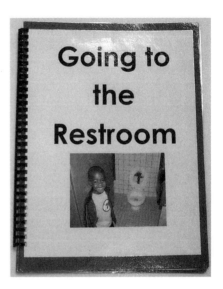

The song "I Gotta Go" on *Brain Boogie Boosters* available at www.ConsciousDiscipline.com provides a fun, helpful hygiene routine for going to the bathroom.

Dismissal Routines

Post your dismissal routine in pictures and follow the same steps each day to minimize chaos and remember homework. Don't forget to end with a goodbye ritual as discussed in Chapter 10. Your dismissal routine might look like this:

1. Transition signal
2. Put away materials
3. Organize materials to take home
4. Bring book bag to your place in the circle
5. Talk quietly with a friend while others join the circle
6. Use the Time Machine to redo teaching moments as needed
7. Goodbye ritual

Arrival Routine

Younger children will benefit from an arrival routine that provides varying numbers of choices depending on their age, temperament and abilities. An arrival routine to depict with your visual routine cards might include:

1. Put personal items in cubbie
2. Put your picture in Safekeeper box (see Chapter 5)
3. Choose a table activity
4. Listen for the "come to circle" song
5. Find a seat on the circle when you hear the song
6. Check to see if you and your friends have enough space

Line Up Routines

Lining up requires safety. Ask children, "Who can show me what it looks like to line up safely?" Pick a child to demonstrate. Notice what he or she does, for example, "She stood up from the floor, pushing off in her own space without touching others. She watched her feet and carefully walked around others without stepping on them. She moved slowly and found her space by the door." Then ask, "Who can show me what it looks like to line up without paying attention to others (ways that might be hurtful)?" Finally ask the class, "What were the differences between the two ways of lining up? Which way felt safer to you?"

Create a predictable routine for lining up. This gives children the necessary structure and limits to ensure an expedient and safe process, avoiding the mad rush to be first. Young children benefit from having a well-defined place to stand when lining up. Use different-colored shoe prints to reinforce colors or different shapes to reinforce the recognition and identification of shapes. Begin the transition with a consistent signal (flicking lights, bell, end of clean-up song, etc.) and then give the command to line up. Your visual routine might include images for:

1. Transition signal (ring a bell)
2. Teacher's cue ("Buddy Bears line up at the door, single file, with your arms at your sides.")
3. Students finding their place in line

4. Checking to make sure both you and your friends have enough room

Or

1. Transition signal (ring a bell)
2. Teacher's cue ("Row 1 line up at the door single file with your arms at your sides. Row 2 …")
3. Students finding their place in line
4. Students answering back: "I'm on red. I'm on blue. I'm on yellow…"
5. Class chants before leaving: "Check my hands, check my feet. I am safe and so are my friends."

Arrival Routine

An arrival routine in an older classroom might look like this:

1. Hang your jacket on the coat rack
2. Put materials in your desk
3. Sign in on the Question of the Day* board
4. Place your "item" in the Safekeeper box
5. Read the morning message from friends
6. Check the Job Board for your job
7. Organize materials and supplies for the day
8. Read a book, write in your journal or make commitment(s) for the day (see Chapter 8)

*The Question of the Day provides a novel way to take attendance by providing an opportunity for discussions, comparisons and graphing. Sample questions for Question of the Day include simple ones such as "Do you like ice cream?" (graph favorite flavors) or more thought-provoking ones such as, "How many acts of kindness do you predict will happen in our School Family today?"

What Can I Do When I Finish?

We talk a lot about what to do during an assignment without ever focusing on what students should do when they finish. Design a "What to do when you're finished" procedure and post the visual routine in your classroom. "What to do activities" could include writing

We Care and Wish-Well notes (see Chapter 14). You could also add challenge questions like: "If each person uses two chopsticks to eat their noodles, how many chopsticks would the girls in our class need to eat their noodles? How many would the boys need? How many will the whole class need?" Use challenge questions that require students to problem solve. An Internet search provides many sites with free puzzles you can use.

You could also create a word challenge by putting an unusual word on the board. When students finish their assignments, they write the word and what they believe it means. Then they look up the word and write the true definition. Finally, they add a drawing or other illustration of the word. You could also use this time for children to create class-made books.

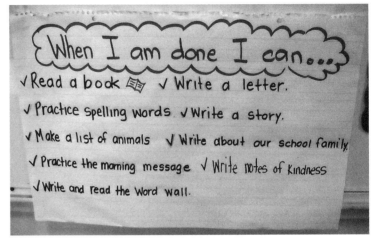

For example, students create a book for a substitute teacher showing all the routines and rituals that are used in your School Family.

Your visual routine for "What to do when you're finished" procedure might look like this:

1. Complete your class work
2. Write Wish-Well and We Care notes
3. Choose a challenge activity, select a book to read or write in your journal quietly at your desk
4. Listen for the signal to wrap it up

Permission Slips

Have students copy the necessary information from the board to fill in the blanks (date, time, cost) on a permission slip. Have them double-check each other's work, and review as a class to make sure the information recorded is correct. This exercise helps students memorize the pertinent information and connects them more to the slip's importance when they take it home for the parent's signature. Designate a box by the door for the children to deposit their signed permission slips as they arrive. Provide a list of class names so they can check they have returned the slip.

Line-Up Routine

As in younger classes, lining up must be practiced with a focus on safety. It may be helpful to role-play lining up safely and unsafely, discussing the differences and creating "lining up" visual rule cards together as a class.

Line up procedures in older classrooms may be longer or shorter, depending on the amount of time remaining. Provide a cue so students know which line-up procedure will come next. For example, if you are going to use the quick sequence, begin with a verbal cue like "snip-snap." Then say, "Find your place in line." Once the standard cue is established, you can then include some false starts before the real cue. You might say, "Wait for the right signal. Bookworm. Silly scissors. Dilly dally. Snip-snap." Change your cues throughout the year, from verbal to nonverbal ("Watch my face and when I blink, line up safely").

If you have time to spare, send children to the line with specific cues or questions. You might say, "Line up if you are wearing red today." You could review the day's lessons, "Raise your hand if you can tell me the state capital." Select the first hand up, and if the answer is correct, say, "Way to go! Get in line." Or you might use the time to learn more about each other: "If you have a pet with fur, line up now."

Class-Made Books
Younger

Individual Routine Books

Create books for individual children who struggle with a particular issue, like the toddler who was having trouble with drop off described earlier in the chapter. Limit to three or four pages or steps for young children.

Lunch Bunch Book

The lunchroom is one of the hardest places for young children to get used to at school. Create a book with step-by-step photos of lunchroom procedures and expectations. Read this book to prepare children for a successful lunchroom experience. The Lunch Bunch Book layout might follow this format:

Page 1: Photo (walking as a class into the lunchroom)
Text: "We walk safely into the lunchroom."

Page 2: Two photos (waiting in line to get a school lunch and sitting down at the table with your lunchbox)
Text: "If I am getting a school lunch, I go wait in line. If I brought a packed lunch, I go sit at the table."

Page 3: Two photos (going through the lunch line and walking to the table)
Text: "I get my tray and carry it to the table. I use both hands and walk."

Continue the book, describing expectations and adding matching photos. Each school lunchroom has different procedures. For example: "If I need help opening my milk, I can raise my hand to ask for help."

Class-Made Books — Older

Older classrooms use the same procedures as above, but with much more detail and autonomy. The expectation is that students will write out the procedures themselves. Sometimes they write the one-sentence procedure on one page, and then write a paragraph explaining in detail what it will look and sound like on the next page. Students can be responsible for taking and printing the pictures needed for the book. Most students are tech-savvy and need little direction on how to do it.

Music & Movement — Younger

One, Two, Buckle My Shoe

Prepare picture cards that follow the routine in the song. Also prepare picture cards that follow the top five routines in your classroom. Play and enjoy "One, Two, Buckle My Shoe" on the *Tony Chestnut*

CD by The Learning Station. After students learn the song, have them put the "buckle my shoe" picture cards in order. Then distribute the classroom routine cards to put in order. Next, create a song to the tune of "One, Two, Buckle My Shoe" for one or more of the routines.

Before long, students will be singing some of your routines. "One, two, if you want a drink; Three, four, line up by the sink; Five, six, breathe while you wait; Seven, eight, drink for five counts; Nine, ten, if I want more, I start over again!"

Watch Me Listen

Sing, "Watch Me Listen," on *Brain Boogie Boosters* by Dr. Becky Bailey and The Learning Station. Then ask what it takes to do a task successfully. Most will answer, "Practice." The more we practice something, the better we can do it. The same is true for classroom routines. Pull out a routine book and say, "When we have trouble with (name the routine), this book helps our brain practice what to do to be successful."

Hula Hoop Game

Hula hoops can be used as a fun way to review and reiterate the procedure for any routine. Before the lesson begins, take a few hula hoops and place dots at random points on them. Also make a card that has the routine's name on it, like "Entering the Classroom." Then split the children into groups of five. Each group chooses a leader and the other four will serve as steps in the procedure. The leader stands at the top of the hula hoop, holding the card that says, "Entering the Classroom." A child stands at each dot a to represent one part of the procedure. At dot one, the student would say, "Enter the classroom" and give a greeting. At dot two, the student would say, "Empty your backpack." At dot three, the student says, "Write the spelling word in the planner." At dot four, the student says, "When finished with your planner, read silently." The leader then organizes the group to illustrate the steps visually. At the end of the designated time, each group shares their routine and illustrated signals with the class.

C = Commitment

I am willing to take a moment to consider the chaotic times in my classroom. I am willing to take time to reflect on children who have trouble with our daily transitions. I now commit to make visual routines for two chaotic class times and for individual children.

Signature _____ **Date** _____

H = Helpful Resources

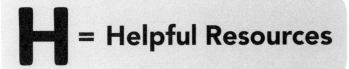

Music

All Ages

***Kindness Counts* by Dr. Becky Bailey and Mr. Al**
Song: "Encouraging Words"

***Brain Boogie Boosters* by Dr. Becky Bailey and The Learning Station**
Songs: "I Gotta Go," "Watch Me Listen"

***Come Join the Circle* by Paulette Meier**
Song: "Come Join the Circle"

***Learning with Hip Hop* by By Mark D. Pencil**
Song: "Following Directions"

126 *Creating the School Family*

Literature — Younger

***Fuzzy Bear Goes to School* by Krisztina Nagy.** Fuzzy bear gets up, gets ready and goes to school. Each page shows how Fuzzy Bear's routine will look and sound.

***No No Yes Yes* by Leslie Patricelli.** This story offers a guide of what's helpful and what is hurtful throughout the school day.

***Quiet Loud* by Leslie Patricelli.** A look at what different areas sound like, like coloring and thinking are activities that sound quiet, while singing and playgrounds are activities that sound loud.

***The Hello Goodbye Window* by Norton Juster.** An arrival and drop off routine book that includes surprises like silly greetings and goodbyes.

Literature — Older

***Monday* by Kerry Smith.** This wordless book shows the daily schedule. Older students can fill in the words themselves and compare Monday's schedule to their own.

Additional Aids

Visual Rules from www.ConsciousDiscipline.com
Shubert worksheets, a free download at www.ConsciousDiscipline.com

Chapter 7

Ways to Be Helpful Boards and Books

I had just painted the inside of my house. Having lived in the southwestern United States for a while, I liked a warm, earthy feel to my home, and the main room's walls had been a light terracotta color for years. However, it was time for change, and I boldly went from terracotta to a warm yellow. My mother came to visit, walked into the house, and the first thing she said was, "Whoever painted missed a spot over here." She immediately found the mistake and pointed it out before commenting on the color, the overall effect, or the change itself.

How many of us spend our days finding fault? We are keen to point out what is wrong with this or that. We are hypervigilant about noticing children whose behavior isn't stellar. It's as if we are living our life on guard, ready and anticipating the next crisis. This is, in part, because we belong to the animal kingdom and have an amygdala in our brain. The amygdala is there to alert us to any sign of danger, which is very useful when a lion is chasing you, but less so when appraising a paint job.

We are the only animals that can choose where we want to put our attention. We are not slaves to our amygdala because we have higher centers in our brains that can appraise situations, modulate the amygdala and allow us to stop and smell the roses. Our orbital frontal lobes can calm the amygdala, giving us the power of choice and free will. We can choose to see the painter's error or to focus on the beauty of yellow sunshine on the walls. Collectively, however, most of us seem to focus on what is wrong. If you don't believe this, just turn on the news. While presenting at a conference in Australia, I was watching a TV show in which they discussed solving various problems. I wondered what I was watching because I found it interesting. It was the evening news! I was surprised to see stories presented with a focus on solutions versus ones focused on violence and trauma. The contrast offered me an "ah-ha" moment about where we place our attention in the United States.

At any given time, in classrooms all over the world, some children are being helpful and some are being hurtful. Which ones get your attention and where do you want to put your focus? Even though most of us would like to focus on solutions, smell the flowers and see the beauty in a situation, we are also unconsciously programmed to see what is wrong. What we focus on, we get more of, and so it behooves us to retrain our eyes to see the love and positivity that surrounds us. We have the potential to help children grow up more inclined to see the positive rather than the negative in life's situations. We can help them develop prosocial and self-regulatory skills, focus their attention on the life they want to live and create mental habits that contribute to the welfare of others. We can do all this for children! However, we must first discipline our own minds to consciously focus on what we want more of.

We can facilitate this process by creating "Ways to Be Helpful" bulletin boards and books, and plastering the school environment with images of what we want children to do. How many class books have you created that focus on what you want children to do that is helpful to the School Family? How many illustrations of those activities do you have in your classroom, the hallways, the cafeteria and bathrooms or on the school bus?

An abundance of research supports developing our power of attention to focus on behaviors we want to see from children instead of those we don't. Dr. Eveline Crone (2008) and her colleagues from the Leiden Brain and Cognition Lab discovered there is a difference in how young children and adults learn from their mistakes. Children 12 years old and younger have brains that learn primarily from positive feedback ("You did it! You read the whole book!"), whereas negative feedback ("You didn't read Chapter 6") scarcely activates the brain at all. This makes sense developmentally. Processing information that you did something inappropriately is more complicated than knowing what you actually did. Learning from mistakes is a more complex task that requires asking yourself what precisely went wrong and what to do about it. Thus, showing children what to do and celebrating their successes is the more brain-compatible way of teaching during the early childhood and elementary years.

Self-talk and Private Inner Speech

Have you ever noticed that you talk to yourself "in your head"? Adults do this all the time. It's called self-talk or private speech. This inner speech allows us to govern ourselves, guide ourselves through complicated tasks and control our behaviors. Only humans have developed this ability. Imagine how you use this self-talk to keep you from eating another doughnut at the front office. It might sound like this: "Come on, Becky, you can pass this by. You're fat enough as it is. One doughnut is a million calories. Just drink more water and keep walking." Self-talk allows us to develop future plans, set goals for ourselves, inhibit our responses (impulse control), achieve those goals and understand the relationship between cause and effect. It increases our free will, giving us access to our executive skills. It frees us from the domineering control of a stimulus-response way of life. In short, the ability to instruct oneself from the inside out helps us stay the course in achieving our goals despite outside distractions.

This skill of self-talk develops through the early childhood years. You can observe it developing in young children. They progress from talking out loud to themselves as preschoolers to gradually talking to themselves subvocally (quiet enough so others cannot hear), and finally talking to themselves in their "mind's voice" at around 12 years old (Barkley, 2005). A three-year-old would reach for a doughnut, slap her hand with the other one, and yell, "NO! NO! Bad girl." A three-year-old's self-talk is said out loud for all to hear. (If you want to become conscious of how you have disciplined your children, just listen to how they discipline themselves aloud.)

Imagine sitting in a staff development class, and all your private thoughts are spoken out loud. As the instructor discusses how to teach long division and fractions, you might shout out, "Did I remember to take the chicken out of the freezer for dinner?" Those who work in preschool and kindergarten easily recognize such behavior. Children will often say something like, "My daddy went to the mailbox in his underwear," out of the blue. By the ninth year, you can see that inner speech is improving but still not fully developed; no matter what you do, some children still whisper the words to themselves during silent sustained reading.

The behavioral changes that inner speech brings about are quite remarkable. It provides children a way to give self-instructions. Before inner speech matures, children are managed mostly by outside events that catch their attention. Their inner control occurs in images, not words. If we say to a child, "Stop running," the image created in his mind is "running." This doesn't help him control the impulse to run. Try it yourself. Right this minute, don't think about the color of your car. What happened? Using images of what you want children to do provides a brain-compatible way to help them manage themselves in conjunction with their developing inner speech. This is why we must paper our schools and classrooms with images of children being kind and helpful to each other.

Remember, in the Conscious Discipline classroom, our job is to keep the children safe, and their job is to help keep it safe (see Chapter 5). In short, their job description is to be helpful. In order to teach them how to do this, we need to do several things. First, we must be willing to use our digital cameras and take pictures of the behaviors we value, as discussed previously (see Chapter 6). Posting photos of expected behaviors throughout your rooms, cafeterias and hallways embeds images into the brains of your students. The children then use these images to guide their behavior; you will see increases in helpfulness, kindness, sharing and caring, as a result. We must also be willing to reflect on our current thinking about helpfulness. Do we want children helping one another be successful, or do we want them to compete with each other in the hope that this will motivate them to be the best? One classroom is based on compassion and the other on competitiveness. The choice is yours.

The Power of Unity: Seeing the Call for Help in Compassionate Classrooms

Compassion is everywhere. It is the world's richest energy source. As we increasingly realize the world is a global village and that each of us are linked interdependently, we need compassion more than ever, not for the sake of altruism but for survival. With one in six Americans going to bed hungry, 1.4 billion people worldwide living in extreme poverty, mounting air pollution, water scarcity and global climate change, it becomes clear we're all in this together and must work together. (U.S. Department of Agriculture, 2008; World Bank, 2008). We must educate children to live compassionately if we are to survive the escalating problems facing our planet. "Compassion," in Conscious Discipline, is defined as a way of living born out of the awareness of our interconnectedness. The School Family, like a healthy home family, is built on compassion.

Compassion suffers miserably at the hands of competition. Compassion is founded upon and seeks to uncover our similarities. It unites us, embraces our differences and is based on shared power. Competition isolates, separates, seeks to make different, divides the winners from the losers and distinguishes the in-crowd from the out-crowd (Fox, 1990). Competition is founded on dominant or conflicted power, as each person seeks more prestige, influence and/or possessions than his peers.

In compassionate classrooms, teachers see children's misbehavior and academic shortfalls as calls for help. A child who hits another child needs help managing her emotions and communicating verbally. A child who fails to understand fractions needs additional or different learning opportunities. When a teacher responds from a compassionate perception, she models that for the children watching. Students then begin to see peers who are having behavior or academic trouble as needing their help. Conversely, if a teacher perceives a child who hits as mean and a child who has trouble with math as lazy, he teaches the class to see these children in a negative light. As a child is perceived negatively, she will have fewer friends, become marginalized and end up victimized and bullied by a system that has zero tolerance for bullying. Compassionate classrooms teach and model what helpfulness looks, sounds and feels like. We do not rely on programs that try to "catch them being good" as a behavioral strategy; we instead train our eyes to see the call for help in others.

The Power of Unity: Building compassionate classrooms and the call for help
Skill: Noticing helpful acts
Structure: Ways to Be Helpful pictures
Value: Compassion

How do we go about teaching children to be helpful? One way is to notice the times they are already doing it. When we wanted to teach a baby the word bottle, we used it in the context of daily actions: "Here is your bottle, hold your bottle, I am fixing your bottle, look at you drinking out of your bottle." With all this repetition, the little one internalizes the concept of bottle. The same is true for helpfulness.

Children, regardless of age, contribute to the welfare of others in some way. A baby may smile at an elderly man in the store and bring joy to them both. A preschooler brings a marker for himself and a friend so both can draw. A school-age child scoots over when the gathering on the floor is too crowded for comfort. These moments of helpfulness and contributing to others are happening all around us. Our job as teachers is to notice them. Often our attention is drawn more to the crying baby, a preschooler who grabs or a school-age kid who practically sits on top of another and refuses to heed a request to move until an elbow jabs him. What we focus on we get more of, and what we focus on is what we value. To change the value system in your classroom from one of competition for attention to one of contributing helpful acts requires that we change our attention system first. The following phrase will help you notice helpfulness: "You (describe what the child did) so (describe how it contributed to others). That was helpful."

Nicholaus was a busy boy. He had a very hard time focusing on his seatwork and was constantly distracted by other events in the room. The task at hand was to measure the cubic centimeters of various shapes. Most of the class was busy measuring and recording. Nicholaus, however, was socializing and repeatedly sharpening his pencil. Bart, his work buddy, signaled Nicholaus to return to his seat. He came immediately and assumed his favorite position, sitting with only one leg in the chair. Bart encouraged him, "Come on, Nick, you can do this. Start with this one. We can do it together." The teacher who was circling around the room noticed this action. Instead of saying to herself, "Thank goodness for Bart! Nicholaus is about to drive me nuts," she walked over and said, "Bart, you helped Nicholaus return to his seat and encouraged him to focus so he could be successful. That was helpful."

It is extremely important that we use these teaching moments to show children how their behavior contributes positively to the welfare of others. Historically, we do this only in regard to negative behaviors. It is common to hear teachers give very specific explanations of children's wrong behavior, for example: "You continue to speak when others are talking. No one else in this room can hear or learn what we came here to learn. Is that nice?" Yet when children offer kindness, caring or helpfulness to one another, we casually comment, "Thank you," or "Good job," if we see it at all. The long-term effect of this treatment is apparent in adulthood, We are very clear about our personal faults while often underestimating our worth and value to others. Start to change this dynamic today by using the positive construction, "You (name action) so (name result). That was helpful," as much as you possibly can.

You will use this language of helpfulness constantly as you teach the jobs to your class and notice each child as s/he attends to his/her job. Using the language of helpfulness helps children become aware of their contributions and self-worth. It also teaches them in context what helpfulness looks like, sounds like and feels like.

The School Family structure that supports the concept of helpfulness is the Ways to Be Helpful Board and/or Book. This structure will be a visual guidepost that reminds your students what it looks like, sounds like and feels like to be a safe, kind and conscientious member of your School Family.

Purpose: The Ways to Be Helpful Boards and Books are created within the classroom to provide children with images of helpful and safe actions. Children take part in creating your Ways to Be Helpful Board/Book in order to define being helpful in clear visual terms, to express the values that are important to them and to strengthen their commitment to helpfulness.

How to set up Ways to Be Helpful Boards and Books: The Ways to Be Helpful go hand in hand with the Visual Rules and Routines discussed in Chapter 6. You can display your ways to be helpful in a variety of forms. It's best to begin the year with a classroom bulletin board that shows ways to be helpful using a combination of art, photographs and words. You can reuse the same photographs from year to year, but it is most beneficial if you take new photos of each classroom's members each year. If "lending supplies to a friend in need" is a way to be helpful in your class, you will want a photograph of one child lending another a piece of paper or a pencil. If "taking turns" is a way to be helpful, you will want to include a photograph of children taking turns. Showing the helpful act visually encodes it in the child's brain, making the visual representations necessary for a child to integrate something into his or her regular behavior.

Some teachers rotate the photos throughout the year and/or bind them in a Ways to Be Helpful Book for the class library. In younger classrooms, it is helpful to leave the bulletin board in place year-round as a strong visual reminder. In older classrooms, you may wish to dismantle the board and turn it into a book after a few months of school.

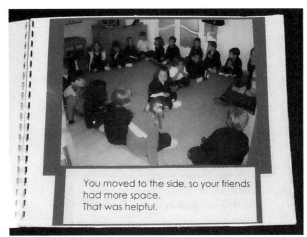

How to introduce Ways to Be Helpful Boards and Books: *Shubert's Helpful Day* will develop the concept of helpful for your students and lay the foundation for your Ways to Be Helpful Boards and Books. Read *Shubert's Helpful Day* and begin a class discussion about what is helpful. Young students might describe helpful as "being nice," but they don't really have a concept of what "being nice" involves. Older students often don't realize that helpful behavior isn't always about complying with the group. Sometimes it's helpful to say, "No, today I want to be by myself," or, "I want to do this instead of that." Girls especially benefit from hearing someone say, "It is helpful to let others know your boundaries. For example, sometimes you might say, 'Sometimes, I want to play with other friends and not just with you.'"

After reading *Shubert's Helpful Day*, go back through the book and list "Mrs. Bookbinder's Class Ways to Be Helpful" on chart paper. Then create "Ways to Be Helpful" for your class. Lead younger children in a discussion about what it looks, sounds and feels like to be helpful, write key terms on chart paper and role-play. Take a photograph of each student doing something from your list of helpful acts. As the school year progresses, take new photographs and rotate the images.

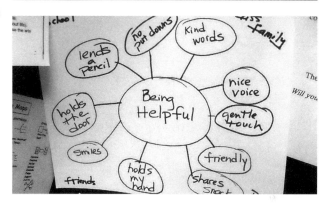

Go over your visual rules from Chapter 6. Show students the card that visually depicts being hurtful. Ask them what you could do in this situation to change your behavior from hurtful to helpful. Show the two choices to be helpful. Let children know that the consequence of being hurtful is to choose a way to be helpful instead.

General Activities
All Ages

Am I being helpful or hurtful?

Write down some typical ways that children are hurtful to each other. You might write, "A child grabs something from another child." Act this out with a child at circle time. Ask the children, "Is that helpful or hurtful?" Then have them think of a helpful way to get the object from the other person. They may say, "Ask for a turn." Write down a list of helpful acts.

Literacy Center

Use the Ways to Be Helpful Board to create a center that builds literacy skills while cementing what helpfulness looks like. Take photos of the children being helpful. Type up short sentences describing each helpful act, for example, "It is helpful to listen during circle time." Start by posting the matching photos and sentences together for children to read with a partner. Later you can remove the sentences, mix them up and have students place them back under the correct picture. After they become familiar with the sentences, copy each one on a sentence strip. Cut apart each sentence and place the pieces in separate Ziploc bags. Have children put the sentence together in a pocket chart.

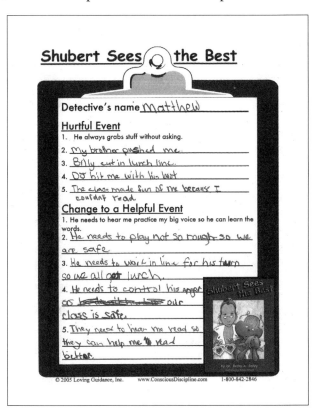

Shubert Sees the Best

In this book, join Shubert as he investigates the problem of name-calling and discovers surprising solutions. Shubert helps children see hurtful behavior from a different point of view, transforming hurtful situations—"He's mean!"—into helpful interactions. Use the free worksheet available at www.ConsciousDiscipline.com to help children transform a hurtful experience into a helpful one.

General Activities
Younger

Heartprints

Read *Heartprints* by P. K. Hallinan. After reading the book, create a bulletin board titled "(School Family Name) Leaves Heartprints." Cut heart shapes out of construction paper and put the hearts in a basket near the board. Explain that when the students notice someone being helpful or kind (leaving a heartprint), they can write the child's name and what happened on a heart and tape it to the bulletin board.

Thank You

Use the story *Thank You* by Betsey Chessen. Before showing the pictures to your class, cover the text with some Post-It cover-up tape . After showing them the pictures, ask them to use the words "You (describe helpful act seen in picture) so (describe result of action)." Do this for every picture in the book. This helps students focus on the helpfulness of each action that is being done. This is a great interactive writing lesson that can span across several days.

General Activities — Older

Scientific Process

The steps in the scientific process are: Ask a question, make a hypothesis, plan a fair test of the hypothesis, perform the test, collect and record data, report your conclusion, then go further. Start by asking the question: "What would happen if we were to use helpfulness all day long?" Have students hypothesize by brainstorming what might happen. Do a fair test by dividing the class into two parts, those who will make a point of being helpful and those who act the way they normally do. Collect feedback about how each group feels at the end of the day and what responses they received from others. Determine the conclusion by analyzing the data. Then challenge students to take it further.

How to Lose All Your Friends

Have students read *How to Lose All Your Friends* by Nancy Carlson. Then think of ways they want their School Family to be. Do they want to lose friends or have friends throughout the year? Make a class book titled "Ways we want our class to be." Give each student a page to complete that says, "I could lose a friend by _____. I would rather win a friend by _____." In the first blank, students fill in something hurtful. In the second blank, they change that behavior to one that is helpful. They then illustrate the helpful choice in the space remaining on the page.

Helpful/Hurtful Plants

This is an amazing experiment. Buy two of the same kind of plant that are approximately the same size. Give the plants the same amount of water and sunlight and have the students name and label the plants. Your "helpful" plant will have a loving name like "Precious," the "hurtful" plant will have a negative name like "Ugly." The only difference is that students tell the helpful plant it is helpful throughout the day and offers it kind words. The students call the hurtful plant names, and tell it that it's mean and hurtful throughout the day. Ask children to write a hypothesis in a journal about what they think will happen with the two plants. Chart the plants' growth for at least two weeks, then have students check their original hypothesis and discuss what they observed. What can this tell us about how our helpful and hurtful acts might impact each other?

Helpful Back Pats

Give students a sheet of plain white paper. Ask them to write their names at the top (they can also decorate it a little). Then tape each child's paper to his or her back. Instruct students to walk around the room noticing each other's kindness and helpfulness. Ask them to silently write a short statement on each other's papers. ("You shared a pencil with me yesterday. That was helpful.") Then they pat their friend on the back and move to another classmate. Play a song or have some other cue so children will know when the allotted time for the activity is over. Then have them go to their seats, remove their papers and read about their own helpfulness. Post the papers on a board or in a book if you choose. (Teacher tip: Give each child his or her own color marker so you can easily identify who is writing which comments.)

Ways to Be Helpful in Our School Family

Use the list generated when you introduced the Ways to Be Helpful structure to create a "Ways to Be Helpful in Our School Family" class book. Take photographs of the children acting out ways to be helpful and bind them together. Create a series of books: Ways to Be Helpful in the Hallway; Ways to Be Helpful on a Field Trip; Ways to Be Helpful at Lunch; Ways to Be Helpful on the Playground; Ways to Be Helpful at Home; etc. These books can complement your Routine Books from Chapter 6.

We Are Helpful

Have each child illustrate a picture that shows him- or herself doing a helpful act. Have them write, "I help my School Family by _____." Take dictation as needed. You can create a different version of this book by taking pictures of each child doing a helpful act, then adding text.

The Helping Book

Read the story *The Hating Book* by Charlotte Zolotow. Make an adaptation of it in your classroom called the "The Helping Book." To begin, have students think of one thing someone in the class did that was helpful. Create a book page using the frame, "(Name) did something helpful. (State the action and its result.). That was helpful." The book can continue all year long, with students adding pages as the helpful acts continue.

The Helpful Hunter

Read *The Honey Hunters* by Francesca Martin. The book describes how different animals hunt and search in different ways. Introduce "The Helpful Hunter" as a job. The Helpful Hunter's class job entails looking for kind acts throughout the day and sharing them at the designated time. Include this job on your Job Board.

School Family Yellow Pages

Create a directory of children's talents to use as a class resource when someone is having difficulty. Photocopy yellow-colored pages (full size or cut in half) printed with, "My name is (Name). I can help with (Helpful skill)." Give each child two to four pages to fill in and illustrate. Provide examples such as, "My name is Lyndsae and I can help with remembering music lyrics. My name is Chris and I can help with drawing. My name is Yvonne and I can help with multiplying." Bind the pages together as your "School Family Yellow Pages" and remind children to use them to seek help when they need it.

Music & Movement — Younger

That Was Helpful

Use "That Was Helpful" on *It Starts in the Heart* available at www.ConsciousDiscipline.com to act out ways to be helpful as you sing and move to the song. Take photos of students acting out the song, and use them to make a book or bulletin board.

Music & Movement — Older

Helpful Circles

Have the students form two circles, one inside of the other. The inside circle faces the outside circle so that the students are paired up. Once paired up, the students look at one another and say one helpful thing that the partner has done, using the formula, "You (action), so (describe impact). That

Chapter 7: Ways to Be Helpful Boards and Books

was helpful." The partner then does the same for that person. After they have shared, rotate the inner circle so that each child will have a new partner. Continue to move the circle several times as time permits or until all students have had the opportunity to offer helpful words to each other. Adding a repetitive, short musical track (20-30 seconds) can help coordinate the movement of the circle.

Encouraging Words

Using the same circle-within-a-circle style as in the previous activity, play the song "Encouraging Words" on the *Kindness Counts* CD. Act out the song with a partner as described in the CD booklet.

C = Commitment

I am willing to consciously focus my attention on noticing helpful acts in my classroom, with my colleagues, and at home with my own family. I will use the following phrase a minimum of three times per day.

"You _____ so _____. That was helpful."

Signature _____   **Date** _____

H = Helpful Resources

Music — All Ages

Kindness Counts **by Dr. Becky Bailey and Mr. Al**
Songs: "Encouraging Words," "Looking for Kindness"

Brain Boogie Boosters **by Dr. Becky Bailey and The Learning Station**
Song: "Team of Two"

It Starts in the Heart **by Jack Hartmann and Dr. Becky Bailey**
Songs: "That Was Helpful," "You Did It!," "Caring Friends," "Look at Me"

Literature — All Ages

Shubert Sees the Best **by Dr. Becky Bailey.** Join Shubert as he investigates the problem of name-calling and discovers surprising solutions. Shubert helps children see hurtful behavior from a different point of view, transforming hurtful situations into helpful interactions.

Thank You **by Betsey Chessen.** This is a picture book that shows what "helpful" looks like in a primary classroom. It gives students a concrete way to see helpful actions.

Mean Jean, The Recess Queen **by Alexis O'Neill and Laura Huliska-Beith.** This book is filled with wonderful language. Everyone at school avoids Mean Jean until one day Katie Sue, the new girl, asks her to play.

The Kissing Hand **by Audrey Penn.** A "Chester" raccoon puppet can be a great tool for pointing out helpful acts in your classroom. You can find a puppet that looks just like Chester at www.folkmanis.com.

Chapter 8

Beginning the Day the Brain Smart Way

Ever had one of those days? You wake up tired. Someone used up the last of the milk for the coffee. Your "Check engine" light flickers on. A brief email turns into a big misunderstanding. Everything that could go wrong, does. As a teacher, you're still supposed to show up at work with a smile on your face to greet children, many who have had their own difficult morning, too.

The transition from home to school can be treacherous for both teachers and children. Several years ago I was visiting a teacher friend who had three wonderful children, ages four, seven and eleven. I was privileged to be there on a school day. The departure time for this family was 7:15 a.m. The four-year-old was up at 5:30, and turned on the television very loud. Since I was sleeping on the couch, I was up early with him. At 6:30, the mother dragged the 11-year-old out of bed, only to see her collapse on the floor complaining. The seven-year-old, notorious for being the "family informant," spent the morning sharing what Daddy did with his new wife at the softball game the night before (unknowingly infuriating my friend). A pleasant 7:15 departure was not looking good.

The 11-year-old made it into the shower and somehow managed to soak the four-year-old, who then ran through the house naked, wet and screaming. That was it. My friend lost it. At the top of her lungs, she bellowed, "I've had about as much of this as I can take!" She began barking orders and pointing: "You get dressed, you no television, and you! I don't know what I will do with you, but I will think of something." At 7:15, amazingly, we all left the house. The four-year-old was dressed, but his clothes were plastered oddly to his body because he did not dry off before dressing. The seven-year-old was crying on the way to the car and the 11-year-old kept repeating, "Whatever." As for me, I felt blessed to have kept breathing through the experience.

The stress of getting up and out of the house is intense for many families. Even in homes with the best of routines, life happens. In many homes, children wake themselves up and dress younger siblings. They feed themselves, if food is available. They walk to the bus stop alone. When children enter the classroom, a lot has already occurred in their lives at home, on the bus and in the halls. The same is true for teachers. It is important to begin the school day the "Brain Smart" way to reenergize, refocus and restart our morning. If we are going to have a successful school day, it is absolutely essential to begin it with activities that will prime the mind-body states of both teachers and students for optimal functioning. The optimal state for learning is relaxed alertness.

The Conscious Discipline Brain Smart Start consists of four activities: An activity to unite, an activity to disengage stress, an activity to connect and an activity to commit. These four activities support our dearest values and provide experiences that help children (and us) shift from a disorganized to an organized internal state. These four activities are designed to create a biochemistry that balances and integrates brain function, mind and body. As noted in Chapter 2, our internal state dictates our behaviors toward one another and our ability to learn. Current research and common sense tell us that if our inner state is peaceful, our view of life is more optimistic and our behavior is more helpful. The Brain Smart Start helps to change our internal state from conflicted to peaceful, so we can experience deeper learning and more cooperative classrooms.

The research in this chapter will give you the foundation necessary to motivate yourself to change how you currently start your day. The activities and lessons will help you begin implementing a Brain Smart Start or help you tweak what you are already doing to maximize the positive potential of each day.

Activity to Unite

Children come to school in many different mind-body states. Some feel happy, others feel sad, many feel anxious and a few feel frustrated. In addition to diverse internal states, their attention is equally scattered. Some are thinking about their upcoming birthday, some about their parents' divorce and others about something that happened on the bus. The goal of the activity to unite is to bring this scattered energy into a more congruent and cohesive whole. It attempts to bring the children and teachers to the same page. Many schools have traditional uniting activities such as the Pledge of Allegiance or a good morning song for younger children. These activities require all students and teachers to stop what they are doing and shift to doing something in unison. Similarly, the activity to unite in the Brain Smart Start involves everyone moving, chanting or singing in unison.

Activity to Disengage the Stress Response

The uniting activity pulls the scattered energy of the group together. Next, we will disengage the stress response. From a biological perspective, our body's basic function is survival, not learning. We are physically and chemically primed to watch for a saber-toothed tiger, even though today's tiger might be a threat from a bully, fear of failing a math quiz or distress over losing a favorite toy. When stressed, the higher centers of the brain shut down in favor of the lower survival centers. When the higher centers shut down, so does all higher-order learning. If your class members remain in a stressed state, their ability to connect with you, each other and the material you are presenting is highly compromised. Not only are stressed children unable to effectively learn, your ability to teach is impaired as you spend much time dealing with outbursts from stressed children who act out in challenging ways.

When we experience stress, a cascade of over 1,400 different biochemicals is released in the body. These hormones and neurotransmitters affect how we perceive, feel and behave. Of all these biochemicals, three are most worth mentioning: adrenaline, catecholamines and cortisol.

Adrenaline decreases deep breathing, eye teaming and whole brain function. It also can give you a boost, much like a cup of coffee. Strong emotions like anger and fear dump a lot of adrenaline into your system, but the adrenaline doesn't stay in the bloodstream long. This is why anger and fear give you a temporary surge of energy, only to leave you feeling like a wet dishrag afterward. Too much adrenaline creates too many ups and downs, and results in burnout. How many teachers go home exhausted and how many children come to school the same way?

Catecholamines are an entire category of neurotransmitters. These particular neurotransmitters deactivate the prefrontal cortex. As we discussed in earlier chapters, the prefrontal cortex is the CEO of the brain and is in charge of concentration, planning, time management, decision making, problem solving, empathy and impulse control (Arnsten, 1998). Stress bathes the brain in catecholamines, essentially deactivating teachers' and children's prefrontal lobes and sending all those wonderful skills down the drain.

Last on our list, cortisol is the big guy when we talk about stress chemicals. Negative emotions fuel higher cortisol levels. Unlike adrenalin, cortisol lingers in the bloodstream for hours, causing longer-lasting results. Cortisol inhibits the immune system and impedes learning and memory. It also increases the transport of fat molecules in the vessels going to the heart, contributing to heart attacks and high-blood pressure (Hannaford, 2010). In adults, constantly misplacing your pocketbook, forgetting where you parked your car and thinking, "Why am I in this room," are wake-up calls from the cortisol in your body. In children, forgetting things they've gone over "a hundred times" and going bonkers during transitions are indicators that cortisol is in play. A child's brain on cortisol has trouble picking up patterns, so the routines that add order to your classroom are not effective for them. Learning is also impossible due to reduced memory capabilities. Essentially, the cortisol released when we're stressed creates both physical and mental absenteeism.

It is absolutely essential to begin the day with stress-reducing activities and take frequent brain breaks throughout the day in order to combat the ill effects of adrenaline, catecholamines, cortisol and the hundreds of other stress biochemicals and their effects. Stretching, breathing, exercising, singing and laughing are all good ways to turn off the stress response and maintain healthy optimal learning states for teachers and students.

Activity to Connect

Once the body begins to relax and the stress response is turned off, true connection with one another is possible. Connection is essential for three reasons:

1. Connection stimulates the impulse control centers in the brain, facilitating children in being helpful, contributing members of their School Family.
2. Connection activates the attention systems in the brain, enhancing children's ability to sustain attention.
3. Cooperation follows connection. With connection, children become willing partners with the teacher, and all learning progresses from this willingness.

Disconnected students are disruptive because of lack of impulse control, low frustration tolerance, inability to sustain attention and decreased self-regulation skills. The biggest problem when attempting to reach out to disconnected children is their resistance to our help. Without a student's willingness to want to solve the problem, the problem is unsolvable. Many teachers make a concerted effort to connect with students using some form of greeting each morning. Teachers foster connections between the students themselves much less frequently. We want them learning quietly, with hands and feet to themselves and backsides in their seats. We seem to think that creating connections between students threatens academic goals. However, research indicates that caring relationships between all parties in schools is necessary for academic success (Wentzel & Watkins, 2002).

Beginning the day with a connection activity between children, and between the teacher and the children, stimulates the impulse control systems of the brain and generates a neurochemical bath that says, "Pay attention, this is fun." Activities to connect differ from activities to unite because they require at least two people to conduct the activity together, and they focus on eye contact, touch, presence and playfulness.

Activity to Commit

The final component to the Brain Smart Start is a verbal commitment. A commitment that is spoken out loud does many things, both psychologically and neurologically. First and foremost, it increases the likelihood of following through on a commitment. Think about this in your own life. Let's say you've been thinking about exercising a bit more to lose some weight. First, you privately ponder this change. From this thinking state, you then progress to talking about it with others. Once you have chatted with friends, you are ready to make a commitment. You might say, "That's it! I'm going to join the gym and exercise more." At this moment of verbal commitment, your chances of actually exercising increase tremendously. Research indicates that making a commitment and focusing our attention activate the planning circuits in the brain's prefrontal cortex (Schwartz & Begley, 2002). Making a commitment and following through also build self-esteem, neurologically bathing the body in feel-good chemicals. These chemicals help focus attention and achieve goals.

Often, we toy with or dance around a commitment instead of actually making one. We might say things like, "I've been thinking about losing some weight," or "I need to get started on my weight loss." We might even get more passionate and say, "I should lose weight." None of these phrases are actually a commitment. When we phrase things in the following ways, we are actually taking a passive, victim approach to managing our lives:

I need to _____
I have to _____
I should _____
I was hoping I could _____
I wish I could _____

Phrases like, "I have to exercise," imply someone else is running your life. Who really says you have to exercise? The hidden context of the language above says, "If external issues, people and events allow, I could possibly move forward with my goals, provided something else does not come up." These phrases hold no power.

Commitments come from claiming our inner power. They are statements that declare, "I will do this regardless of external events." I encourage people to use the phrase "I'm going to _____" with themselves and with their students. "I'm going to_____" is an internal declaration of the willingness and ability to be true to yourself. For children, these internal declarations help activate and develop executive skills.

150 *Creating the School Family*

Commitments in your Brain Smart Start can be independent, such as writing individual commitments in journals, or in a group, like stating together, "Today I will be helpful at least one time." You could also speak your commitment in the form of a class chant, such as: "Today I'm going to have listening ears, kind words, no put-downs, the right to pass and gentle touches treating everyone as I would like to be treated." Once you have made your commitment, the brain is prepped for a day of increased self-regulated learning.

The Benefits of the Brain Smart Start

By using the Brain Smart Start, both you and your children will be ready for an exciting day of learning. It's one thing to talk about creating a safe classroom where children feel a sense of security and belonging. It is another thing to provide activities so that children can experience what safety and connection feel like internally. Starting the day the Brain Smart way creates the potential to achieve the following:

1. An organized, stress-reduced body
2. Focused attention
3. An integrated mind, body and brain for optimal learning
4. A positive internal state that facilitates the brain's ability to pick up patterns
5. A connection with others and the feeling that "I am part of something bigger than myself"
6. An activated prefrontal lobe, bringing impulse control, empathy, problem solving and all higher thinking skills online
7. A personal commitment to be the best "you" possible

Yeah, But I Don't Have Time!

Mrs. James was a third-grade teacher in a school that was beginning to implement Conscious Discipline. A Loving Guidance Associate explained the Brain Smart Start and demonstrated some activities. Mrs. James didn't buy in one bit! In her mind she believed, "My children have a lot to accomplish in third grade. This is not kindergarten and I do not have time to sing and carry on with this feel-good nonsense." However, Mrs. James was a team player and, to be honest, she wanted the approval of the principal. So, she reluctantly started her day the Brain Smart way. Lo and behold, her days seemed easier. Still, she didn't attribute this to the Brain Smart Start; she believed the children were becoming better adjusted as the year progressed. Then her principal was transferred to another school. The new principal wasn't familiar with Conscious Discipline, and as soon as the former principal was gone, so was the Brain Smart Start. Mrs. James's class soon became unruly and agitated. To her surprise, her own fuse felt shorter, too. She and the class just didn't feel right, the number of discipline situations increased, the amount of teaching she could accomplish in a day declined and the students' productivity also declined. The children begged her to return to the Brain Smart Start from day one. After a week of frustration, she was more than willing to agree with them. These days Mrs. James can't say enough good things about the Brain Smart Start. She calls herself a "convert" and swears by its effectiveness. Her comment to others teachers is simple: "You don't have time not to do it."

The Power of Becoming Brain Smart: The optimal state for learning is one of relaxed alertness
Skills: Activities for uniting, reducing stress, connecting and committing
Structure: Brain Smart Start routine
Value: Safety

The Brain Smart Start is a scientifically based way to maintain optimal learning states during daily transitions. The biggest transition for schools is the start of the day; however, transitions occur throughout the day. There are transitions to and from specials (music, art, physical education). There are transitions for lunch, toileting, rest time and between subject areas. Following each transition, think of your job as helping children organize, relax and be motivated to refocus their attention on the task at hand. You will achieve all of this by using the Brain Smart Start.

Many teachers who work in early childhood education or the early elementary grades are familiar with transition songs and signals. These songs and signals are wonderful tools to help the children move from point A to point B. If you already use these transition tools, start thinking of their purpose as something bigger than a prompt (flashing lights), reminder ("It's time to clean up") or song. Instead, think in terms of activities to unite (sing the song after flashing the lights), reduce stress (follow me in being a S.T.A.R.), connect (high five a friend) and commit (say, "We can do it!" to a friend). Switching from a simple prompt to a Brain Smart activity designed to promote optimal brain development will yield immediate positive results. Think of one transition in your school that is difficult for the children, and transform it into a Brain Smart transition, as in the following example.

Current Transition Routine:	New Brain Smart Transition Routine:
Signal by the teacher: "1-2-3, eyes on me. Red group, go to the reading table." The teacher arrives, shows the book that is the center of the lesson, and reminds children to keep their hands and feet to themselves, their bottoms in their chairs and their eyes on the teacher.	Signal by the teacher: "1-2-3, eyes on me. Red group members, raise your hands and say, 'I am going to the reading table.'" At the reading table, give one child a little lotion on his or her hand and rub it in while singing, "Passing the lotion, passing the lotion, passing the lotion to my friend right now." The children then pass the lotion from one child to another, singing in unison. At the conclusion of the passing game, instruct the children to S.T.A.R. (Smile, Take a deep breath, And, Relax) while smelling the lotion on their hands.

At Fern Creek Elementary School, the Brain Smart Start routine starts as soon as the children arrive on campus. Twenty percent of the students arrive by bus from the homeless shelter. The remaining 80 percent come from high-poverty areas. For many children, the transition to school is very difficult. They arrive hungry, tired, hurt and angry. Children are first greeted on the bus with a "call and response" chant. The adult greeter says the first line, and the children on the bus respond back with the second line.

Adult: "This is Fern Creek, what do you say?"
Students: "We're going to have a great day."
Adult: "We'll work hard to keep you safe."
Students: "We will help in every way."

Then the adult leads them in being a S.T.A.R. together. The greeting ends with the adult making any necessary announcements and saying, "Have a great day!"

Once the children leave the bus, five different adults greet them in a delightful, organized way before they arrive at their classrooms. The greetings are as simple as high fives and hugs. The teachers are taught to read faces and body language. Children who are tense are encouraged to take a deep breath with the teacher as the teacher says, "Breathe with me. You're safe." The teachers love this morning routine because the children's learning state begins to change before they ever arrive in class. Review the above morning routine, which starts on the bus, and see if you can identify the parts of the Brain Smart Start.

Activity to unite_____
Activity to disengage stress_____
Activity to connect_____
Activity to commit_____

Mr. Bartlett's second-grade class begins arriving in a scattered format starting at 8:15. Some children come straight to class, others go to breakfast first, and some start their day with reading interventions. He does not have all students in one place until around 9:00. At this time, he gathers the children together for their Brain Smart Start of the day. He starts with movement and music, using the song "It's Brain Smart Time" from the *Kindness Counts* CD. This song is designed to include an activity to unite, disengage stress and connect. Once students finish the song, they then conduct a commitment rap they created:

> I will listen, use kind words and commit to quality work
> If someone gets in my face, I will calm down in the Safe Place
> My power comes from working it out, there's no need to scream or shout
> Mr. Bartlett's School Family takes care of you and me!

E = Environmental Structure: Brain Smart Routine

The Brain Smart Start includes an activity to unite, to disengage stress, to connect and to commit. An activity (or activities) that combines all of these qualities creates a brain state that is optimal for learning, cooperation and success.

Creating the School Family

Purpose: The Brain Smart Start has two core purposes:

1. Helping teachers and children make the transition from home to school
2. Maximizing teaching time by reducing the amount of time wasted during other daily transitions.

In the simplest terms, the Brain Smart Start prepares the brain for a successful day of learning. The Brain Smart breaks you take throughout the day help to keep stress levels low and attention, connection and learning levels high.

How to set up your Brain Smart Start: The Brain Smart Start is essentially a routine that includes the components of uniting, disengaging stress, connecting and committing. Choose from the activities below (or activities you design yourself) to create a clear daily routine that includes the uniting, disengaging stress, connecting and committing components. You may choose to add a visual way to manage the Brain Smart Start using flip charts, choice cubes or a spinner. In younger classrooms, select a routine that has minimal variation in order to strengthen the pattern. Primary and younger children are accustomed to having circle time in their classrooms at least once if not twice a day, and this provides an ideal time to conduct your Brain Smart activities. Older grades benefit from more variety and can manage their Brain Smart Start themselves, using the tools mentioned above (chart, cubes, spinner). In older classrooms, you can conduct your Brain Smart Start with a morning circle or have the children stand by their desks. Starting the day in a circle is preferred because everyone is able to see everyone else, like a healthy family starting its day around the breakfast table.

How to introduce the Brain Smart Start: Begin your Brain Smart Start on the first day of school. Plan your routine in advance, paying attention to each category of uniting, disengaging the stress response, connecting and committing. One activity might incorporate several of the components. For example, the song "Get Ready" on *It Starts in the Heart*

CD incorporates the first three components of the Brain Smart Start as it directs children to unite, disengage the stress response and connect. The Activities section below provides ideas for each component of your routine.

It is helpful at the beginning of the year to use the same song for a week or longer to reinforce the pattern. As the year progresses and you become more comfortable with each of the components, you will feel empowered to be more spontaneous and add variation to the activities. Older students benefit from switching activities with some frequency to keep things fresh and novel. Older students can also be responsible for learning, tracking and changing many of the activities themselves.

Eventually, it will also be beneficial to lead a discussion about why you do your Brain Smart Start together. Students can compare how they feel before and after they do their Brain Smart Start. Simply asking children to rate their internal state on a scale of 1-5 can provide a good gauge of your routine's impact, and this helps raise children's self-awareness. For example, you can say, "On a scale of 1-5, how awake and ready to learn do you feel this morning? Write that number on your paper." Gather together and conduct your Brain Smart Start, then ask, "Now, on a scale of 1-5, how awake and ready to learn do you feel after your Brain Smart Start? Write that number on your paper." In older classrooms, you would also share the brain information discussed earlier in this chapter and throughout this book.

Below are examples of activities you can use as part of your Brain Smart Start routine. Many activities will embody multiple qualities of uniting, connecting, disengaging the stress response and committing.

General Activities — All Ages

School Family Song or Chant

If you have created a School Family song or chant (see Chapter 10), this can also serve as your activity to unite. Your School Family song or chant may also incorporate your class commitment, in which case it would also fulfill the commitment activity.

I Love You Rituals

I wrote the book *I Love You Rituals* to build the healthy connections that foster cooperation and learning. Favorite rituals from the *I Love You Rituals* book include "Peter, Peter Pumpkin Eater," "Twinkle, Twinkle, Little Star" and "A Wonderful Woman." The *Songs for I Love You Rituals, Vol. 1 and Vol. 2*, music CDs contain some rituals that match up with the book, plus some new ones. You can introduce I Love You Rituals either as whole group or with a partner. All of the I Love You Rituals will fulfill the connection component of the Brain Smart Start and are essential for the developing brains of children eight years old and younger.

Mix and Mingle Learning

As a review, give half the students a card with a vocabulary word or a question on it. Give the other half cards with the answer or definition on it. A younger example might be the word "elephant" on one card and a picture of an elephant on another. An older example might include "4x9" on one card and "36" on another. Students stand up and find their correct partner. Once they find their partner, they greet each other in some way. This activity connects.

Pencil Stretches

Have students face one another. Each will put a pencil between their pointer finger and their partner's pointer finger. Have them stretch in different ways, with one arm up, one arm down, bending and stretching. Variation: Have students hold their pencils together while doing a dance to a song like "YMCA." This activity connects and disengages the stress response.

Active Calming Techniques

Active calming techniques are a sure way to disengage the stress response. The four core active calming techniques of Conscious Discipline are S.T.A.R., drain, balloon and pretzel. S.T.A.R. is an acronym for Smile, Take a deep breath And Relax. For the drain technique, extend both arms straight out in front of you, tensing all the arm, shoulder and face muscles as tightly as possible. Exhale slowly making a "sssshhh" sound and release the contraction, draining out the stress. For the balloon, place your hands on top of your head and interlace your fingers. Breathe in and raise your hands off your head. Take additional deep breaths as you raise your arms, blowing up an imaginary balloon over your head. Release the air in the balloon by pursing your lips and exhaling slowly, making a "pbpbpbpbpb" sound. For the pretzel, stand or sit and cross your right leg over your left leg at the ankles. Now, put your arms out in front of you and cross your right wrist over your left. Turn your hands so your thumbs are pointing down, put your palms together and interlace your fingers. Bend your elbows out and gently turn your hands down and toward your body until they rest on the center of your chest. Put your tongue on the roof of your mouth. Relax and breathe in this position for a few minutes. You will be noticeably calmer after that time (Hannaford, 2005). These activities need to be done daily and whenever the children are mildly stressed. Regular practice with active calming techniques prepares children to successfully use them in the Safe Place when they are intensely upset. These activities disengage the stress response and are also helpful for staff meetings.

Cross Crawl

Stand or sit. Simultaneously put your right hand across your body toward your left knee while you raise up your knee. Repeat the same motion using the left hand on the right knee. Repeat for about two minutes with or without music. Crossing the midline of the body in this manner integrates the hemispheres of the brain and has a calming effect. This activity disengages the stress response.

Brain Smart Choices for Connection and Calming

Fill one cube from the Brain Smart Choices for Connection and Calming (from Loving Guidance) with the Active Calming cards and the other cube with the I Love You Ritual cards provided with the set. At the beginning of the activity, have students clap their hands on their legs and say, "Let's rock," then make a rolling motion with their arms and say, "and roll." Roll the cubes. Students then perform the active calming technique and the I Love You Ritual that lands facing up. Thorough instructions for conducting all the activities and rituals are included in the set. This activity connects, unites and disengages the stress response.

Arm Raise Pair and Share

Ask everyone in the class to stand up. Inhale while raising your arms above your head. Exhale while slowly lowering your arms. Now say, "Turn to your neighbor and _____," asking them to share either a learning-related item or something from their personal life. You might say, "Share three examples of how we use mercury in real life," or, "Tell your partner one thing you did last weekend." This activity connects and disengages the stress response.

If—Then Breathing

Say to students, "If you are ready for ____, then ____," naming the next activity and then asking them to do something that shows their readiness. You might say, "If you are ready for snack time, then take a deep breath and exhale slowly to the count to five," or, "If you're ready for science, then stand on one foot and take three deep breaths." This activity disengages the stress response.

Safekeeper Ritual

Include your Safekeeper ritual from Chapter 5 as part of your activity to commit. You are committing to keep them safe and they are committing to help keep the classroom safe.

Class Agreements

Recite the class agreements you made in Chapter 6 daily (pg 116). Add a motion for each commitment, making a rhythmic chant. Remember to post a visual representation of these agreements in a prime location to help the children be successful. This activity unites and commits.

Individual Commitments

Have students write a commitment beginning with the words, "I'm going to" each day. Guide students

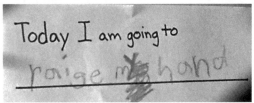

> **Individual Committments:**
>
> Some students will have difficulty keeping their individual commitments. First, check to see that the commitment is specific, narrow in scope and realistic. If commitments are still an issue, have students self-evaluate several times throughout the day (after specials, after lunch, etc.). The more often the students check in with their commitment, the more likely they will be successful with them. Remember to remove your judgments about their success or failure. It is their judgments that matter, not yours.

to create commitments that are stated in the positive and are specific, narrow in scope and realistic. For example, "I won't hit anyone" becomes "Today, I'm going to use words to ask for what I want," and "I'm going to eat healthier" becomes "Today, I'm going to eat all my vegetables at lunch." Older students can write their commitments in their planners or journals. Younger students can choose from a series of commitment sentence strips you have created for them. Make certain students of all ages use the format, "Today, I'm going to _____." At the end of the day, invite students to evaluate their commitment to themselves with either, "I did it!" or "Oops! I'll try again tomorrow." This activity commits.

Music & Movement
All Ages

It's Brain Smart Time

"It's Brain Smart Time" on *Kindness Counts* is the perfect Brain Smart Start theme song! This song will unite, connect and disengage stress, so all you need to do is make a commitment to fulfill all four requirements. It is a fun, energetic song for transitions and brain breaks, too.

It Starts in the Heart

Play "It Starts in the Heart" from the CD by the same title. If you all hold hands and lift your arms above your head when you hear "Build a Bridge," this song fulfills two of the four components: unite and connect.

This Is My School Family

Play "This Is My School Family" on *It Starts in the Heart*, create movements for the lyrics that aren't self-explanatory and follow the lyrics for the ones that are ("Hug with a friend," etc.). This song will unite and connect.

Good Morning

Follow along and create movements that work with the song "Good Morning" on *It Starts in the Heart* CD. This song will unite, connect and disengage stress.

Greetings

"Greetings" on *Brain Boogie Boosters* unites and connects.

We Are a Family

"We Are a Family" on *Learning to Love* by Jack Hartmann includes sign language for the lyrics in the CD booklet. Teach students a few of the basic signs before you begin. This song unites.

I'm a Helpful Person

"I'm a Helpful Person" in *Songs for I Love You Rituals, Vol. 2* will meet three of the four components: uniting, connecting and committing. You can randomly hand out puzzle pieces that fit together in matching pairs and have children use them to find their partner. This eliminates children being left without a partner or having their feelings hurt. If there are an odd number of children, take a puzzle piece yourself and partner up with a student.

We Are Family

"We Are Family" by Sister Sledge is a pop culture family song. There are many karaoke versions that will give you the music of the song, or you can play the original. Ask students to adapt the words of the song to fit their School Family, for example:

> We are family
> I got all my classmates with me!
> We are family
> Come on everybody and see!
> We are family!

Mix, Pair and Share

Have the students stand up. Start some music. As the music plays, students walk around the room. When you stop the music, the students grab a person nearby and tell them a fact about a given subject. Once they have shared the fact, they greet each other in some way (high five, etc.). Start the music again, and they find a new partner to repeat the process with. Make this a memory-building activity in older classrooms by selecting a time later in the day for students to restate their facts and do the greetings they did earlier with their partners.

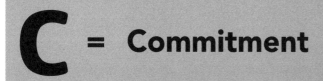

C = Commitment

I am going to start off my personal day in the Brain Smart way. I am going to unite with others in my household or my creator. I am going to reduce the stress by stretching and breathing. I am going to authentically connect with others or my creator. I am going to commit to one thing for this most precious day.

Signature _____ **Date** _____

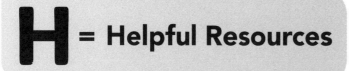

H = Helpful Resources

Music — All Ages

Brain Boogie Boosters **by Dr. Becky Bailey and The Learning Station**
Songs: "Greetings," "Friends Connect"

It Starts in the Heart **by Dr. Becky Bailey and Jack Hartmann**
Songs: "My School Family," "I Wish You Well" (English and Spanish), "Friendship Chant," "Welcome," "People to People" (English and Spanish)

Kindness Counts **by Dr. Becky Bailey and Mr. Al**
Song: "It's Brain Smart Time"

Songs for I Love You Rituals, Vol. 1 and Vol. 2 **by Dr. Becky Bailey and Mar Harman**
Song: All songs

Learning to Love **by Jack Hartmann**
Song: "We Are a Family"

Tony Chestnut **by The Learning Station**
Song: "Tony Chestnut"

We Are Family **by Sister Sledge**
Song: "We Are Family"

Learning with Hip Hop **by Mark D. Pencil**
Song: "Following Directions"

Literature

I Love You Rituals **by Dr. Becky Bailey.** This book is full of classroom and family rituals that build connection and foster cooperation. Many of the activities fill more than one component of the Brain Smart Start.

Additional Aids

Brain Smart Choices for Calming and Connection from www.ConsciousDiscipline.com
Yoga Pretzels by Tara Guber, Leah Kalish and Sophie Fatus
I Calm Safe Place Mat from www.ConsciousDiscipline.com

Chapter 9

Safe Place

In December 2004, Lisa Simms died in a horseback riding accident. Her third-grade daughter, Madeline, attended a Conscious Discipline S.T.A.R. School. Michael Simms, Madeline's father, wrote the following letter to the school about his efforts to move through his own grief and help his daughter:

> *In this time of my losing my wife, and my children's mother . . . we are all trying to make sense of aspects of the accident. Sadly I often can only console the girls with the truth and reality. It hurts and creates a loneliness that I wish on no one.*
>
> *Only a week now from the accident, I felt the importance of getting the girls back into a semblance of the schedule that we enjoyed prior to their mother's passing. We talked about when we might be ready to go back to school, and as you can imagine the girls had good excuses to put it off and delay. During the day after the Celebration of Lisa's life, I let Madeline know that the next day (Friday) she would need to be prepared for school.*
>
> *As we were driving to school, I was talking to her and reminded her that*

Mrs. Matthews was so looking forward to her return . . . that the children were anxious to see her and comfort her. My concern was that she would be overcome with a wave of grief that we all seem to be weathering these days.

She reminded me, to alleviate my concerns, that she had a "Safe Place" in her classroom. I asked her about it… thinking that it was more of a "time-out" space. She explained that it was a place that she could go at any time to settle her emotions and that in the Safe Place there were exercises that she had learned to get her emotions, be it anger, sadness or as we say, "sassiness" under control. Obviously, I was floored . . . and very grateful to know that she saw a place at the school as a haven for the mess that she is having to weather at the age of seven.

I had, to this point, considered the Safe Place in her classrooms as a bit hokey. But I saw in her eyes that she knew she could get though the day at school knowing that she had a refuge.

Thank you for creating that zone that has and will provide her with the comfort she will need to process the passing of her mother while she gets back on track. . . . I sure wish our work places had safe zones.

Thank you.

Regards,
Michael H. Simms

The Safe Place is a structure that concretely embodies our philosophy and commitment to creating safe learning environments for children. Stressful situations throw us into the lower centers of our brain where we can only access survival skills. Whether we are four years old or 40, we find ourselves attacking, defending, hiding and lying when we operate from the lower centers of the brain. Unless we consciously intervene in our own minds, our reaction will be some version of the infamous fight-or-flight response. The Safe Place provides this intervention for us, empowering us with self-regulatory strategies.

We see fight-or-flight responses in the classroom every day. Shakena comes to school distraught and buries her head in her arms on her desk, refusing to participate. Danny is anxious about an upcoming quiz, so he yells at his reading partner. Kim's feelings are hurt so she shoves Mackenzie, then looks right at you and says he fell over by himself. Children experience a multitude of stressors. Unless we teach them how to self-regulate and calm themselves, there will be some sort of negative physical, verbal or psychological outcome. Furthermore, it is impossible for new learning to occur when a child is stressed or distraught. (As we learned in previous chapters, learning is a higher-order brain function, and a stressed child is operating from the lower centers of the brain.)

The good news is that even the youngest children can be taught simple breathing activities that help calm the brain and the body. As adults, we carry our Safe Place with us in our minds. Ideally, when stress hits, we calm ourselves to move from the brain's fight-or-flight lower centers to its reason-and-wisdom higher centers. Once in the higher centers, we can respond with self-control, responsibility and problem solving. Children require assistance with the calming process, and the Safe Place is the learning center for teaching emotional control and self-regulation.

The Safe Place represents a sacred space where children are instructed, encouraged and supported in attending to their own emotional upsets through self-regulating activities. It is a voluntary structure they are free to use as needed, and can use as long as needed. I use the word *sacred* in describing the Safe Place to signify the trust and respect required from the adult so the Safe Place can successfully fulfill its function for the children.

Recently, a teacher approached me with excitement and said, "I just felt safe enough to implement a Safe Place in my classroom." I was somewhat surprised because I knew she had embraced Conscious Discipline and had been implementing it in her classroom for over a year and a half. I released my judgment of how it's supposed to be done and celebrated the joy she was feeling. I responded, "Good for you! How is it working?"

Her response was typical of what I have heard from teachers and parents across the nation: "It's wonderful! You wouldn't believe what's happening in my classroom. I introduced the Safe Place on Monday and Tuesday. No one had used it by Wednesday of the next week. Then on Thursday, one of my students came to school very sad because his dog had died. I used this moment to reintroduce the Safe Place in the context of this child's life. The child went to the Safe Place that morning and visited it occasionally for the next two days. The empathy and understanding offered by other children was greater than I could have imagined or thought possible from this particular class. After that, other children have used it as needed. Even my most difficult student, who tends to blow up when frustrated, went to the Safe Place and did some breathing activities. To my surprise, he then came back to his seat and finished his work. All the fears and *what ifs* that kept me from implementing the Safe Place dissipated. I had been thinking, *What if they try to get out of doing work?* and *What if they won't go when needed?* and *What if they stay in it all day?* I am so glad I finally let go of enough fear to come from my heart, and trust the children and myself. My classroom has changed a lot, but I think it might be me who has changed the most in my respect for the children."

The Power of Perception

The Safe Place is the self-regulation structure that combines the Conscious Discipline skill of composure and our power of perception. Composure is our ability to remain or regain our calm in difficult situations. Perception is how we choose to see certain situations. Our internal state and our perception are intricately linked. When we are upset, it is easy to make a mountain out of a molehill with how we "see" the event at the time. Once we have calmed ourselves down, we are able to more accurately perceive the molehill that triggered us. We must develop our internal Safe Place and internalize composure skills before we can teach them to children. This requires becoming aware of our personal triggers, choosing internal dialogue that is calming instead of inflammatory and intentionally making choices different from our habitual ones. Only then can we effectively teach children to use the classroom Safe Place to regain calm.

Upset (the loss of composure) comes from resisting what is occurring. Common thoughts that resist the moment include, "Children shouldn't talk to adults like they do. I would never talk to my parents like that." "This road work shouldn't take five years, look at those workers just standing around." We are only able to practice authentic composure when we stop demanding that events occur and people act in prescribed ways. This authentic composure radiates from within us and sends an energetic communication to others that translates into a sense of "all is well." This energetic communication is felt by children and broadcasts a beam of love that says, "You are safe." It also allows us to access the higher centers of our brain so that we can solve problems, see from another's point of view and communicate effectively.

 I find that meditating, exercise and walking in nature help me locate my inner Safe Place.

During these times, I'm able to access a sense of peace that soothes my soul. My goal is to go through life remembering this soothing inner peace, drawing from its wisdom to accept what is and moving forward with solutions. However, if your life is anything like mine, you more often feel frantic than filled with blissful peace. My mind is jammed with thoughts of phone calls to make, upcoming workshops, stacks of correspondence, deadlines for writing and lists for groceries. My details may be different from yours, but I'm sure many of your days are similar in tone.

We all have demands of time and circumstance. Peace comes from choosing, through the power of perception, to allow life to unfold rather than attempting to force it into our mold of what "should be" based on our past experiences and current judgments. It requires that we let each moment, each item on our to-do list and each conflict in our life exist just as it is. For me, it all comes back to the serenity prayer:

> Grant me the serenity to accept the things that I cannot change,
> The courage to change the things I can,
> And the wisdom to know the difference.

Our example teaches children how to perceive others and how to communicate upset. When we operate from an internal Safe Place where we perceive peace in the face of difficulty and disruption, we will teach children to practice peace in their lives. If we operate from the perception that Terrence is kicking the desk just to annoy us and the teacher's assistant should have finished organizing the worksheets already, then we teach our children to snap to judgment and negate the moment. Negating the moment says the moment is not good enough and neither are you. To feel good enough on the inside, we must let life be good enough on the outside. It is our choice to see a situation with acceptance or judgment. My hope for all of us is that we choose to maintain our quiet center today and remember the Safe Place within that is waiting to be called upon.

In one very high-risk school, the staff perceived a fifth grader named Dylan to be nothing but trouble. This school's mobility rate was 82 percent, but Dylan had defied the statistics by staying at the school for four years.

The school had just begun using Conscious Discipline, but only one fifth-grade teacher, Ms. Harris, was interested in implementing it. Fortunately for Dylan, Ms. Harris was his teacher. Recognizing an opportunity to teach, she put Dylan in charge of devising a School Family song or chant. He worked with a group of classmates to create a rap called "Got your back, no need to slack." She also taught Dylan about the brain, helping him redefine "power" as being composed enough to handle life situations, rather than his previous definition in which dominance equaled power. She introduced the Safe Place as a place he could go to collect his power through composure. She said to him, "Almost everyone in this school expects you to stay in trouble. They believe you're a troublemaker. They are telling you who you are. Is that what you want? Do you want all these people telling you who you are or do you want to take back your power by showing them who you really are?" She asked him to think about it and let her know his answer at the end of the week.

During that week, Ms. Harris invited a friend of hers to the class. He had come from a violent home and had been in jail, but then he redefined himself through karate. He explained how his life had been out of control and how he struggled to be somebody. Eventually he had realized that without self-control, he would never achieve his goals. At the end of the week, Dylan went to Ms. Harris and said, "What do you want me to do?" She wisely responded, "It is not what I want that matters. It's what you want and who you want to be that counts." After this dialogue and some intense work on his part, Dylan became the poster child for the Safe Place. He made a video for the school, demonstrating how to know when you need it ("When you're dissed or stressed"), what to do when you arrive ("Hang out, breathe and chill") and the benefits of going ("It's tight"). Dylan empowered himself by practicing breathing techniques at times when he would normally have exploded, and he helped others do the same.

Ms. Claire was a first-grade teacher in south Florida. At the beginning of the year, one of her students had a tough time separating from his mother. She used this difficult time as a means for teaching the Safe Place. One day when he arrived in the class very sad, she said, "Carson's face is looking like this (she demonstrated), tears are coming down his face like this (she traced pretend tears down her own face), what do you think he is feeling?" In unison most said, "Sad." Then she said, "He's having a hard time because he misses his mommy. We have a place in the classroom to help you when you are having hard times. It's called the Safe Place." She took Carson over to the Safe Place and held his hand while she showed the various things that were available to help him calm down. Then she said, "What could we add to the Safe Place that would help Carson?" The children decided that some drawing materials would be nice so he could draw a picture for his mother. They also thought a photo of his family in an album might be helpful. Carson continued to use the Safe Place extensively during the first week of school. By the third week, he was the resident expert and helped others learn how to use the Safe Place for themselves.

The Safe Place Teaches, Time Out Punishes

When first presented with the concept of the Safe Place, teachers often confuse it with Time Out. The two practices are philosophically and practically different in their goals and strategies. The Safe Place comes from a constructivist and humanistic perspective, and uses times of upset as teaching moments so children can acquire new active calming skills. Time Out comes from a behaviorist perspective, seeks to punish and is based on the following common beliefs:

- Teachers are in charge of children's behavior.
- Children need external motivation to change, and external force is reliable for governing behavior.
- One size fits all.
- Children want to be a part of what is happening in the classroom, and removal from classroom activities creates discomfort and motivates them to stop a specific behavior.
- Children already know how to change their "bad" behavior (i.e., teaching additional skills is unnecessary).
- Upset in the classroom disrupts the learning process and needs to be eliminated.
- The length of a child's stay in Time Out should be related to the child's age and the severity of the offense committed.

During my teaching years, it quickly became clear that when I used Time Out, the same children were repeatedly stuck there. It also struck me that these particular children appeared uninterested in being part of the class activities, so removal didn't create the desired discomfort. I also realized I didn't feel in my heart that I was making a difference or being helpful in these children's lives. It felt like, "This is not who I am," and the incongruence I experienced was more than my teacher's soul could take. I felt disconnected from my children, my career and ultimately myself. I created the Safe Place based on the following beliefs:

- Children want to be successful, they want to belong and they want to feel safe. Helping children meet these needs generates intrinsic (internal) motivation to change.
- What is helpful to one child may not be helpful to another.
- When feeling powerless, children tend to withdraw or act out. Powerlessness comes from feeling out of control due to internal situations (perceptions) or external situations (triggers).
- Children want to feel in control of themselves, but may not know this is possible. They may not know how to regain or maintain self-control. Feeling out of control is frightening.
- The internal desire for self-control, belonging and competence motivates children to make positive decisions when they feel genuinely cared for and supported.
- Upset is an opportunity to teach self-control strategies and is a part of your social-emotional curriculum.
- Choice is important. Children elect to go to the Safe Place. They choose strategies they find helpful. However, the teacher may also take an out-of-control child to the Safe Place if the child's behavior is a threat to him/herself and others.

Because the idea of Time Out is so ingrained in our current mindset, it is important to set aside every notion that might connect Time Out to the Safe Place and start with a clean slate. On the most basic level, the intent of these two classroom structures is completely different. The parents of the children in your classroom may also need some assistance separating the Safe Place from Time Out. Belinda Lorch, a Certified Conscious Discipline Instructor, created the letter below and distributes it to parents the same week she teaches the Safe Place in her classroom. This type of letter is also helpful when explaining your choice to utilize a Safe Place to colleagues who may still be using Time Out:

To Whom It May Concern,

I am enclosing this information for you so that you may understand what the "Safe Place" is. We started using the Safe Place in school this week. Children have learned that if they are upset, sad, mad, crying or are just having a difficult time and need to remove themselves from the activity, they can go to the Safe Place. The child can go there to regain composure using deep breathing techniques they've learned (S.T.A.R., drain, balloon or pretzel). As soon as they regain composure, they go back to the task at hand. In the Safe Place, I keep a stress ball to squeeze, a small stuffed animal to hug, a notebook (so the children can draw a picture of how mad, sad, etc. they feel), icons to remind them how to do deep breathing, and a Friends and Family board in the classroom. The Friends and Family board can be a science board, bulletin board, small photo album or just pictures on a piece of poster board. The children are encouraged to bring in a picture of their family and friends so that during the day, if they are missing their parents, etc. they can go to the Friends and Family board to look at a picture of their family. It's comforting to see a picture of someone you care about during the day.

*I would be happy to answer any questions you may have about these structures. Feel free to contact me anytime. You may also go to **www.ConsciousDiscipline.com** to find out more.*

Wishing you well,
Belinda Lorch

E = Environmental Structure: The Safe Place

Simply put, the Safe Place is a learning center where children can go to change their inner state from upset to peaceful and composed. It is your classroom's self-regulation tool, and research proves that self-regulation is the prerequisite skill needed to create safe, effective learning environments. There are four steps to self-regulation: 1) *I Calm*, calming down; 2) *I Feel*, naming the feeling that has generated the out-of-control inner state; 3) *I Choose*, selecting a strategy to change the feeling to a desired state, and 4) *I Solve*, solving the problem that triggered the feeling.

Therefore, your Safe Place will consist of the following:

1. A comfortable physical structure to sit on or in (beanbag, chair, soft pillows).
2. I Calm activities that consist of the four Conscious Discipline breathing icons (S.T.A.R., Drain, Balloon, Pretzel) and the I Calm Safe Place Mat.

3. I Feel activities that allow the child to see the facial expressions of different feelings so they can identify the name of the feeling. This could be the Conscious Discipline Feeling Buddies kit, or the Conscious Discipline feeling chart that can be downloaded from www.ConsciousDiscipline.com.
4. I Choose Board showing the activity choices available to assist children in making decisions that promote organization and integration of the brain. Some children may require individualized choice charts.
5. A Safe Place Case, to hold all the items mentioned on the choice board discussed in number four. If a squeeze ball is a calming choice, you would place it in the Safe Place Case. If journal writing is a choice, place writing materials in the case also.

Purpose: The purpose of the Safe Place is to provide a specific location in the classroom where children can choose to go to calm down when they feel any sort of upset. Traditionally, we have perceived behavior as bad or good. Conscious Discipline advocates that a person's behavior is either extending love or calling for love. If behavior is calm, cooperative and helpful, the person is extending love. If behavior is disorganized, oppositional, withdrawn or generally hurtful, then the person is calling for love. When children are calling for love, the Safe Place is a helpful option. Real-life examples of children calling for love/help include:

- Missing mom/dad/guardian
- Feeling overwhelmed with class events
- Frustration with social conflicts
- Sadness over life events (death, divorce, sick relative or pet)
- Anger over classroom responsibilities and expectations
- Disappointment with outcomes (no permission slip equals no field trip)
- Feeling tired from lack of sleep
- Having a bad day for unexplained reasons (biorhythms)
- Just needing a moment

As one 3-year-old child so brilliantly put it, "You go to the Safe Place when you are sad, mad, tired, missing your mom or just having a bad day."

How to set up a Safe Place: The basic design of your Safe Place consists of a physical structure and a series of activities and tools that enable children to change their inner states from upset to calm.

Begin by selecting a cozy corner or quiet area for your Safe Place. This location should reduce distractions but allow for a view of the classroom. This view is essential because the Safe Place is part of the classroom, not like Time Out when you are removed from the group. Once you have selected a location for your Safe Place, you will need to outfit it with hardware and software.

Physical Structure: A beanbag chair makes an excellent physical structure for your Safe Place because it is soft, inviting and almost hugs you when you sit in it. Alternately, you or your students may choose to decorate a Safe Place chair, put down a special rug or stack up soft pillows. The Safe Place for toddlers must be big enough for both the adult and the child, as they will go together most of the time. The hardware in a Safe Place can be as original as the classroom that uses it. I've seen a sixth-grade classroom use a donated recliner and a second-grade teacher fill a claw-footed bathtub with blankets and pillows. The look and feel of the Safe Place is one of warmth, invitation and comfort, regardless of the hardware you select.

I Calm tools: The most essential software for your Safe Place is the four Conscious Discipline breathing strategies. These four skills are the S.T.A.R., balloon, drain and pretzel. They are the first strategies you will teach children, and are handily

Teacher Tip:

If space is an issue, create a portable Safe Place. One physical education teacher purchased a push light in the shape of a star and used that as a portable Safe Place. An after-school program in Utah used a carpet square with a star printed on it.

displayed on the I Calm Safe Place Mat from Loving Guidance. These exercises turn off the stress response in the body and integrate the hemispheres of the brain. If you have implemented the Brain Smart Start of the day, you will have already introduced these skills to the children. The repeated use of these activities during slightly stressful times will make them accessible to children (with prompting) when their feelings are more intense.

S.T.A.R: S.T.A.R. is an acronym for deep, conscious belly breathing: <u>S</u>mile, <u>T</u>ake a deep breath (breathe with your belly going out), <u>A</u>nd (holding the breath momentarily), <u>R</u>elax (exhale slowly, with your belly going in). This "belly in, belly out" breathing encourages children to move their diaphragms. The general rule is: If the diaphragm is not moving, the brain is not thinking.

Ballooning: Ballooning is a pretend exercise in blowing up a balloon. Raise your arms up, interlace your fingers and rest them on top of your head. Now, inhale several breaths of air, moving your hands upward with each puff of air. When your lungs are full and your arms are extended in a round shape above your head, release the air out of your "balloon" by pursing your lips and blowing the air out. Making the "ppppbbbbbb" sound with your lips accentuates the imaginary image, slows down your exhale and provides enjoyment, especially for young children.

Draining: Draining combines muscle relaxation and belly breathing. Ask the children to extend both arms out in front of their bodies with their fists tightly balled up. Instruct them to inhale, hold their breath and tighten the muscles in their arms, hands, face, chest and shoulders. Give the en-

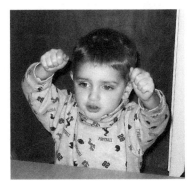

176 *Creating the School Family*

couragement, "Tight, tight, tighter," then tell them to exhale while releasing all the muscle tension in their body, washing the stress down the drain with a "ssshh" sound, which slows down the exhale.

Pretzel: The pretzel is similar to a "hook up" in Brain Gym or the "eagle pose" in yoga. To do the pretzel, have the children cross their legs. Extend their arms forward with the thumbs pointing down and the backs of their palms touching each other. Now cross their arms at the wrist and interlace their fingers.

Next, pull both hands in toward the heart and eventually rest them under the chin. Finally, have children put their tongues on the roofs of their mouths and breathe. This posture equally stimulates both hemispheres of the brain, the motor coordination system and the vestibular system. It turns off the fight-or-flight response and brings the system into a coherent state that facilitates focus, learning and memory (Hannaford, 2005). You can also do the pretzel sitting down. Simply cross your legs from a seated position and perform the rest of the activity as described.

I Feel tools: When a child acts out his or her emotions, we generally call it a discipline problem. We act out our emotions when we become the emotion instead of feel it. There is a big difference between the statements " I am angry" and "I feel angry." "I am angry" is overwhelming; I have lost my identity and become this attacking being. "I feel angry" separates me from the feeling; I am now Becky who feels angry. That simple act of consciously separating me as an individual from the intense emotion I am feeling is essential for emotional regulation. A child cannot manage a feeling without this separation, which happens automatically when we are able to name it. As soon as a feeling is named, there are two entities, the child and the child's feelings.

> **Teacher Tip:**
> You can teach older children these relaxation techniques all at one time and practice them during class meetings throughout the first couple of weeks of school. For younger children, introduce one technique at a time. Use the children's reactions and application of the techniques to judge how quickly you can introduce the next one. It may take one week of practice on each technique before your children are ready to learn another one.

The I Feel tools in your Safe Place can be the I Feel chart downloaded from the Conscious Discipline website or the I Feel Feeling Buddies Kit offered by www.ConsciousDiscipline.com. The I Feel Kit is a series of gingerbread dolls that have different emotions on their faces. The children learn how to identify their feeling, separate themselves from it (the doll they are holding) and soothe it ("You're safe, you can handle this"). As they soothe their feeling buddy, they soothe their own feelings and learn constructive language that will eventually become their inner speech for self-regulation and self-healing.

I Choose tools: It is essential to provide children with visual options of activities they can choose to help self-regulate. Many teachers worry that children will stay "too long" in the Safe Place. Teaching and providing specific activities through an I Choose Board from www.ConsciousDiscipline.com or creating your own I Choose Chart will facilitate students' processing of emotions so they can reenter the classroom ready to learn.

The I Choose Board from www.ConsciousDiscipline.com provides images of different feelings and a mirror to help children identify their feelings. It then provides strategy choices to help them change their inner state to one of calm. The prompts on the board are "I feel ____. I choose _____." The child selects the feeling that represents his/her inner state, and then chooses the strategy to use to self-regulate. You will place the materials for conducting the strategies listed on the board in your Safe Place Case.

You may also create an I Choose Chart that shows the choices available to the children. These may include reading a book, writing in a journal, squeezing a ball, focusing on a wave bottle and hugging a stuffed animal. The choices you offer will be determined by the unique needs of the class and individual children. Place the choices listed on the chart in your Safe Place Case.

Additional tools: As you build your Safe Place, the hardware and software listed above are an absolute necessity. You may also want to consider the following items to include in your Safe Place, and to change them as your students change from year to year.

Visual prompts: Visual prompts in the form of photographs or icons are essential for the success of your Safe Place. Children under seven encode information visually; they govern their behavior with internal images rather than words. For this reason, visual icons of the strategies you expect students to use in the Safe Place are essential. At the very least, the four basic breathing strategies should be posted. Download the art for these icons at ConsciousDiscipline.com and take pictures of children doing these and other calming activities. Place these images in a Safe Place book and on your Safe Place's walls.

Safe Place Case: The Safe Place Case is a box or case with items that can help children return to a peaceful inner state. These might include a CD player or MP3 player with soothing music and headphones, pictures of family members, stuffed animals, lotion, a wave bottle, writing materials, a small blanket or beach towel, and a stress-relieving ball.

Start off the year with a few items in the case, then add others you think would help students who frequently visit the Safe Place. Involve the students by asking them, "What would help you feel calmer and more peaceful in your body?" Utilize their ideas, especially when they have special needs or sensory integration issues.

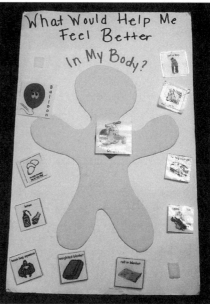

Whether or not your children have special needs, the children who frequent the Safe Place do have issues in their young lives. Composure is a reflection of a balanced nervous system. Often, children who visit the Safe Place regularly are overwhelmed. Some children require detective work to discern which strategies will calm their nervous systems. Different children will need different input to help them meet the goal for future learning. Keep sight of the goal: to help children learn how to calm and organize themselves. Watch what the child seeks in the natural environment, use your intuitive wisdom and think in terms of the senses (touch, sight, sound, smell) to help you select the most effective items for your Safe Place Case. Be careful not to put too many items in your Safe Place or it will become overwhelming.

Teacher Tip:

Elizabeth Montero-Cefalo, a Loving Guidance Associate and brilliant teacher of children with special needs, shared how she would observe her children with autism carefully to uncover what might help them calm down. Watching as Jonathan went to the sink and turned the water on and off, on and off, she decided that a wave bottle might help him in the Safe Place. Sure enough, it did! Later, another child with autism entered her School Family. She gave him a wave bottle the first time he went to the Safe Place, and he threw it at her. Everyone is different. Observation is the key to finding what calming tools will work for which children.

Journaling: Include a journal in the Safe Place. Younger children will draw their feelings, while older students will often provide elaborate narratives. Instruct older students to fold their page in half for privacy, and leave it in the journal. Assure them you are the only person who will read it, and only for their safety. Let them know

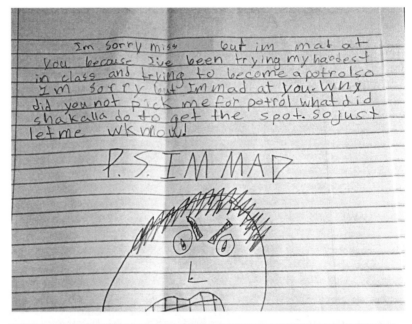

Teacher Tip:

Be prepared! Some entries in the journal may concern you and how unfair, mean, stubborn, etc., you are. Remember to not take these comments personally; they are a way to work through their feelings.

180 *Creating the School Family*

their thoughts will remain private and there will be no punishment associated with the journal.

Safe Place Pass: Children two to five years old and those with special needs will benefit from a Safe Place Pass. The Safe Place Pass is a 3 x 7-inch laminated card with the four Conscious Discipline Safe Place Icons printed on it. You can make a Safe Place Pass on your own or use the pre-made template on the Make-N-Take CDrom from Loving Guidance. If a child shows signs of distress, the teacher can give the child the Safe Place Pass to assist him/her to the Safe Place. The pass serves as a helpful reminder to use the Safe Place and also reminds children to do the breathing strategies when they arrive there.

Friends and Family Board: This structure provides children with the opportunity to display their family pictures in the classroom. Putting the Friends and Family Board and the Safe Place near each other is helpful. Children can then be comforted by looking at photos of their friends and family while visiting the Safe Place (see also Chapter 4).

Touch: An infant's sensory system is immature and calms to the deep, firm pressure of swaddling. Individuals under stress and those who have immature sensory processing systems will respond favorably to deep pressure in much the same way as infants. Children who fit this description are easily distracted, hyperactive or lacking in concentration skills. These children might like tightness around their bodies (like wearing bike shorts) or they may prefer heaviness (like lying under beanbag animals). Swaddling-type activities (like the hot dog game explained in the Activities section below) are helpful for these children, as is including these items in your Safe Place:

- Blankets
- Weighted beanbags, stuffed animals, pillows and lap animals
- Lap table for writing

Vibration is another way to offer calming touch. Vibration activates touch receptors to foster calming. Vibration tools and activities may benefit children who chew on things (including their shirts), bite, are picky eaters, dislike having their teeth brushed or face washed, have Autism Spectrum Disorder or pervasive developmental delay, are toddlers in the sensory motor stages of play, have been tube fed, have discomfort in the mouth because of teething or TMJ, or demonstrate self-injurious behaviors. You can locate vibrating tools by searching "sensory integration tools" on the Internet.

Sight: We already discussed the importance of posting visual aids of the four active calming strategies in your Safe Place. In addition, consider that most classrooms are designed to be visually stimulating. They have loudly patterned carpets, pictures everywhere, vivid colors and bright fluorescent lighting. For many children, this environment is stimulating and delightful, but for some, it can overload their systems.

Marcus was in kindergarten. He was okay in his very busy, very beautiful classroom until there was a lot of movement. During transitions and clean up, he would run around the room like a banshee. The teacher spent enormous amounts of energy trying to control him, and they both were completely worn out by the end of the day. Marcus, the teacher and I made a plan that involved Marcus going to the Safe Place just before a transition or other time when lots of movement occurred. Once most of the movement had dissipated, Marcus would leave the Safe Place and rejoin the class. We practiced the plan, and then Marcus tried it by himself. Initially our plan failed because Marcus had difficulty rejoining the class. So we added a buddy to assist Marcus in leaving the Safe Place and catching up on his responsibilities (cleaning up, lining up, etc.). The revised plan was very successful.

Sound: Music affects the whole body. As soon as I hear the scary music in the movie theater, I cover my eyes and my whole body tenses. I generally don't open them and relax until I get an "all clear" nudge from my movie partner. Soothing music, on the other hand, has a powerful organizing effect on the brain and body. Soothing music at test time has been shown to improve test scores (Cokerton, Moore, & Norman 1997), probably because it reduces cortisol levels in the body, thereby reducing stress (Malyarenko, 1996). The following are examples of sound items to consider for your Safe Place:

- CD player or MP3 player and headphones
- Soothing music or nature sounds
- Rap, drumming or other music with a strong beat
  (helps organize the brains of children with attention issues)
- A recording of a parent's voice saying, for example, "Hi (child's name). I want you to know you are safe. Ms//Mr. (teacher's name) will keep you safe and help

you learn until (activity that signals the end of the day, like getting home on the bus). Keep breathing and calming yourself. You can handle this. I love you and will see you soon."

Dada was a curly-haired boy who had just entered Ms. Fullerton's first-grade classroom. He was from Nigeria and did not speak English. Dada was scared, so Ms. Fullerton emailed me asking for ideas to help him feel safer. I offered several ideas, and she chose to ask Dada's parents to record a message in his native language. Ms. Fullerton felt strongly that hearing his native language would be helpful, if not essential, for Dada's adjustment.

Since no one could communicate with the family at that time, Ms. Fullerton demonstrated what she wanted the mother to do in hopes the nonverbal message would be received. She pushed the record button and said, "Talk into the microphone and speak loudly enough so that your son can hear. He can play it back during the day. So just talk." Then she played the recording back. She rewound, pressed the button and offered the microphone to the mother. It appeared the demonstration was successful, as the mother began talking into the microphone.

Ms. Fullerton put the recording in the Safe Place and showed Dada how to use the cassette player. About two weeks later, Ms. Fullerton emailed me about her success with Dada. She said putting the mom's voice in the Safe Place was brilliant. She was so sold on the idea that she began telling everyone, "You have to do this!"

Later that year, Ms. Fullerton met a bilingual person from the same part of Nigeria and asked for a translation of the cassette. The translator said, "I'm not sure, but it roughly translates as 'Speak into the microphone and talk loud for your son to hear. He will play it during the day. Keep speaking.'" When Ms. Fullerton heard this, she laughed herself silly. The words themselves were not as important as the intent of his mother's heart.

Smell: While cleaning my closet after my mother passed away, I came across one of her blouses. The first thing I did was bring it to my face in hopes of smelling my mother's scent. Smell is important for bonding and emotional security. Babies find comfort in the scent of family members and in their own body odors (which helps explain why toddlers grow especially attached to their blankets and stuffed animals).

Smell is underutilized in the learning environment and can be a wonderful asset to your Safe Place for some children. Research suggests that peppermint, basil, lemon, cinnamon and rosemary enhance mental alertness. Lavender, chamomile, orange and rose calm nerves and encourage relaxation (Jensen, 2000). Smell can be utilized in the Safe Place with scratch-and-sniff stickers, aromatherapy sprays and scented lotions.

Label scented lotions with "boo boo cream," "concentration cream" and "cranky cream." (Pre-made labels are available on the *Make-N-Take* CDrom from Loving Guidance.) Children can use these lotions themselves or you can use them with a child. Ask the child, "Would you like some concentration cream, boo boo cream or cranky cream?" Once the child makes a selection, put the lotion on his/her hand and rub it in with a deep hand massage. Sing the following songs:

Tune: "Good-Bye Song"
    Bye-bye crankies.
    Bye-bye crankies.
    Bye-bye crankies.
    It's time for you to go.

Tune: "Good-Bye Song"
    No more boo boos.
    No more boo boos.
    No more boo boos.
    It's time for you to heal.

Tune: "Have You Ever Seen a Lassie"
    It's time to concentrate, concentrate, concentrate.
    It's time to concentrate, and start your work!

Safe Place Agreements: It can require an enormous amount of faith to trust that children will use the Safe Place constructively when they need it; however, it is essential that you trust them to do so. The Safe Place Agreements, the final component for your Safe Place, are a set of rules that may be helpful in alleviating your discomfort and helping children regulate their Safe Place usage.

The Safe Place Agreements may vary from classroom to classroom. Older classes may have input on the agreements, while teachers of younger classrooms will develop the agreements themselves. Post your agreements in the Safe Place for all to see or create a class book. Regardless of age, the Safe Place Agreements will be similar to the following:

- Anyone can choose to go to the Safe Place at any time. You can stay as long as you want and return to the planned activities when you are ready.

- An adult can suggest that the Safe Place would be helpful. "James, your face is going like this. (Demonstrate) You arms are tense like this. (Demonstrate) Your body is telling me you might be feeling angry. Are you willing to go to the Safe Place and see if something there might help you feel better?" (As time goes by, you might simply say, "Do you think the Safe Place would be helpful?" or "What could you do right now to help yourself calm down?")
- Friends can suggest you go to the Safe Place. Brainstorm phrases children could say when suggesting a friend use the Safe Place.
- If you are in the Safe Place and someone else needs to go there, be willing to solve the problem. Often children have solved this by returning to the class and letting the new person in, by sharing the Safe Place or by pulling a pillow to another area to make a temporary second Safe Place.
- The teacher can take you to the Safe Place. In volatile situations, children will need to be restrained for safety reasons. Respond to these situations per your school's protocol, and with a focus on calming yourself by being a S.T.A.R. Say to yourself silently, "I'm safe, keep breathing, I can handle this." As you begin to feel your body relax, the child's body will start to relax also. As s/he begins to calm down, say aloud, "You're safe. Breathe with me. You can handle this." Once somewhat settled, you can help him/her identify the feeling and move to making choices.

The best way to teach it is to use it.

Teacher Tip:

Don't be surprised if no one in older classrooms mentions stuffed animal-type things; older students do not like to admit that they like that "baby stuff." Putting one or two soft animals in the Safe Place is still completely appropriate. Many students will use them to feel better.

When teaching the expectations, invite students to practice. If you notice someone is not following the procedures, say, "Your face is telling me you feel better. Go back to your area and get started," or, "The procedure at the Safe Place is to _____, or _____, or _____. Which are you choosing?"

How to introduce the Safe Place:

A teacher emailed me and said her four-

> **Teacher Tip:**
>
> With younger children and toddlers, especially those who are out of control, it is vital that you demonstrate using the Safe Place in this manner:
>
> - Take the upset child with you to the Safe Place and use your body as a calming instrument.
>
> - Hold the child (if s/he is out of control) or have the child snuggle in your lap.
>
> - Start actively calming yourself by being a S.T.A.R. Take at least three calming deep breaths. Consciously relax your body. Bring your entire focus inward to create the state you want the child to achieve.
>
> - From this very calm state, open your heart by picturing a precious moment and then generating an internal state of gratitude.
>
> - Finally, imagine you are breathing that energy out of your heart to the child. Once the child's body begins to relax (you will feel it "give"), say in a soothing voice, "You're safe. I've got you. Breathe with me; you can do it. That's it, you're doing it. You are calming down."
>
> - Once the child is calm, you may want to place a stuffed animal in his/her lap and sing the following I Love You Ritual (from the *I Love You Rituals* book and the *Songs for I Love You Rituals, Vol. 1* music CD):
>
>   > Snuggle up children in your Safe Place.
>   > You can go there to have your own space.
>   > When you feel scared and want to be hugged
>   > You can cuddle yourself and the bear with a hug.

year-old children must be too young to use the Safe Place. She said that they would hit a friend, then run to the Safe Place as if it were a base in a game of tag. I responded that this indicated she had not sufficiently taught the Safe Place. After several more emails, she wrote, "I did it. I taught the Safe Place. One afternoon, I was so frustrated that my blood was about to boil. I am somewhat embarrassed to say this, but I completely lost it. I put my hands on my hips and screamed, 'That's it! I have had it!' Then I stomped over to the Safe Place, flopped into the beanbag and began squeezing a stress ball and breathing. As I looked up, I saw 18 sets of eyes staring at me. Shortly after my recovery, a little girl named Tyler put her hands firmly on her hips, screamed loudly, 'That's it! I have had it!,' and proceeded to imitate me. One by one that afternoon, each child took turns assuming the hands-on-the-hips position, saying those infamous words and going to the Safe Place. They finally got what the Safe Place was for. Since then, they use it everyday. To my surprise, they're willing to go, and deeply want to stay calm and organized just like me."

There are basically two different approaches to introducing the Safe Place. One option is to plan lessons to introduce it during the first weeks of school. Another option is to wait for an opportunity when a child needs the Safe Place, and use that as a teaching moment.

Regardless of how you introduce the Safe Place, your top priorities are instruction for the breathing techniques; examples for when and how to use the Safe Place (brainstorm these together, especially in older classrooms); and the Safe Place Agreements.

One fourth-grade teacher, Cindy Larrabee, would prepare a lesson plan, put the structure in her classroom and wait for a child to ask about it. For the Safe Place, she set up a chair and cushions, put the icons on the wall, filled up her Safe Place Case and turned the sign around so the center was not labeled. One day, a student asked, "What do we use this for?" and Cindy began the lesson. In another fourth-grade classroom, the teacher cordoned off the Safe Place with "Under Construction" signs. After she taught the four core breathing techniques (S.T.A.R., balloon, drain, pretzel), she led a discussion about how everyone sometimes feels angry, sad or upset. She then asked students to brainstorm different things they do to help themselves feel better. Over the next few days, she added the appropriate items from this discussion into the Safe Place. Then she introduced the Safe Place and set forth the Safe Place Agreements. She then declared construction complete on the Safe Place and opened it for use in the classroom.

One kindergarten teacher roped off her Safe Place with yellow crepe paper. She waited until students learned two of the four core breathing activities (S.T.A.R., balloon, drain, pretzel), and then gathered the class at the Safe Place. She then explained that Safe Place helps you calm down when you feel sad, angry or frustrated. She asked if anyone had ever been to a ribbon-cutting ceremony, had them practice the breathing techniques, did a drum roll and then cut the tape, saying, "Now the Safe Place is open!" Then she entered the Safe Place, took out the Safe Place Case, and taught them how to use the calming strategies. Later she followed up by reading *Shubert Is a S.T.A.R.* and singing "Snuggle Up" from the *Songs for I Love You Rituals* CD.

Regardless of how you choose to introduce your Safe Place, you must teach students the purpose of it and how to use it, just like you would teach them about the block area or a science lab. You can do this through modeling, teaching moments, literature, songs and role playing.

There are many helpful activities for teaching children how and when to use the Safe Place. The following will help you get started. Remember, one of the best ways to teach the Safe Place is to use it yourself. The next time you start "losing it" in class, walk over to the Safe Place and practice active calming instead.

Shubert Is a S.T.A.R.

In this story Shubert is having a yucky day. Mrs. Bookbinder uses Shubert's upset as an opportunity to teach the class about active calming and the Safe Place. As you read, ask children to show you what their faces would look like if they came to school feeling angry. Repeat Mrs. Bookbinder's words, "You seem to be having a hard start this morning. Your body is telling me you might be feeling mad," then practice breathing your way from bug crazy mad to oozy doozy caterpillar calm. Use your Shubert worksheets to lead the class in additional calming activities for both younger and older children. These can be downloaded from www.ConsciousDiscipline.com.

Brain Smart Cubes

Load the Brain Smart Choices cubes from Loving Guidance with active calming strategies. Take turns tossing the cube and then practicing the strategy that shows on top. This is a great activity for "in-between" times when you have a few spare moments. Older students can make up their own breathing techniques or research yoga poses to add to the existing dice cards. Keep a cube loaded with activities in the Safe Place for individual use.

I Calm

The I Calm Safe Place Mat mentioned in the Environmental Structures section on p. 175 provides a huggable, touchable representation of the four core active calming techniques in Conscious Discipline: S.T.A.R., drain, balloon and pretzel. Hold the mat up during your Brain Smart Start and ask children to choose which active calming technique they would like to practice. (You may want to turn this into a classroom job.)

I Choose

The I Choose Board from Loving Guidance is an activity that empowers children to name their emotion and then choose an activity that will assist them in regaining their composure. It comes with extensive instructions for use, and was discussed earlier in the Environmental Structures section on p. 178 of this chapter. In small groups, have students discuss a past scenario or create a make-believe one. Then ask them to discern the feeling and choice they might choose, using the board as a helpful tool.

I Feel

As mentioned in Environmental Structures, the I Feel Feeling Buddies Kit includes eight feeling buddies representing the following emotions: angry, frustrated, scared, anxious, sad, disappointed, happy and calm. It also comes with classroom songs and activities for all ages, and a DVD showing how to conduct them. The I Feel Kit teaches children and adults how to separate becoming their emotions from feeling their emotions, and how to soothe their emotions in ways that allow them simultaneously to "be" and to be constructively managed.

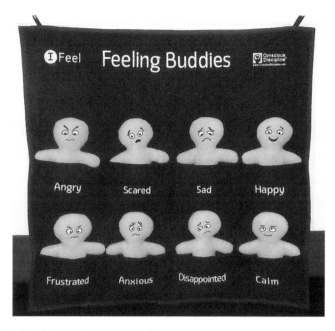

Demonstrate how to use the buddies during small group time. Integrate them into your literacy program by asking, "Which of these feelings (point to the buddies) do you think the character in the story was feeling?"

General Activities — Younger

Today I Feel Silly and Other Moods That Make My Day

This book by Jamie Lee Curtis is the story of a young girl and the different moods she experiences. It is a great way to open a discussion about the different feelings that may prompt going to the Safe Place. Lead a conversation about different moods your students experience and things they can do to calm themselves. Extend this activity to creating a class-made book about the ways your students calm themselves.

Hot Dog Game

Swaddling young children is helpful, as discussed in the "Touch" section of Environmental Structure. The hot dog (or burrito) game from the *I Love You Rituals* book is one way to help young children, especially those with special needs, to experience the benefits of swaddling. You will need a baby blanket or a beach towel to conduct this activity.

Lay the blanket flat on the floor. This is your bun (or tortilla). Say, "I'm going to pretend this blanket is a hot dog bun and you are a hot dog. Lie down here on the bun. (Have the child lie across one end of the blanket.) Boy, I'm hungry! I would love a hot dog. Look! I see a hot dog right in front of me. I need to put on some ketchup." Pretend to squirt ketchup on the child and spread it all around (massage the child with deep pressure). "I want some mustard." Continue to pretend by adding as many things as the child desires. (If you are making a burrito, massage in spices, cheese, salsa, etc., in much the same manner.) Now, roll up the child in the towel/blanket. Be sure that the child's head and feet remain uncovered. Place the child in your lap and pretend to gobble him or her up with delight. You can play the game with one child while the others play along, using dolls or stuffed animals and blankets.

General Activities — Older

How Are You Peeling? Foods with Moods

Written by Saxton Freymann and Joost Elffers, this book is great for introducing different feelings to older students. By the time students arrive in fourth and fifth grade, they know the basic feelings like happy, angry, mad and sad. This story also includes insecure, amused, frustrated and attacked. Explore what's behind the emotions you're feeling, talk about what it feels like to experience different emotions and role-play ways to calm and recover.

Amelia's Notebook

Amelia's Notebook by Marissa Moss is about journaling styles and is a great way to introduce journaling as a Safe Place activity. In this story Amelia records everything in her notebook. She explains her feelings and why they are important. The pictures are crazy and keep the students engaged with the journal entries.

Role-Play with "What If" Cards

Create "what if" scenario cards based on situations students have experienced or witnessed (such as not being chosen for a part or becoming frustrated with an assignment). During a group activity time, set out a variety of coping and relaxation tools, or pictures that represent those tools. Have children take turns reading the "what if" cards. As each card is read, discuss what tools might help in that situation. Honor all responses. There is no right or wrong answer because individual children will benefit from using one tool over another.

Breathing and Brain Connections

When working with older children, the active calming techniques used in the Safe Place and described in *Shubert Is a S.T.A.R.* can be taught from a scientific standpoint. Tell them that when they are able to S.T.A.R. and repeat the process three times, they will disconnect the "fight-or-flight" stress response and calm their bodies. You may also share with them that research shows that deep breathing before and during a test empowers them to do their best. The *Becoming Brain Smart Presenter's Series* from Loving Guidance has slides and handouts meant for teaching the Conscious Discipline Brain Model to adults, but you can easily use a pared-down version of these materials with older students. Relate Shubert's experience to common events in your classroom (social exclusion, running late, etc.), share information about what happens when the brain is under stress and role-play situations that might get children into and out of the Safe Place.

Class-Made Books — All Ages

What Bugs Us Book

Help children become self-aware by asking them to record things that bug (upset) them, and help them problem-solve by recording solutions to these situations. Pre-print a piece of paper with a line down the center and "It bugs me when _____" on the left half and "When I feel _____, I can _____" on the right half. Instruct students to draw a picture of something that bugs them on the left side of the paper. Model what you are asking them to do by drawing an example yourself. With younger children, ask what their pictures are about and fill in the blank for them. Older children can complete the sentence themselves.

Share "what bugs you" during circle time or class meeting time, then share solutions for whatever that is. Active calming with the four breathing strategies and utilizing the Safe Place should be at the top of your solutions list. At the end of the discussion, have children draw their favorite solution on the right-hand side of the page and fill in the blanks. (Assist younger children as needed.)

> **Teacher Tip:**
>
> A picture is worth a thousand words – As an addition to the What Bugs Us book, take photographs to go along with each child's drawing and description. For young children, the photos may be expression pictures of how they look before and after the activity to calm. Older children may want to photograph an acted version of what bugs them and then take a photo that shows them using the calming techniques.

Now, gather up the papers, add a page that says, "When something bugs me, I can go to the Safe Place to S.T.A.R., drain, balloon or pretzel until I feel calm again," and bind the pages into a book. Allow students to check out the book and read it with their home families.

When I Feel Angry Book

Use the following sentence stems to help each student write a page for a "When I feel angry" book:

> **When I feel angry, sometimes I want to (old action).**
> **(Picture the child demonstrating the emotion).**
> **But I can choose differently. I can choose to (new skill).**
> **(Picture the child doing the calming technique listed).**

Class-Made Books
Younger

What We Do in the Safe Place

Use the frame below to create an instructional aid for your classroom's Safe Place. Photograph students doing each of the activities listed page by page in the book. You can have multiple students in one photo to ensure all students' images are included. Once you laminate and bind the book, keep it in your Safe Place as a helpful reminder.

> **Page 1:** I go to the Safe Place when I feel:
> **Page 2:** mad
> **Page 3:** sad
> **Page 4:** frustrated
> **Page 5:** like I'm missing my mom or dad

Page 6: I can calm down in the Safe Place by doing the S.T.A.R.
Page 7: Balloon
Page 8: Drain
Page 9: Pretzel
Page 10: I feel calm now!
Page 11: Now I can do my work.

When _____ Gets Angry

Read *When Sophie Gets Angry … Really Really Angry* by Molly Bang and create a personalized class book of the same theme. Use your School Family name in place of "Sophie" and create a book full of calming reminders. Photocopy the sentence below on a page for every student. Ask students to illustrate themselves calming down and help them fill in the blanks with their own words. Alternately, you could photograph each child doing his or her calming strategy.

When <u>(child's name)</u> gets angry, <u>(child's name)</u> can <u>(activity)</u> to calm down.

Class-Made Books

Older

Our Feel Good Book

Use *The Feel Good Book* by Todd Parr to create your own book of feel-good activities that will serve as self-made calming behavior plans for the students. After reading the story, have the students share different things they do to help themselves feel better. Stress the importance of using school-appropriate techniques. For example, students might suggest running or leaving the area. These strategies are acceptable so long as you set clear, acceptable limits, such as, "You can leave the area after getting the teacher's approval." Once you have a sizable list of appropriate activities, tell students to select one of the strategies you've discussed. This will be their "Calming Behavior Plan." Then have each student write up and illustrate his or her plan in detail on a page for the class book. Laminate and bind the book together, then put it in the Safe Place. When the students use the Safe Place, encourage them to read and follow their calming behavior plan.

Teacher Tip:

Remember, naming a feeling provides conscious awareness. With this consciousness, regulation becomes possible.

C = Commitment

I am willing to trust children enough to set up a Safe Place in our classroom. If I feel a child may be using the Safe Place to avoid a class activity, I will reframe my thoughts about the situation so that I can choose to see the child as calling for help. I will start implementing the Safe Place in my life, school and classroom by:

- Being willing to learn and use relaxation techniques so that I can manage my own upsets and model helpful practices for my students
- Choosing to do at least two of the activities in this chapter with my class
- Introducing songs to my class that will help teach them to relax
- Downloading the breathing icons from www.ConsciousDiscipline.com

Signature _____ **Date** _____

H = Helpful Resources

Music CDs

All Ages

I Love You Rituals, Volumes 1 and 2 **by Dr. Becky Bailey and Mar Harman**
Song: All songs

It Starts in the Heart **by Jack Hartmann and Dr. Becky Bailey**
Songs: "S.T.A.R. Song," "All Together"

Kindness Counts **by Dr. Becky Bailey and Mr. Al**
Songs: "Stop in the Name of Love," "Safe Keeper," "You Can Relax Now"

Brain Boogie Boosters **by The Learning Station and Dr. Becky Bailey**
Songs: "Calm Your Brain," "Peace Like a River," "Safe and Calm"

Hello World **by Red Grammer**
Songs: "When I Get a Feeling," "I Want You to Listen"

Getting to Know Myself **by Hap Palmer**
Songs: "Feelings," "What Do People Do"

Literature

Younger

Knuffle Bunny: A Cautionary Tale **by Mo Willem.** This book explores the difficulties of communication with a preverbal child. Young Trixie starts to cry when she loses her stuffed animal and grows frustrated when she can't explain what happened to her father.

The Boy Who Didn't Want to be Sad **by Rob Goldblatt.** A boy who doesn't want to be sad tries eliminating all sources of sadness from his life, including toys (they can get broken), pets (they can't live forever), friends (what if they don't call?) and even his own family (sometimes they get mad at him). Ultimately, he realizes that all sources of sadness are also his sources of happiness, and he reclaims them.

***A Terrible Thing Happened - A Story for Children Who Have Witnessed Violence or Trauma* by Margaret M. Holmes and Sasha J. Mudlaff.** The "terrible thing" is not named in the book. Instead, the focus is on how Sherman first tries to forget about what happened until it is just too hard. Fortunately, a wise adult helps him move through his big feelings.

Literature
Older

***The Pain and the Great One* by Judy Blume.** This book follows sibling rivalry between a sister and her younger brother. The book is divided into two parts, one told from the viewpoint of each child. It is a humorous look at the mixture of emotions shared by young siblings.

Additional Aids

I Calm Safe Place Mat from www.ConsciousDiscipline.com
I Feel Feeling Buddies Kit from www.ConsciousDiscipline.com
I Choose Board from www.ConsciousDiscipline.com
Yoga Pretzels by Tara Guber, Leah Kalish and Sophie Fatus

School Family Make-N-Take CDrom from www.ConsciousDiscipline.com
(Safe Place Pass, etc.)
CASEL website: http://www.casel.org/sel/prevention.php
Brain Smart Choices for Calming and Connection from www.ConsciousDiscipline.com

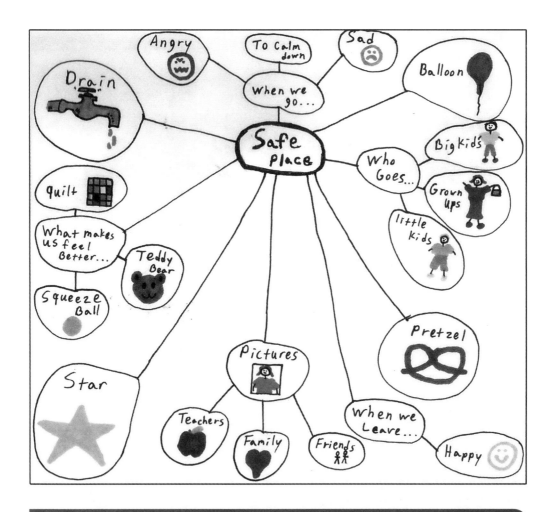

Teacher Tip:

Teach children when to go to the Safe Place and how to calm themselves when they get there. Remember, each child is unique and will find different strategies to be soothing.

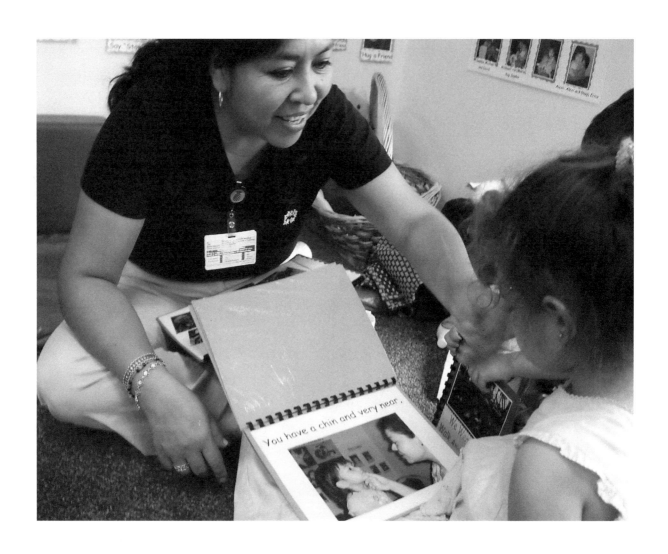

Chapter 10

School Family Rituals

Angel was in third grade and about to become a big brother. The class had been wishing Angel's mom well during the months of her pregnancy. Angel had brought a picture of his mom to put on the Friends and Family Board, along with a copy of the sonogram photo to show off his baby sister who was still in her tummy. Angel was excited about his new sister Maria but also a bit scared about the birth. He would be staying with his grandparents during the delivery and was worried about the changes in the family that were sure to come. Mr. Bartlett, his teacher, was the big brother in his own family, so he knew the big brother role well; he also knew the power of rituals to soothe anxiety and mark life transitions. He decided to start a class-made book titled "Advice for Being a Big Brother." All the students were excited about the project. Anyone who was a big brother or a big sister, had a big brother or big sister, or hoped to have one or be one, was asked to write a piece of advice in the book. The class gave Angel the book the day after Maria's birth, and he read it many times that day. Some of the advice he received was:

> **Never poke the baby in the eye or push on the hole on the top of her head.**
> **Keep things that she can swallow away, especially popped balloons.**
> **When the poop stinks, try not to scream and run away.**
> **You have to hold the head up or the baby's neck will break.**

This simple School Family ritual did wonders for Angel, his mom and his father. It did wonders for his School Family as well. It brought the class together in a spirit of caring, encouraged meaningful writing and allowed each child to share his or her wisdom, which was deeply appreciated.

Angel's School Family ritual shows the power very small acts have to make a huge difference in people's lives. Schools often feel so pressured to be on task every minute that teachers and principals think there's no time to create a School Family. I would say we can no longer afford not to create School Families. This one ritual had profound personal and educational effects. Writing these notes

Benefits of Creating a School Family through ritual.

- Was integrated into the existing curriculum so no academic time was lost.
- Was meaningful and encouraging to students, thereby enhancing the intrinsic motivation to improve their writing skills.
- Created a strong bond between home and school.
- Strengthened a sense of belonging among classmates, creating more willingness to adhere to the class agreements.
- Created an optimal internal learning state for every member in the class through the experience of caring for another person. This internal coherency prepares children to learn more.
- Helped children see the world from another's point of view, increasing their perspective-taking and empathy skills.
- Expressed the values of the classroom in a concrete manner.

Creating Rituals Vs. Establishing Routines

Rituals and routines are different, even though a ritual contains a routine within it. The purpose of a ritual is connection. The purpose of a routine is predictability.

Think of a holiday you share with your family such as Thanksgiving. Within this holiday, there is predictability (routines such as eating at Grandma's house and arriving around noon) and connecting moments (rituals such as taking turns sharing something you are grateful for while at the dinner table). Now, think of your daily morning routine at home. We generally develop routine habits such as showering, getting dressed, eating while listening to or reading the morning news and heading out the door. Many of us also add a connecting ritual like giving our partner a kiss goodbye. Schools also have morning routines. If we choose, we can add a connecting ritual to our school's routine as well. That goodbye kiss at home fosters connections that last a lifetime, but the time invested in the ritual itself is minimal. The same can be accomplished in our schools by offering a hug or a high five with eye contact as each student enters the classroom.

When connecting with children through rituals, it is helpful to include four key components: eye contact, touch, presence and a playful setting. Rituals can be led by the adult or can be conducted between small groups of children or as a large group. It is often helpful to involve your students in creating your classroom rituals. Some classrooms use a lot of chants in their rituals, some use symbolic props like star wands and puppets, and some use activities that involve much physical movement. The rituals you use in your classroom each year will be as varied and unique as the students within it. The only steadfast "rule" is to hold true to the goal of creating an authentic connection.

Think about your usual classroom routines. Which of these could you enhance by adding a ritual within it? Perhaps a greeting ritual could accentuate your morning routine or adding a playful ritual could reduce test-taking stress. One fourth-grade student brought in a stuffed chicken that played the chicken dance song when you pushed its wing. The class created a ritual around it, singing, "We will do our best when we take the test," while doing the chicken dance. It was a great stress reducer before testing, and several other fourth-grade classrooms eventually picked up the idea and joined in.

The Gift of a Ritual

Rituals are the events—big events like holidays or small ones like a kiss goodbye—that connect us and provide texture and meaning in life. Rites of passage, from losing a tooth to getting a driver's license, mark time, create wonderful memories and define us as individuals and as community members. Healing rituals like Band-Aids for real and imagined boo-boos, and funerals for the death of loved ones help move us through difficult times. There is no more profound form of human bonding than shared experience. Rituals affirm our connection to one another. They provide the following much-needed services in our lives, families and schools:

- Rituals bestow a protected space and time to stop and reflect on life transformation. They mentally slow down the hectic pace of life.
- Rituals give us a place to be playful, to explore the meaning of life and to rework and rebuild relationships. Play is essential for all development.
- Rituals embrace both change and consistency at the same time. This makes them a perfect "brain food." Rituals perfectly balance soothing the lower centers of the brain with consistency and stimulating the higher centers with novelty.
- Rituals help us preserve human ties, even during times of conflict and intense turmoil. They are a bonding agent, like glue, that holds us together.
- Rituals allow us to create new relationship patterns, rules, roles and opportunities. They promote positive changes in how we interact and in those we interact with.
- Rituals help us initiate healing from loss. Today's children are facing more trauma and in larger numbers. Many experience the shattered trust and broken promises of divorce, for example. Unacknowledged loss turns to anger. Rituals help repair this dysfunction.
- Rituals express our values and beliefs, and help us learn more about each other while promoting the celebration of our accomplishments and life transitions (Imber-Black & Roberts, 1992; Imber-Black, Roberts & Whiting, 2003).

FRIDAY SING!

Once we shift from the factory model of education to the School Family model, rituals become a significant part of the classroom. Rituals become the bond that holds the School Family together in shared, meaningful experiences. They are essential for children who arrive in school without the intangible assets of "family privilege" mentioned in Chapter 2. For those possessing family privilege, they strengthen the relationship between home and school. Rituals provide challenging children (and those that share a classroom with them) with a medium to heal, change and rework relationships so academic learning is the main focus instead of policing for safety. Rituals become a strong alternative to expulsion and suspension. They bond children to the school, helping them engage in the social life and learning processes of school instead of driving them away.

Relationship-Resistant Children

The capacity and desire to form healthy emotional relationships with one another is related to the organization and function of specific parts of the brain. Just as our brain allows us to see, hear, talk and move, it also allows us to care for and love each other (or not). During infancy and the first years of life, we develop systems that enable us to form and maintain the emotional relationships that allow us to care, support and help one another instead of distrust, hurt and harm another. Experiences during this early, vulnerable period are critical to shaping our capacity for intimate and healthy emotional relationships. Caring, sharing, empathizing, inhibiting aggression, expanding the capacity to love and all other characteristics of healthy, productive human beings are related to the core attachment formed in infancy (Perry, 1996). When children who lack attachment enter prekindergarten programs and move through the educational system, they act out in diverse ways, disrupting learning and sometimes entire schools. They utilize a disproportionate amount of educational resources at extreme financial cost. Without appropriate intervention, they will drop out of school. They then continue to act out their pain, often through substance abuse, violence and other weights on society.

How do you recognize these children? You already know them. These children have problems with eye contact, touch, play and presence/engagement (sustained attention):

Eye contact: *Gianno would enter the classroom with his head down, rarely making eye contact. Sometimes he seemed to be staring right through me. I eventually realized that his attention span was as fleeting as his ability to sustain and enjoy eye contact. Because he didn't focus on faces like the other children, he seemed to miss the social cues necessary for healthy relationships. The school psychologist put him on a reward point system for his attention problems. It did nothing but create paperwork for me, and I still felt there was a precious child in there that I couldn't reach.*

Touch: *Heavenly had successfully irritated every child in the classroom with her hurtful behaviors. She was odd in her response to touch. She would sometimes lean against me as if asking for affection or connection. However, every time I reached out to touch her, she would withdraw. Her touch with the other children was aggressive. A "hello" could easily be a hip bump or an elbow to the gut. She was put on a behavioral plan that rewarded for keeping her hands and feet to herself. At times, she was successful and achieved the rewards offered, but she never really advanced socially or academically.*

Playful situations: *Daquan entered the school during prekindergarten, at which time teachers noticed he would mess with materials instead of engaging. His play skills were delayed and abnormal, and he seemed unaware of other children and their feelings. In later grades his academic lags continued largely unnoticed, but his behavioral problems achieved celebrity status. By fourth grade, he was two grade levels behind in reading and was being suspended more and more often. According to all his teachers, Daquan never really engaged with other children or the schoolwork. He had trouble playing during recess, working cooperatively in groups and truly getting along with peers. His attention and activity level was as scattered as his academic record. He seemed to have an odd laugh, would find weird things funny and leave things that are typically funny at his age unnoticed.*

Presence: *Sara was as anxious as they come, but you would not know it because she kept herself very busy. She was busy walking around the room. She was busy fiddling with stuff at her desk. She was busy aggravating others. It seemed that when she was calm, alert and attentive, she would suddenly pop out of that state and do something hurtful or disruptive. She was diagnosed with ADHD and was put on medication during the last part of the year. The medication helped reduce her busyness, but her ability to engage with others and the learning process was still a problem.*

Children who are at risk of becoming relationship-reluctant or relationship-resistant generally have trouble with eye contact, touch, playful situations and presence. We can glimpse some understanding of these children's experience in our own lives. Think of a time when you have felt hurt by and extremely angry with someone you love. When you walk in the house, your tendency is not to make eye contact. You probably avoid it at all cost. If the person reaches out to hug you, you almost instinctively jerk away from the touch. Your mind is busy replaying the injustices you perceive, so your presence and engagement is severely limited. Your sense of humor went out the window with your willingness to reconnect. This is the state of mind many of these children live in all day, every day.

The most seriously hurting children view friendly, helpful adults with deep distrust. Expecting rejection, they defend against it and attempt to control life instead of engage with it. They pull away from affection. The greater the depth of relationship hunger, the more controlling of people and situations these children will be. Their attention will be focused on protecting themselves and outwitting others instead of learning their ABCs. They seek to manipulate and control attention instead of offering the vulnerability and trust required for connection. Their willingness to be cooperative, compliant or solve problems is nonexistent. Unless we address the needs of relationship-resistant children, we will continue to

- Utilize nearly 90 percent of school resources on a few children, without success.
- Constantly see the same children for most of the referrals, suspensions and expulsions (we often refer to them as "frequent fliers" or "serial offenders").
- Leave children with repeatedly low standardized test scores behind, regardless of the curricular remediation offered.
- Add to the teacher's role those of a counselor, cop, corrections officer and con artist detector.
- Stress teachers to such a degree that they leave the field of education, costing billions of dollars annually.
- Fail in our educational mission to teach all children to become productive members of society.
- Cost taxpayers enormous amounts of money in terms of academic remediation, special education, juvenile delinquency and, eventually, criminal behavior.

The rituals embedded in the School Family are essential for pulling relationship-resistant and relationship-reluctant children back from the brink of unwitting self-destruction. The rituals included in this chapter and the *I Love You Rituals* book are helpful for connecting all children, but they were specifically designed to help transform relationship-reluctant children into resilient children who become functioning members of a classroom and society.

Power of Unity

Your classroom has a culture. Your school has a culture. All cultures create rituals, including our educational cultures. The trick is to create and conduct rituals consciously. There are many different ritual styles, some of which are no more reassuring than the "have a nice day" offered by a bored clerk at the clothing store. To be successful, your rituals must be authentic expressions of togetherness and joy. The following are different ritual styles. Think about the kinds of rituals that are promoted in your school and classroom, the type of rituals you experienced growing up, and the ones you've created for your family.

1. Minimized rituals: These rituals are not emphasized. Academic achievement is the goal. Little attention is placed on the whole child, specifically social and emotional intelligence. Holidays and birthdays might be celebrated if time permits, work is complete and the children have earned the break by demonstrating good behavior.

2. Interrupted rituals: Interrupted rituals usually indicate some sort of crisis has taken precedence. This crisis could be the changing of teachers, long-term illness of a teacher, a push by the county or state for immediate program changes, natural disasters, bomb threats and human tragedy.

3. Rigid rituals: Rigid rituals are created by the teacher and are done the same way year after year, regardless of the makeup of the classroom. Trying something new is out of the question. Everyone's role is highly prescribed. The emphasis is on doing the ritual correctly instead of connecting. Those who do the ritual "wrong" are excluded from the activity. Playfulness and humor are lacking.

4. Imbalanced rituals: Imbalanced rituals occur in classrooms that conduct only a small range of rituals. Instead of having good morning rituals, absent child rituals and such, only holidays and birthdays are emphasized. Sometimes the curriculum is driven by holidays, with November focusing on Thanksgiving and so on. These rituals usually represent one ethnic heritage more than balance among all.

5. Obligatory rituals: Obligatory rituals exist because they "should." They lack true connection and consciousness. The good morning song is sung as a way to start the day, not as a way to connect. Children toss their Safekeeper figure into a bucket without the conscious commitment to contribute to class success. Teachers do not pause to talk about the meaning of helpfulness or take the time to consciously connect the class. Rituals feel more like routines that mark the passage of time instead of meaningful events. A tired flight attendant routinely saying goodbye to 300 people exiting a 747 is an example of an obligatory ritual.

6. Authentic rituals: Authentic rituals are true, conscious rituals. The teacher and students jointly create them. They evolve out of the family framework constructed by the teacher. Authentic rituals are flexible, capturing and reflecting the current needs of the members of the community. They offer a sense of continuity and connectedness throughout time. Authentic rituals bring cohesiveness to the School Family. They emerge and dissolve with spontaneity and delight. They help establish relationships, mark life changes, heal wounds from hurtful experiences, voice the beliefs of the School Family and celebrate life itself.

Much research shows that "survival of the fittest" simply doesn't hold true; it is the most connected who thrive. Relationships are necessary for us to survive, learn, work, love and live in harmony with one another, and rituals are key to creating healthy relationships. A detailed review of literature finds that the creation of supportive learning environments increases student engagement and attachment to school, and that these factors significantly influence student academic performance (Osterman, 2000). As you create your School Family, keep a keen eye on places where routines can be enhanced with the authentic rituals that will enrich your classroom with connection.

The power of unity: We are all in this together
Skill: Consciousness and mindfulness
Structure: School Family rituals
Value: Compassion

Rituals create connection and connection is the key to creating the willingness to cooperate and solve problems. Every disconnected student provides the opportunity for many teaching moments for connection. The key is to see and seize these opportunities.

I once visited a classroom in North Carolina that consisted of a large number of disconnected children who were, as you may guess, extremely out of control and disruptive. I arrived just as they transitioned from circle time to center time. Typical center activities were available for them. As I interacted with children at each center, I took every possible moment to build a connection with eye contact, touch, presence and a playful situation. At the play-dough area, I began making eyeglasses out of my play dough. My attempts to hold the play-dough glasses to my face brought their attention to my eyes. I used that moment to say, "The better to see you, my precious ones." That led into some peek-a-boo moments, followed by my fingers walking up a child's arm. As my fingers walked up her arm, I chanted, "I'm walking, I'm looking, I'm looking, for YOU!" Instead of using the play dough to make shapes and talk about them, I took the moment to create a connection with these relationship-reluctant children.

In a fifth-grade classroom in Arizona, I was able to connect with one very disconnected student whose dad had recently been incarcerated. I began by saying, "If your dad was sitting here right now, what would you want to say to him?" The student thought for a moment and he said, "I would tell him I loved him and be safe so he could come back home." I asked him to make some movements to go with that statement. His movements included "I love you" in sign language, followed by pointing to the class Safe Place and ending with both of his hands coming together. I mirrored his motions and added some tweaks. We both made the "I love you" sign, we both touched our hearts to represent a Safe Place, and then we did a hammer-up/hammer-down fist bump. We co-created a ritual he could do each time he was missing his dad or thinking of him. Later that day, he looked up from his desk and sent me the "I love you" sign. I responded with touching my heart and walked over to his desk and did a hammer-up/hammer-down fist bump. After this reassuring connection, a small light came to his face, and he went on with his math work.

> Children who seek attention are afraid of connection.

Once you grasp the power of seeking connection rather than giving attention, you will see opportunities for connection throughout the day. As I've stated many times before, the connection we seek involves eye contact, touch, presence and a playful situation. All the activities in my *I Love You Rituals* book are designed to make these specific types of connections.

> **Teacher Tip:**
> Some cultures have different rules for eye contact; however, they are all relative to context. No culture has rules against eye contact in playful situations.

Rituals are a very fluid environmental structure; there is no one "thing" to set up or one lesson to teach. The following, however, are the top ten rituals that will help you create a culture of connection and caring, where the willingness to engage, cooperate and solve problems becomes the soil for a bully-proof environment and academic success. These core rituals can be used with any age group.

1. Greeting ritual: Select a location where you will stand every morning to greet the children. Greet them both nonverbally and verbally. Nonverbally, you can greet with your eyes or with a touch. Verbally, you can say, "Hello, good morning, I'm glad you're here today," or "I was waiting to say hello to you." Part of the greeting ritual may be to have children notice a morning message written by a classmate. You may also use props like a greeting apron or tie to give children a choice about how they would like to be greeted.

> **Teacher Tip:**
> Put the greetings below on a greeting apron, tie or poster on the front door, and ask children, "How would you like to be greeted today?" You can also use the template on the *Make-N-Take* CDrom from Loving Guidance to make a greeting apron with many other options like skunk, butterfly, snowman and fish greetings.
>
> | Picture | Action |
> |---|---|
> | Hand | Handshake |
> | Five | High five |
> | Heart | Hug |
> | Smiley face | Smile |

2. School Family song: Each classroom creates a School Family song or chant that showcases the values of the classroom. You will sing it daily at specified times. The following represents one School Family song. Several examples are below.

"You Are My School Family" (tune: "You Are My Sunshine")
You are my family,
My School Family.
I feel happy,
When we are here.
I hope you know, friends,
How much I like you! (make eye contact and point to a friend)
When we're apart,
I'll keep you in my heart! (cross hands over your heart)

Ms. Levitt's class chant
"We are intelligent thinkers who persevere through difficult obstacles. We show compassion to people around us. We practice self-discipline in our work and actions. Together we can help each other make the world a better place."

Mrs. McKenzie's Physical Education classroom rap
In this class our work is play (sidestep left, sidestep right),
If you have fun you've won, I say (interlock fingers and do the arm wave)!
So jump right in and have a ball (jump and pretend to dribble a ball),
But sit down quietly when freeze is called (sit on circle with legs crossed).
Now I'm your teacher (point thumbs to self),
I may seem tough (hands on hips),
That's because I care so much (hands over heart, make eye contact with every student).
I want you to be the best you can be (point to students and give a thumbs up),
And make your dreams a reality (do the sign language for dream)!

3. Connecting and Appreciation rituals: At specified times during the day, take time for connecting and appreciation rituals. Connecting rituals are activities that ask children to consciously touch one another, make eye contact and be playful. Two appropriate times for a connecting ritual are during the Brain Smart Start routine in the morning and during the closing rituals at the end of the day. *I Love You Rituals* is a book of 79 connecting activities that can be used with young children (3-8 years old). They can be sent home as homework and used in your reading buddy program to involve older children striving to move from relationship-reluctance to resilience. Appreciation rituals are verbal and written expressions of caring and helpfulness. The following are two examples of I Love You Rituals:

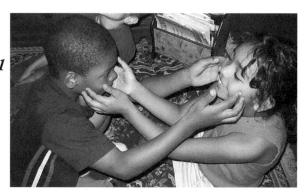

"Peter Peter"
I Love You Rituals, page 62 and
Songs for I Love You Rituals, Volume 1
Peter, Peter, Pumpkin Eater,
Had a friend he loved to greet.
Treated her/him with kind respect,
And in the morning hugged her/his neck.

Story Hand
I Love You Rituals, page 167
Tell the child, "It's story time." The child will probably think you're going to read a book. Instead, take his/her hand and tell a reassuring or encouraging story about a success, concern or event in the child's day.

Start with the pinky finger, giving it a nice massage and saying, "This little finger wanted to learn how to ride a two-wheel bicycle." (The story you tell will be based on the child's life; I am using the success story of learning to ride a bike as an example.) Go to the next finger and give it a massage, saying, "This finger was a little afraid that he might fall off." Continue to the next finger, saying, "But this finger said, 'I can do it. I just know I can.'" At the index finger, continue with the story, "So he decided to try and try again." Finally, massage the thumb and say excitedly, "Did he do it? Did he do it?" Then tuck the thumb into the palm of the child's hand and make a reassuring or "you did it"–type statement: "No problem. All the fingers knew she/he would do it all the time."

4. **Wish Well ritual:** The wish well ritual creates coherent classrooms. It involves creating a calm, loving internal state and then "sending" that feeling to others. Wishing well is a three-step process: 1) Take a deep breath in, 2) put your hands on your heart while filling your heart with love, and 3) send that love out to others while opening your arms and exhaling. Older children can use specific mental images to help them create that loving, wish well feeling. When first teaching children to wish well, help them "fill their hearts with love" by telling them to picture something precious.  Offer age-appropriate examples and share something you might think of lovingly. You can also share research about quantum physics and/or the healing effects of prayer and meditation in older classrooms, as appropriate.

Utilize the simple, yet powerful act of wishing well as a part of many School Family rituals and activities and as a stand-alone ritual. Wish well for students who are absent, for people we feel concern for, when students are upset for any reason, for local or global situations students feel concerned about and whenever students are struggling with a task. If Shanita is having trouble reading aloud, the teacher instructs, "Shanita needs our help. Let's take a deep breath and wish her well." If a news headline has upset children, take a moment: "Several of you brought in current event articles about the people who lost their lives and homes in the earthquake over the weekend. Let's take a deep breath and wish those people well."

5. Absent Child rituals: Lead your School Family in brainstorming things they could do for a child who is absent. The message you want to send is, "We noticed you were gone, we missed you, and we're glad you're back." Some classes make cards or poems. Others write songs. The following are examples of a song and a chant you could use:

"We Missed You" (Tune: "Frère Jacques")
    We missed (name).
    We missed (name).
    Yes we did! Yes we did!
    Glad that (name)'s back.
    Glad that (name)'s back.
    Now we're all together.
    Now we're all together.

"You've Been Gone"
    You've been gone and you've been missed.
    Where would you like your welcome back kiss? (Use a puppet or wand to give a kiss.)

6. Welcome New Child rituals: I have frequently said, "Teachers are always pregnant, they just don't know when the next child is coming." With the increased mobility of our society, children leave and enter new schools frequently. It is helpful to mark these life transitions with welcoming rituals. Your class can develop the ritual. A second-grade classroom made t-shirts at the beginning of the year. Children decorated the t-shirts with their handprints and made extras with all the children's handprints in case a new child joined the class. When a new child came, the t-shirt was presented during a welcoming ceremony the children helped design.

7. Moving Child rituals: Just as children come, they also leave. Rituals are helpful in marking the transition as children move to new schools. One first-grade class decided they would make a goodbye video for the child leaving. Similar to the process of recording "best wishes" for the bride and groom at a wedding, the children had the opportunity to say something to the child on camera and record footage of the school and classroom.

8. Life Change and Holiday rituals: Life changes include birthdays, deaths, graduations, the birth of new siblings and losing teeth. Most classrooms mark these transitions in some way. Design a series of fun and/or reassuring rituals for these occasions. If you include holiday rituals, make sure you include diverse cultures and the ways they celebrate holidays.

9. Goodbye rituals: As the school day draws to an end, another critical transition occurs. Children end their time as students and teachers end their time as teachers. Many teachers close the day with a report from the Kindness Recorder (a classroom job suggested in Chapter 11) and a song. They then send each child off with a personal goodbye. One kindergarten teacher says something like, "Tomorrow, I'll see your smile, crocodile," and gives a hug. She has a different saying for each week of school. Another teacher has the entire classroom hold hands in a circle and say goodbye with a "hand hug." While holding hands, she gently squeezes the hand to her right, that person squeezes the hand next to him, and the hand hug moves all the way around the circle and back to her.

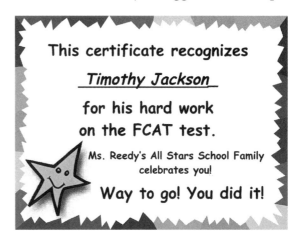

10. Testing rituals: With increasing emphasis placed on testing, testing rituals are extremely helpful for creating a more coherent brain-body state. In one school, the principal brings each teacher a rose one week before the state achievement tests. In front of the class, the principal presents the rose and says, "Mrs. Luther, you've worked hard all year teaching these students. They are ready for the upcoming test. You can relax knowing you have prepared them well." In the same school, kindergarten children write "You can do it" notes to the older students and hold a parade two days before the test. A second-grade teacher involves parents by asking each family to write a note to their child. After the test, each child is presented with a "you did it" certificate and the note from home. The chicken dance celebration discussed earlier in this chapter provides another fun way to relieve stress and connect before a test.

A = Activities

General Activities — All Ages

End-of-Year Rituals

Generally, children begin to act out toward the end of the year. Some are excited about summer, some are sad about leaving their School Family and some are angry that the safety they found at school will be gone. To help soothe this unsettled state, use transition rituals. Some schools create, "I will remember" class books. Others write a book to the upcoming class about what their grade is like. One teacher uses the form to the right to help children create a helpful "about me" page to give to next year's teacher.

Yet another teacher combines music and a class-made book for her classroom's goodbye rituals. She introduces the song, "Love Is a Circle" on *Kindness Counts*, about a month before the school year ends. After singing the song for about a week, she goes around the circle and has each child complete the sentence, "I will remember _____," sharing one thing they will remember about the year in her classroom. About a week later, she gives each child a circle-shaped piece of paper and has them write what they will remember, then illustrate their page. To make the book's cover, she enlists an adult to stand on a stepstool and take a photo of the class standing in a circle with their arms around each other (including the teacher). She then makes copies of the book and presents one to each student on the last day of school.

**Madelyn Pryor's
Things you should know about me...**

I am feeling EXCITED about kindergarten. It'll be FUN.
One thing that I am really good at is DOING TRICKS ON THE MONKEY BARS. But I may need help with TYING MY SHOES.
One thing that I feel a little worried about is NOTHING.
I feel excited about GOING TO THE NEW PLAYGROUND AT KINDERGARTEN.
I hope that my kindergarten teacher is NICE, HELPING THE CLASS LEARN STUFF.
If I feel upset or sad, GOING TO THE SAFE PLACE will help me feel better. If I'm upset I can FIND A FRIEND TO TALK TO.
One thing I didn't like doing at lab school was WHEN THERE WAS A LOT OF READING BECAUSE IT MIGHT BE TRICKY BUT I DID IT ANYWAY. One thing I loved to do at lab school was PLAY ON THE PLAYGROUND.
When I grow up, I want to be A SINGER.

Begin your end-of-year rituals when the children clearly know the school year is ending. The rituals generally start earlier for older students and later for the younger ones.

I See Song

The "I See Song" is a ritual of noticing. It allows each child to be seen by the teacher and receive individual attention in a group setting. Young children struggle to get enough attention to sustain them when they are in group settings. This ritual is one of the ways teachers can begin to meet the needs of young children in group care. In the song, the teacher describes what she or he sees the children doing. It is important not to mention jewelry, glasses or clothing. The song is about valuing and seeing the child, not the "stuff."

"I See Song" (tune: "Frère Jacques")
"Hello (state child's name)." Children echo the sentence sung.
"I see (state child's name)." Children echo the sentence sung.
"Her hands are going like this!" (Demonstrate hand positions)
Children echo and copy the movements.
"Her legs are going like this!" (Demonstrate the leg positions)
Children echo and copy the movements.

Welcome to School Ritual

The first time the children come to school, give them this poem with a teddy bear. Any time a new student enrolls, have the class present him or her with the same poem and teddy bear.

Welcome to Kindergarten
Here's a teddy bear
To let you know that I'll be there
To keep you safe and watch you grow,
To help you learn the things you need to know,
To help you when you don't know how,
To clap for you when you take a bow,
To give you time to play each day,
To listen to what you have to say,

To celebrate when you read books,
To taste all the yummy things you cook,
To help you learn to think and do,
I'm looking forward to the time I will spend with you!

General Activities
Older

Beginning of the Year

Before school begins, create a ritual for bringing the class together. Use the School Family name and induct each student into the School Family. Make this time very ceremonious, like when they introduce new players on popular reality TV shows. "The tribe has come together to form this family. We shall call this family (School Family Names)." Have students introduce themselves and share one or two things about themselves. End with the same type of ceremonious ending, "The Tribe has spoken—now it's time to get back to work."

> **Teacher Tip:**
> Some classrooms choose a symbolic item to designate whose turn it is to speak. One third-grade teacher travels all over the world on his time off from school, and during his travels he picks up hats. Each year the School Family chooses one hat to be their symbol. They pass the hat around as they introduce themselves.

Honoring Ritual

Hold an honoring ceremony each month. In this ceremony, the school family gives "shout outs" to each other. At the beginning of the month, put a slip of paper with each child's name on it in a hat. Each student chooses another's name randomly from the hat and notices the things that student does during the month. At the shout-out ceremony, the students offer each other shout outs. They can give homemade certificates or just a verbal "I'm giving this shout out to (name) because I noticed that they (what they did). This helps our School Family by (how it helps)."

> **Teacher Tip:**
> Eat lunch with your children once a month and do your shout-out ceremony then. You can include special music and other activities to help celebrate together.

Jack-Be-Noodle

Draw and cut out or buy pre-made cutouts of children. Glue one to each page in the book for every child in the class, leaving the arms unglued so they are moveable. Then glue a photo of each child's head

Class-Made Books
Younger

onto the head of the cutout. Put a heart sticker where the heart would be. Add the following text to each page, mimicking the words to the "Jack Be Noodle" song on *Songs for I Love You Rituals, Volume 2*:

(Name) be noodle
(Name) be quick
(Name) come over and hug me quick. (Fold the arms in as you read.)

Humpty Dumpty

Cut out ovals about six inches high for each child. Draw a brick wall and write the poem below on a piece of paper. Photocopy it so each child has a page. Fill in the child's name, and the child's name starting with a "D" to personalize a page for each child. For example, "Becky, Decky sat on a wall,"

_____ , _____ sat on a wall,
_____ , _____ had a great fall.
All the king's horses and all the queen's men,
Could put _____ together again!

Read the "Humpty Dumpty" I Love You Ritual. Pass out the ovals, have children tear up pieces of white paper and glue them to the ovals. Tell them they are putting Humpty back together again! Then pass out the poem pages and have them glue their Humpty Dumpty on the wall. Bind the pages into a book.

Music & Movement — Younger

I Love You Rituals Books

Have children act out a variety of rituals from the *I Love You Rituals* book and take photographs of them. Use the photographs to create class books for your library. These books are also excellent keepsakes to send home for special events or at the end of the year.

Chapter 10: School Family Rituals

Music & Movement

Older

Songs for I Love You Rituals, Vol. 1 and Vol. 2

All of the songs on these albums make wonderful rituals for your School Family; most can be done with partners or in groups of several students, and most have movements that are self-explanatory. "Good-bye Rituals" on *Songs for I Love You Rituals, Vol. 1* is a great way to end the day. It's only one minute long, so you can fit it in when you are running short on time. The hand motions to this song are:

See you later, alligator / after awhile, crocodile (Extend your arms and clap so it looks like an alligator or crocodile opening and closing its mouth)
So long, King Kong (Beat your chest with your fists)
What's the deal, white seal? (Hold elbows up and clap your hands together)
Toot-a-loo, kangaroo (Bounce up and down like a kangaroo)
See you soon, raccoon (Hold both hands in the shape of an "o" around your eyes and look around)
Come again, little hen (Flap arms at the side like chicken wings)
See you there, teddy bear (Hold arms to body like a hug)
What's the word, blackbird? (Hold hand to ear like you're listening for something)
Good-bye, gotta fly (Lock thumbs together and have them fly away like a bird)

Clapping games

Clapping games make great connecting rituals for children who may feel they're "too old" for I Love You Rituals. A couple to try are:

"Miss Mary Mack"
Miss Mary Mack, Mack, Mack
All dressed in black, black, black,
With shiny buttons, buttons, buttons
All down her back, back, back.
She asked her mother, mother, mother,
For fifty cents, cents, cents,
To see the elephant, elephant, elephant
Jump over the fence, fence, fence.
He jumped so high, high, high,
He reached the sky, sky, sky,

And he never came back, back, back,
'Til the end of July, 'ly, 'ly.

"Cinderella Dressed in Yella"
Cinderella, dressed in yella,
Went upstairs to kiss a fella,
Made a mistake, kissed a snake,
How many doctors will it take?

Once your students are comfortable with the games, challenge them to change the words to make them fit your School Family name. Use these personalized clapping games for your end-of-day and other rituals.

C = Commitment

I commit to consciously implement at least two rituals during this school year. The two I will start with:
1. Wish You Well
2. HOPE circle

Signature Maureen E. Goder   **Date** August 6, 2014

H = Helpful Resources

Songs for I Love You Rituals, Vol. 1 and Vol. 2 **by Dr. Becky Bailey and Mar Harman**
Songs: All

Music — All Ages

Kindness Counts **by Dr. Becky Bailey and Mr. Al**
Songs: "Love Is a Circle"

Literature — All Ages

Shubert's New Friend **by Dr. Becky Bailey.** Shubert's new classmate is not what they expected. Watch as Mrs. Bookbinder helps them see things from a different perspective and see their "welcoming a new student" ritual in action.

Literature — Younger

Goodnight Moon **by Margaret Wise Brown.** This classic tale shows the mother and child saying goodnight to everything in the room as part of their bedtime ritual.
The Kissing Hand **by Audrey Penn.** Chester's mother teaches him the kissing-hand ritual as a way to adjust to being at school.

If someone is gone for three days we call their house and sing the "Wish Well" song.

Teacher Tip:

There are many ways to implement the wish well ritual. Something as simple as calling to leave a voice mail message for the child/family connects the home and school in a wonderful partnership.

Chapter 11

Classroom Jobs

Maria is three years old. She attends a preschool that uses Conscious Discipline. Every day when her mother picks her up from school, they greet each other with joy and the following ritual. Maria sees her mother and runs to hide. Mom says, "Where's my girl? I've been waiting all day to see her brown eyes, her black hair and her ten fingers." As Mom describes her little girl, she walks around looking for Maria. When she finds her, Mom exclaims, "There you are," and scoops her up in her arms. As they giggle and laugh together, Mom says, "I'm going to say hello to your nose (then she kisses it). I'm going to say hello to your hand (then she kisses it)." Before they leave the preschool, Mom requests, "Show me your favorite thing you did today." Every day Maria shows her the same thing. She leads her mom to the Job Board, points to her picture and says, "I did my job," beaming with pride.

Maria demonstrates and communicates the deep universal need to be of service. Among the many aspects that give life meaning and promote self-worth, contribution is one of the most rewarding. We all seek, on some level, to make a difference and live a life of purpose. Neuroscience emphasizes that our brains develop through meaningful social interactions (Jensen, 2000). Psychologists tell us we must balance our needs for survival, safety and belonging with our need for power (Glasser, 1998). In essence, this research tells us what Maria already knew at three years: We need each other, and we need each other to do our part in contributing to the whole of humankind. We are not meant to be completely independent nor dependent, but to give and receive in mutual interdependence. As we give to others, we strengthen ourselves. As we receive from others, we allow them to grow. Being of service is not an option; it is a biological imperative that is required for optimal brain development (Cacioppo, Visser & Pickett, 2005). Every kind act, every contribution we make reanimates our own life force.

All major religions and spiritual traditions tell us that we serve the divine through caring for each other. The Talmud states, "All men are responsible for each other." Jesus taught, "That which you do to the least of these, my brethren, you do unto me." In Islam, Number 13 of Imam An-Nawawi's Forty Hadiths states, "None of you [truly] believes until he wishes for his brother what he wishes for himself." Theologies of service to others are also found in Buddhism, Taoism and Native American wisdom. Caring and contributing to others opens our hearts to something greater than ourselves and allows the vulnerability of our own spirit to surface. Science and religion tell us we are energetically interdependent. The journey of the "self" is inherently tied to the journey of the "other." To raise our self-worth, we must turn away from relying on external sources of power such as money, status, material goods and physical appearance and shift to internal empowerment that relies on universal truths such as "give and it is returned tenfold unto you." This way of viewing self-worth puts the need to be a contributing, caring, compassionate person at the heart of the School Family.

Meaningful Contributions

I remember arriving at a workshop in Sarasota, Florida. My trunk was full of handouts and heavy boxes of books and CDs to sell. My sales helper, a heavy-set woman in her early 50s, had brought her 14-year-old son with her. He was busily playing with a hand-held computer game as his mother loaded and unloaded the very heavy boxes. It amazed me that she didn't ask him for help and that he didn't offer to help. The sad part for me is not bemoaning the work ethic of the next generation, but that this budding adolescent didn't know how much the world needs him. He did not know that he mattered, that he made a difference. He was separate from his own life force.

Years ago, farm life depended on children doing their share of the labor. Without their contributions, the family could not survive. As society shifted from agriculture to manufacturing to information technology, children began to be seen more as a liability than an asset. News headlines now calculate how much money each child will cost to raise. The numbers are staggering. It seems our priceless children now have a price tag.

Some parents, rushed for time and feeling guilty, find it easier to do chores themselves or hire someone than to systematically teach and rely on their children. Some children are raising themselves, lacking the necessary supervision to learn how to contribute to family life. To balance these and other cultural trends, Conscious Discipline provides children the opportunity to be significant contributors to others through meaningful classroom responsibilities called "School Family Jobs." Each student in the classroom has a job. If you have 25 children, you will have 25 jobs. These jobs contribute to the educational process in a number of ways.

[handwritten: 90 is too many]

[handwritten: Children learn:]

1. Students are empowered to co-create their classrooms with the teacher. Power and responsibility are a mated pair. The people with power share the responsibility. Conversely, the people with the responsibilities share power. So, power and responsibility in the School Family are dispersed and shared among all its members.
2. The classroom becomes a microcosm of a democratic culture. The students experience the reality that freedom comes with responsibilities. They are encouraged to practice being responsible classroom citizens.
3. Children experience what constitutes a "job" and come to learn the meaning of job descriptions. This becomes a foundation for even the youngest child to begin understanding what Mom, Grandma and Dad do when they go to work. As children grow, they can relate better to academic units on careers and community helpers, eventually leading to understanding career options.
4. Children learn that for a community to be successful, each person must do his or her part. They experience firsthand that each person in a community—regardless of race, creed, color, ability or disability—is an essential, valuable part of the whole.
5. Children learn that everyone has unique gifts, regardless of academic, physical, social or emotional limitations. Sharing their gifts mirrors the self-sustaining, interdependent system of unity in nature.
6. Each class job provides students with the opportunity to practice reading, writing, math, social studies and science in the meaningful context of daily living.

So Much To Do!

When teachers first hear that every child in the classroom has a job, some of them gasp. Providing a job for every student seems a bit much at first. However, the payoff in your classroom is huge, for both you and the students. I receive three or four emails per month from teachers singing praise for "a job for each student." The email below is from a second-grade teacher in Iowa.

> *I first heard about Conscious Discipline and the School Family notion at a state conference. I was attentive and it seemed to make sense. However, when I heard about providing a job for each of my students, it seemed overwhelming. I thought to myself, "How will I ever come up with 29 jobs?" Up until this conference, I had some jobs in my room, usually five total. I would have the students earn those jobs like rewards. As Dr. Bailey explained how this approach promotes specialness, "the good kids get the goods," it hit home! Some children would feel special while others wouldn't. Now, a year later, I think to myself, "How did I ever run my classroom without having a job for every student?" The class runs itself. The children love the jobs and take pride in doing them.*

A job for every student will require an initial time investment to list the necessary jobs, routines and rituals that keep your classroom running smoothly, flesh out the job descriptions, organize a Job Board to visually represent the jobs, teach the jobs to the students and notice/encourage students as they compete in their jobs successfully. Once the initial instruction is complete, the children will guide each other as they rotate jobs. By the third week of job use, you will likely notice that a burden has been lifted from you and that the children thrive on the opportunity to be responsible.

Power of Unity

In Conscious Discipline, the organization of the classroom is aligned with the universal principle of nature: unity. Nature is a self-sustaining, self-nourishing, interdependent system where each tiny part contributes to the functioning of the whole. The School Family is designed around this same power of unity, which states, "We are all in this together." It therefore behooves us to help and encourage one another. A job for every student is the structure that enables each child to offer service to the functioning of the class. Encouragement is the skill that adults can use to focus the class on the concept of unity by highlighting the contributions each child makes to others and the group.

Power of unity: We are all in this together
Skill: Encouragement
Structure: Job Board
Value: Responsibility

Very powerful teaching moments will naturally occur as children learn their individual jobs for the classroom. The following are three common moments I encourage you to maximize for learning.

"**Almost**" **moments:** As with learning any new skill, your students will experience a learning curve and make mistakes. Some children will learn their jobs and perform them with care and expertise; others will struggle and lack focused attention. Children who halfway wash the table, swing the door handle back and forth while holding the door open or water the plant by drowning it need our encouragement and additional instruction. We could easily choose to see these as imperfect moments that require us to point out their mistakes, lecture them about the value of good work or give their job to someone who does it better. Alternately, we could seize these as the perfect moments to encourage, refocus the child to his or her potential, build esteem and teach the proper procedures for washing a table thoroughly, holding a door safely and watering a plant. We can do this by enthusiastically saying, "You almost did it! All you need now is to _____." Fill in the blank with more detailed verbal instructions, accompanied by a specific demonstration of how you want the finished job to look. You could also take pictures of what a clean table looks like or how much water is needed for the plant. Then ask the children to reflect on their accomplishments relative to the goal you have set.

Early childhood classrooms require this type of teaching with great frequency. It's not until around nine years old that children become concerned about the product of their work rather than the process of it. For example, a young child cleaning a table will lose himself in the soap and sponge instead of focusing on a spotless tabletop. A young child might delight in pouring the water, not realizing she has flooded the plant and dripped all over the floor. Our job is to continue to coach and encourage children through this developmental process instead of holding strict standards and expecting them to reach them.

Chapter 11: Classroom Jobs

Have you ever noticed how young children love to help, from carrying the dishes to washing the car? Over time, we get frustrated with the additional mess they create in the name of "helping." We either take over the task or become impatient with their ability to do it right. It is helpful in these moments to remember that the journey from process to product takes at least nine years developmentally. If you can continue to encourage them to achieve more of the desired standards of quality by saying, "You almost got it! Try this one more thing," you both will complete that first decade of life with peace of mind and a willingness to be helpful.

"You Did It" moments: There will be times the child accomplishes what you asked. These are the "you did it" moments when we celebrate their accomplishments and achievements. These precious moments provide an opportunity for us to celebrate children and highlight for them exactly what they did to achieve a goal. If a child was successful in washing down the table, you might say, "You did it! You washed down the table using the sponge and moving your hands in circle motions like this (demonstrate) until the whole table was clean." If a child was successful in holding the door open, you might say, "You did it, you held the door open and watched each of your friends as they walked by you. You even gave a smile to many so you could say, 'hi,' without talking." By saying, "You did it," we celebrate the children. By describing what they accomplished and how they accomplished it, we focus their attention on the process and scaffold ways for them to increase their expertise in the area.

As you read this, you might think, "Well naturally, that makes sense." As much sense as this makes, it's not what happens in practice. We tend to judge or generalize rather than offer authentic praise for the child's accomplishment. When we say, "Good job," or, "Thank you for cleaning the table," we are actually judging instead of celebrating. Our judgments shift children's focus from the process of the task to pleasing the teacher. When we shift from helping them attend to the process to having them attend to pleasing us, we lose our scaffolding ability. We are then raising a child who does a job to obtain our approval rather than for the self-satisfaction of doing the job well.

We also tend to generalize our judgments instead of describing. Instead of describing how they washed the table, we generalize by commenting, "Yesterday you cleaned the table so well, what happened to you today?" Or we might end up assigning character traits like, "Becky has trouble with watering plants. I'm looking for someone who is paying attention and sitting up straight, and who I know will do a good job with the plants." The result is discouraged children who feel criticized instead of encouraged children who are making progress.

"It Helps Our School Family by _____" moments: There will be moments where a child or children refuse to do their job. This can mean a number of things. Ask yourself the following reflection questions to discern what might help the child be more successful.

Good Questions to exceptions

- Is this a chronic situation or an infrequent event? We've all had "one of those days." Children have them, too! If the behavior is infrequent, have the child ask others for help. Let the child know that it's his or her responsibility to find a substitute for that day.
- Is the job meaningful? Was the job meaningful to the workings of the class or did you make it up because you were short one job per child?
- Do the children know how this particular job helps the School Family? If not, lead a discussion about how the classroom jobs help the School Family. When you see a child doing his job say, "Michael, you are holding the door open so everyone in the room can walk out safely and calmly without worrying the door will hit them."
- Ask children why they do their job. Young children will say, "To give a cup at snack time." You must extend this concept beyond the immediate act by saying, "Yes, you give a cup so everyone can have a drink and not feel thirsty during snack time."

E = Environmental Structure: Job Board

Meaningful contributions to others are an essential part of healthy development. A job for every student is a vital way to give children the opportunity to contribute to the group welfare. These jobs are managed using a Job Board. The Job Board becomes a tangible structure representing your class commitment to encourage and help one another.

Purpose: The purpose of the Job Board is to organize, manage and visually represent a classroom job for every student.

How to set up your classroom jobs: Much of your set-up for the classroom jobs can be accomplished by purchasing the School Family Job Set, which includes illustrated job cards, a vinyl pocket board that hangs on the wall and job descriptions for each job. You can also make your Job Board from scratch.

> **Teacher Tip:**
> To make your own Job Board, take photos of each area or piece of equipment used to do each job. Post the photos on the wall or on a board and label each photo with the job name. Place a Velcro dot next to each picture. Next, take a photo of each student and place the other side of the Velcro dots on the back of each photo, so you can easily attach and move the photos to a new job each week.

The first step in setting up your Job Board is to select the jobs your class will perform. You will need one job per student in your class (18 students equals 18 jobs). Individual jobs will generally fall into three categories: chores, routines and rituals.

Every classroom demands a certain number of necessary tasks such as attendance, lunch count and stacking chairs at the end of the day. These tasks can be thought of as chores.

Routines are daily procedures that promote predictability in the classroom. You have an arrival routine, a lining-up routine, a bathroom routine, a clean-up routine and many more. A school day is a complex script of successive routines that children learn and master in order to be successful, as discussed in Chapter 6.

Rituals are activities that center on connection, caring and respect, as discussed in Chapter 10. Once you establish your rituals, you will want to assign classroom jobs to manage them. Using the family as the metaphor for the classroom can help us create classroom rituals and the jobs that will help manage them. Family members send cards to sick relatives, so you might want a "We Care" job in your classroom. The We Care person would draw a picture, write a note, and so on for sick classmates. Family members greet relatives at the door, so you might want the "Greeter" to be another class job.

As you create your job list, think about the chores, routines and rituals that help your classroom operate smoothly and with connection. Each class will have a unique job list, just like every family is a unique expression of the love that creates it. The following will assist you with creating your own unique list:

1. Brainstorm a list of classroom chores and routines you are doing everyday. Then check the box beside the tasks you are willing to hand over to the children. For example:

- ☐ Arrival
- ☐ Breakfast
- ☐ Quieting the class/attention routine
- ☐ Pencil/marker routines
- ☐ "What to do when you are through"
- ☐ Rest routine
- ☐ Coming to circle
- ☐ Observing good hygiene
  (restrooms, diapers, hands, etc.)
- ☐ Late work
- ☐ Distributing materials
- ☐ _____

- ☐ Late arrival/tardy/absent
- ☐ Dismissal/departure
- ☐ Emergency routines
- ☐ Lining-up routines
- ☐ Attendance/lunch count
- ☐ Movement of paper/supplies
- ☐ Safe place routine
- ☐ Headings on papers
- ☐ Turning in papers
- ☐ _____
- ☐ _____

Next, do the same for the classroom rituals.

- ☐ Absent children
- ☐ Wish well
- ☐ Moving/leaving child
- ☐ We Care ritual
- ☐ School Family song/motto/chant
- ☐ Morning message
- ☐ Safekeeper ritual
- ☐ _____

- ☐ Greeting visitors
- ☐ New child
- ☐ Testing rituals
- ☐ Connection and appreciation rituals
- ☐ Life change/holiday
- ☐ Community news
- ☐ _____

Add and subtract marks on your list until the number of checks is equal to the number of children in your class. You now have your job list!

2. Create your job descriptions by writing down behavioral expectations for each of the chores, routines and rituals you checked above. Consider these steps for teaching a job as you write:

Step 1 Explain: State, explain, model and demonstrate the chore/routine/ritual.
Step 2 Rehearse: Rehearse and practice the chore/routine/ritual.
Step 3 Reinforce: Notice children who are successful.
Step 4 Manage: Prompt, remind and encourage children as they complete their chore/routine/ritual.

The following is a series of job descriptions to help you get started:

The Safekeeper job always belongs to the teacher. It is the teacher's job to keep the classroom safe for all children to learn and grow. Activities and rituals for introducing the Safekeeper are provided in Chapter 5.

The Greeter greets students as they come into the classroom in the morning and also greets visitors who enter the classroom. Teach children exactly how to greet others and what to say. You might teach this process:

- When a visitor comes to the room, walk to the door.
- Look the person in the eye, and say, "Welcome to Ms. Bailey's classroom. My name is Riley. How can I help you?"
- Some classrooms may have a sign-in book for visitors. In that case, the greeter would instruct guests to sign in.

The Goodbye Wisher selects a goodbye ritual and sends students off at the end of the day.

The Absent Child Helper writes notes, songs or poems for those students who are absent. This can be one person's job or there may be several absent child helpers. Mrs. Hepler created a class book to teach this job description to her kindergarten students. When the book was finished, she sent it home so that the children could read it with their parents. Several pages from this book are pictured here.

The Problem Solver helps solve classroom problems that arise (being locked out of the classroom, running short on supplies). This person also assists when someone is using the *I Solve* Time Machine. (The *I Solve* Time Machine is a way of going back in time and changing hurtful situations into helpful communications; it is discussed in Chapter 12.)

The Clean-up Announcer goes around the room announcing it is time to clean up. He or she decides the manner of announcement. He or she will show the class how to announce

232 *Creating the School Family*

clean-up time on Monday and will continue with that procedure all week. The announcer might use a clean-up wand, chant, light-flicker or other helpful means of prompting. Alternately, you could decide on the procedure and it will remain the same throughout the year.

The Encourager has specific sayings, both verbal and written, to offer to those who need encouragement. The sayings are, "You can do it. Keep breathing. You can handle this." For younger children, the encourager is in charge of the We Care bag. The We Care bag can consist of hand lotion, a teddy bear, a squeeze star and a small blanket. When a young child is upset, the encourager can give her/him the bag and say, "I want you to know we care. Will anything in this bag help?"

The Line Helper assists the teacher by reminding students to stay in line, keep their hands to themselves and be safe. You will teach the line helper what to say and how to say it. This job's main purpose is to be a helpful reminder, not a police officer. Sample sayings to teach include, "Stay together so we are all safe," "Remember our class job is to help keep the class safe," and "Remember to walk with hands by your sides."

The Morning Message Writer writes a message on the board (or a specified location such as a white board or computer screen) from the heart to start off the day with inspiration. Younger children can draw a picture of well-wishing or use sentence strips. Older students might want to use inspirational quotes from historic figures such as Martin Luther King, Jr. You may want to stock some inspirational quote books as resources.

The S.T.A.R. Helper reminds children to be a S.T.A.R., which means to <u>S</u>mile, <u>T</u>ake a deep breath, <u>A</u>nd <u>R</u>elax. This person might have a star wand, star light or star cape as accessories to help with the job. You will need to teach the student what to say, how to say it and when to offer this assistance.

The Kindness Recorder watches for kind acts in the classroom and records them either by writing them in a journal, by putting one artificial flower in a vase, or putting a heart on the kindness tree as a symbol for each kind act. The method of recording kind acts will vary depending on the developmental age of the child. Younger children, those with special needs and toddlers will need assistance and props to successfully accomplish their job.

Chapter 11: Classroom Jobs 233

The Attention Helper assists the teacher is getting the class's attention and keeping the volume down. The most successful attention helper methods come from the class itself, so brainstorm the way your class would like to be reminded to pay attention. One class decided they would like the person to flick the lights. Another class created giant red lips glued to a paint-stirring stick, and the helper moved through the room with it as a signal to stop, close your mouth, look and listen.

The Researcher looks up information needed by the class or teacher. This may require going to the library, using class books, asking resource people (janitor, principal), using the computer or announcing what page something is on when the class loses track.

The First-Aid Giver walks the wounded to the nurse and supplies Band-Aids and moral support following accidents and hurt feelings, using phrases like, "I'm going to walk with you to the nurse so you will not be alone" and "Here is a Band-Aid. Would you like some help putting it on?"

The Floor, Wall and Window Monitor checks to make sure trash is picked up and the floors are clean from excess debris. If some artwork or poster falls off the wall, this person will secure it back in its original place. You may wish to create a checklist or take photos of what a "clean" classroom looks like to help with this job's success.

Now that you have selected your jobs and created job descriptions, it is time to manage them. You must use a visual means of displaying the jobs, such as the Job Boards described earlier in the chapter. You can make your own Job Board or purchase the School Family Job Set from Loving Guidance. Older students can use a simple written list on a dry-erase board. The Job Board-style you select must allow you to rotate the students through the different jobs and modify jobs as students come and go, as new jobs are needed and as the jobs naturally evolve over time. The School Family Job Set and the handmade examples pictured all meet successful Job Board requirements.

Regardless of what board style you use, make sure you put your job as the Safekeeper in the first position on the board. Place your picture and name in this pocket. Your job will not change unless you have a student teacher or a long-term substitute.

How to introduce the Job Board: Introducing the Conscious Discipline Safekeeper job description as presented in Chapter 5 is also a great time to show the children your Job Board. Reiterate to them that, "My job is to keep you safe," and place your picture or icon in the Safekeeper position on the Job Board. Follow up by saying, "Your job is to help keep the class safe, and you will do this in a number of ways in our School Family. One way you will keep the class safe is to contribute to the running of our classroom and helping each other to be successful. Each person in this class is important, valuable and needed to help our School Family reach its greatest potential. So, each person in our School Family will have a job."

> **Teacher Tip:**
> For very young children and children with disabilities, it is helpful to display the jobs individually rather than on one big Job Board. Place the individual job visuals at the location where the job is performed. For example, Jaynese was the wagon puller; his job was to pull the wagon filled with toys to the playground. At the beginning of the year, his teacher mounted a clear pocket on the back of the wagon. Jaynese knew his job was to pull the wagon because his photo was inside the pocket that week.

You may choose to directly teach the children their jobs during specific class meetings, circle time or large group instruction, or you may choose to introduce each job as the need for it arises in the classroom.

Typically speaking, for younger children it is best to directly teach the jobs in circle time or during small group lessons. For older students, it is more effective to assign and teach them as the need arises. You will know best what is most comfortable for you and your classroom.

1. Introducing the jobs during circle time/group instruction. All children benefit from discussing the duties of each job, seeing those duties demonstrated and role-playing. Teachers who thrive on structure, or who work with very young children or children with exceptional needs, will find the greatest success when they directly teach each job as a lesson. Show the job icon, state the job description, demonstrate the job responsibilities and then practice with the children until they are successful. Even with this degree of direct teaching, the children will still need prompting and hands-on assistance. I have found that developmentally younger children are more successful and enjoy the job more when they have appropriate props (hats, aprons, gloves, etc.) that accompany the job.

Tailor your job duties to the developmental level of the children in your classroom. In one fourth-grade classroom I visited, the greeter welcomed me at the door, shook my hand, introduced herself and asked me to sign the guest book. I didn't know if I'd entered a classroom or a bed and breakfast! In a toddler classroom, Tasha was the greeter. Her caregiver said, "Look, Tasha, we have a visitor. It's time to do your job. Go get your greeter hat." Tasha's face lit up with a glow that could melt road rage, put on a Hershey's Kiss hat and greeted me by handing me a chocolate kiss, taking my hand and walking me over to an adult.

2. Instructing as the need arises. Vicky Hepler, a kindergarten teacher in Florida, takes photos of each student during home visits and pre-assigns the jobs before school starts. She begins the year with the Job Board, the job cards and the student photos already in place. She then introduces each job as the need for it arises in the classroom.

The first time someone needs a Band-Aid, Mrs. Hepler introduces the First-Aid Giver. She tells the children that the First-Aid Giver uses the We Care Kit. The We Care Kit is a bag that contains a bear to be used if someone needs to cuddle, Band-Aids for boo-boos, a bottle of lotion called "cranky cream" for someone who may be feeling upset, and heart stickers to let the children know they are loved.

Mrs. Hepler shows the children the contents of the bag and explains the use for each item. Early on in her teaching, she discovered that most hurt children want to put on their own Band-Aids. So Mrs. Hepler now teaches the First-Aid Giver to say, "Do you want some help or do you want to put it on yourself?" This trains children to ask for help and also to ask others what is helpful for them personally.

When Mrs. Hepler first notices someone being kind, she introduces the Kindness Recorder. This job involves seeing and recording random acts of kindness in the classroom. Since young children are just learning to write, she devised symbolic ways of recording kindness. She has her students place an artificial flower in a flowerpot. Other teachers have children place a felt heart on a felt tree. Whatever system you use, demonstrate your system by first doing it yourself.

3. Providing enough time to learn the jobs. It usually takes the full first week of school to introduce the jobs, and a second week for children to successfully accomplish their jobs, so the jobs remain the same for the first two weeks. After that, students will change jobs weekly. When the time to rotate jobs comes, each child teaches the next child his/her job specifics. To manage this rotation, simply move the pictures or names on your Job Board.

Around the second week of school, you will also want to begin teaching the concept of contribution, what it means to have a job and the importance of each person doing his/her part in the School Family. The end of this chapter includes activities that are helpful in this task. Choose the activities that fit your personality and your classroom.

By week three, all your classroom jobs are in place and each student is able to experience the importance of his/her job as a contribution to the School Family. At this time, you may see that a certain job is not really needed. If this happens, look for another job that needs to be done and adjust your Job Board accordingly. Keep in mind that the Job Board is not static; it should change throughout the year according to the needs of your classroom.

Ms. Brown, a kindergarten teacher, reports, "Before long, our backpack hooks weren't holding all the backpacks. It was not safe by the sink area because the backpacks crowded the floor there. I had noticed that the Book Monitor was not called upon often because this class was careful about returning books to the shelf. I presented the situation at morning meeting and asked what we could do in order to solve the problem with the backpacks. The class suggested that the Book Monitor become the Safety Monitor. Now this person helps keep the backpacks clear of walkways so no one trips."

By week four, you will likely notice that you are required to do less maintenance in the classroom. You will see how the children thrive on contributing to the School Family because making a difference is the core of self-worth. Often, children are capable of more than we give them credit for and will feel empowered when they contribute to the group's welfare. You will also find that as you empower children, you also empower yourself because what we offer to others, we strengthen within ourselves.

At the Loving Guidance office, we have a Job Board for our weekly contributions to the office. The jobs include such things as Kindness Recorder, Wish Well Person, Friday Lunch Helper, and so on. One job, the Secretary, is the dreaded one. The Secretary is responsible for taking notes at our weekly staff meetings. When we shift our names on the board from week to week, we eventually began to hear a moan in the room whenever someone found their picture on the Secretary slot. The same may happen with children's jobs, so be ready to transform this into a teaching moment. We revisited the importance of note taking for those who may be absent, for record keeping, for clarification and for its value toward accomplishing our goals as a company. Now, instead of the dreaded moan, we hear willing sighs and occasional giggles and jokes.

The power of unity: We are all in this together
Skill: Interdependence
Structure: Job Board
Value: Contribution, responsibility

General Activities — All Ages

We Are All Connected

Use an "energy ball" (available from Loving Guidance and others) to show students we are all connected. An energy ball is a small ball with two metal strips that demonstrate a closed circuit. Two or more people touching the metal strips and touching each other will close the circuit, demonstrating conductivity as the current flows through the people, causing the ball to light up. Demonstrate to the class that when everyone holds hands, the light stays on, but if one person lets go, the light goes out. Relate the conductivity of the energy ball to the connectedness of the School Family. If someone doesn't complete a classroom job, then the light in the School Family goes out. This helps make an abstract thought (we are all connected) more concrete for children. Follow up this activity by singing "This Little Light of Mine" or making a book of ways each person "keeps the light on in the School Family."

Community Workers

Invite community workers and/or parents into the classroom to share with the children what they do in their jobs. When you are talking about community helpers or other jobs, relate that information to the class. Help children understand the importance of jobs, how each job has a job description and how well each person either contributes benefits to or weakens the team, classroom or system.

Family Interviews

Ask the children what they know about the work their family members do. Then have them ask their family for more they would like to know. In addition, you might have them bring a drawing from home or a job description they wrote for their parents' or guardians' jobs.

Meet the Work Force

Take a tour of the school. On the tour, focus on locations your students will be going to and people they need to know. Introduce the secretaries, the principal, the persons making and serving food in the cafeteria, the janitors and others. Tell students who they will meet and how to behave before entering each area. For example: "When we enter the office, we will be meeting Mrs. Stanson and Ms. Reynolds. Our job is to walk carefully with our hands at our sides and maintain quiet, just like this (demonstrate). Now, you try it." Have the workers say a sentence or two about their job and take pictures at each location. Print the photos and place them on your Friends and Family Board or in a class book titled "School Jobs."

Inside–Outside Circles

Have students choose a job for the week. Once they have their jobs, they form two circles, one inside of the other. Have the inner circle face the outer circle, so that students match up in pairs (one from the inner circle with one from the outer). Each student then describes his or her job duties in detail. After the job description is complete, rotate and repeat until all students have shared their job duties.

Jobs Quiz

Before the students arrive, write each job name on a separate sheet of blank paper. When they arrive, have them choose one of these and write on it one of that job's duties. Then rotate to another paper and write one of its duties on that paper. Rotate four or five times. When finished with the rotations, form small groups so the students can check the job descriptions on each sheet for accuracy and understanding.

Sequencing

Divide students into small groups of four or five. Write a job on an index card. Next, have students write each of the steps needed to complete that job on a separate card (one step per card). Have each group exchange their cards with another group who will then put the steps in the proper sequence to perform the job successfully.

Class-Made Books — Younger

Job Picture Book

Create class books to explain job descriptions visually. For example, your "How We Notice Acts of Kindness" book would have photographs of the children acting out the following text:

- The Kindness Recorder's job is to notice when someone does something kind.
- Whenever they notice an act of kindness, you put a heart on the Kindness Tree.
- Then you record the name of the person who was kind in the Kindness Book.
- At the end of the day, the Kindness Recorder counts the hearts and reads the names.

Teacher Tip:
A Kindness Tree template and instructions can be found on the *Make-N-Take* CDrom from Loving Guidance.

My Job Matters

After being in school for about six weeks, create a book about the importance of each job. The children will write and illustrate the job they have the week you create the book. Use the following phrase on each page: "My job is _____. This job helps my School Family by _____."

Let Your Light Shine

Give each child a light bulb-shaped piece of paper. Have them write and illustrate what they do to keep the light on in our School Family. (This is ideal to do after using the energy ball activity described earlier.) Remind them their answers should be related to School Family jobs, but they are not limited to jobs alone.

Job Description Book

Begin by having students write a job description, in collaboration or individually, for each job in your classroom. Students can then illustrate the page in a number of ways, by taking photos, adding drawings or gluing related objects to the page. Place these books in the library for reading and as a resource.

Jobs Matter

After the children are familiar with the song "Jobs Matter" from *Kindness Counts*, ask them to list all the jobs mentioned in the song and their job descriptions. Conduct a discussion of why jobs matter. (This could evolve into a class-made book, "My Job Matters," as mentioned previously in this chapter.) You could also compare the jobs mentioned in the song with the jobs utilized in the class.

We All Count

The chorus of the song "We All Count" on *Kindness Counts* says, "We all count in so many ways, doing our part, each and every day. We need each other, every sister and brother, because we all count." Using the chorus as a jumping-off point, discuss with the children what this means to them. Ask them, "How and why do we need each other?" This brainstorming and discussion time could lead to a writing exercise for older children.

Class-made Songs and Chants

Songs and chants have been used throughout time and in many venues to encourage people to unite around a common purpose or belief. Your class can create their own song or chant by adapting classic songs to fit their theme.

"Work Together" (tune: "I've Been Working on the Railroad")
We know how to work together
To get the whole job done.
We know what it takes to prosper,
It takes everyone.
Doing what we know is needed,
We help each other out.
Our School Family is a strong team.
You can hear us shout:
We will get the whole job done
One for all and all for one!

"Class Jobs" (tune: "Sound Off")
I don't know what you've been told,
Our School Family shines like gold.
We're a family that has heart,
Each of us will do our part!
Class jobs 1 – 2
Class jobs 3 – 4
Class jobs 1 – 2 – 3 – 4!

C = Commitment

I am willing to begin the process of creating jobs for all members of my classroom. I will begin by making the job list that was presented in this chapter. I understand the first step in completing a task is to begin the process.

Signature _____ Date _____

H = Helpful Resources

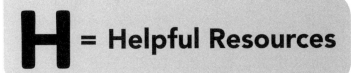

Music

All Ages

It Starts In the Heart **by Dr. Becky Bailey and Jack Hartmann**
Songs: "That Was Helpful," "You Did It!"

Kindness Counts **by Mr. Al and Dr. Becky Bailey**
Songs: "We All Count," "Jobs Matter," "In Every One of Us"

Hello World **by Red Grammer**
Songs: "We're All in This Together," "On the Day You Were Born"

Be Bop Your Best **by Red Grammer**
Songs: "Responsibility," "Perseverance"

Sesame Street Platinum
Song: "People in Your Neighborhood"

***Anna Moo Crackers* by Anna Moo**
Song: "Everyone Counts"

Literature — Younger

***You Can Count on Me Learning About Responsibility* by Regina G. Burch.** The little girl in this book demonstrates the importance of being responsible, chanting "You can count on me!"

***The Important Book* by Margaret Wise Brown.** This book has wonderful repetitive language and celebrates the importance of being you. This book can lead to a discussion on what we contribute to the School Family and how doing our jobs contributes to the whole group.

***Jobs People Do* by Christopher Maynard.** This book shares the many jobs people do in our world by showing children photographed in the uniform or typical outfit for each job.

***Guess Who* by Margaret Miller.** A child is asked who delivers the mail, gives haircuts, flies an airplane, and performs other important tasks. Each question has several different answers from which to choose.

Literature — Older

***Help Wanted: Riddles About Jobs* by Larry Adler.** This book is a fun way for students to read about different jobs in the world beyond school.

***50 American Heroes Every Kid Should Meet* by Dennis Denenberg.** Explore the jobs and lives of 50 incredible people including Thomas Jefferson, Mary McLeod Bethume, Yo Yo Ma and many others.

***Kid's Guide to Service Projects* by Barbara Lewis.** Describes a variety of opportunities for youngsters to participate in successful community service.

Additional Aids — All Ages

School Family Job Set from www.ConsciousDiscipline.com
School Family Make-N-Take CDrom from www.ConsciousDiscipline.com

Teacher Tip:

Adding props to the classroom jobs helps young children to be successful and increases the joy they experience while contributing to the welfare of the class.

246 *Creating the School Family*

Chapter 12

Time Machine

While first writing this book, I was attempting to get a house rezoned to use as an office building for Loving Guidance. My city is known for its strict code requirements and difficult city managers. The house under consideration was a beautifully landscaped Florida home with a huge 300-year-old oak tree on the property. The city code, which was designed for corporate developers who strip the land of all vegetation, states you must plant oak trees every so many feet apart on the property. It would be impossible, if not ridiculous, for me to plant 15 small trees under the canopy of the large oak because there would be room for them to grow, and I had no intention of cutting down my ancient oak to plant 15 baby trees. No matter how fervently I reasoned with them, the city representatives insisted, "This is the code." It didn't take long for me to lose it. I was not interested in being a S.T.A.R.—I was more passionate about being a nut! I ranted, raved and finally blurted, "I can't believe you can sleep at night, drawing a salary for being this stupid." At the time, I felt justified in every word I said. By evening, I couldn't believe how horrible I had been to this city worker who was just doing his job. The conversation played over and over in my head. I wished for an adult Time Machine to re-do and improve my communication.

How many times have we said to ourselves, "I wish I could take back those words?" How often have we replayed conversations in our minds, trying out new words with different outcomes? How would our lives have been different if we had learned how to deal with conflict effectively at an early age?

The Problem with Conflict

The health of any entity, whether of an individual, family or school, can be seen as a function of its ability to resolve conflicts. More often than not, we expend more energy avoiding or demanding that problems go away than we do actually solving them.

Emotional and behavioral problems result from our deficiencies in the handling of conflict, be it inner conflict, conflict with other people or conflict surrounding life circumstances. Most of us are unaware that the way we attempt to solve our inner conflicts is also how we try to solve outer ones. Emotional problems are not produced by our needs; we all have needs. Emotional problems result from how we go about getting our needs met. Conflict resolution patterns, like language, are initially learned from our family of origin. Often, the patterns that were suitable and essential for survival in our family are not appropriate in schools. This is true for both students and teachers.

One teacher attending the Advanced Conscious Discipline Institute (affectionately known as CD2) shared that in her family, attempts to resolve conflict included the following: screaming at each other, throwing objects, walking off in a steamy silence that lasted for days, or getting drunk. She concluded by saying, "We ended up spending all our energy in avoiding conflicts instead of solving them. I remember the day my dad said to my mom, 'I don't want you watching Phil Donahue on television, he's just a rabble rouser.'" My sister and I prayed Mom would obey so we could all avoid the screaming, throwing and deadly silence. I understand now why it was so important to me that my own children do as they were told; I was afraid of what I might do if conflict arose from their lack of obedience. The same was true at school. I kept looking for the magic consequence that would make sure conflict never occurred in the first place. Gummy bears for good behavior and loss of recess for bad behavior were my mainstays until Conscious Discipline. Now, I'm finally learning to manage my emotions and resolve conflict healthily rather than pouring all my energy into avoiding it."

The *I Solve: Conflict Resolution Time Machine* is designed to help teach children conflict resolution skills and provide a structured procedure to help adults safely overcome skill deficiencies they might have from their own upbringing. It provides concrete steps and gives specific language for helpful, healthy ways to meet our needs.

Bully Prevention: Teaching Children to be Assertive

Children constantly struggle to establish boundaries with other children. These interpersonal conflicts are wonderful opportunities to teach them to use an assertive voice to set healthy boundaries that will serve them throughout their lives. In all relationships, we teach others how to treat us. People who seem doubtful or unsure invite others to boss them around and "help," even when help isn't wanted or needed. People who appear extremely confident and in control send the message, "Leave me alone, I'm fine," even when their world is falling apart.

On the other hand, some people act with assertiveness and set boundaries for behaviors they consider appropriate, safe and permissible. Assertiveness empowers them to say no to behaviors that are hurtful and yes to helpful, supportive actions. Assertiveness is the medium through which adults and children model and teach respect for themselves and each other. The bully-victim dynamic can thrive only in an environment that lacks assertiveness. When you teach children to assertively set limits, you teach respect and encourage personal power. When children use these skills, bullying drastically decreases.

Aggressive behavior in children begins early in life. According to maternal reports, 80 percent of 17-month-olds have already engaged in some form of aggression toward other children (Tremblay, Hartup, & Archer, 2005). The general progression is from physical aggression to verbal aggression to social aggression. Physical aggression involves hitting, kicking and pushing. Verbal aggression takes the form of name calling, insults and threats. Social aggression has to do with excluding and hurting others by manipulating relationships. Examples of social aggression include spreading rumors, exclusion, telling lies to hurt others and statements like, "We don't like her, do we?" Generally speaking, boys are more physically aggressive and girls are more socially aggressive, with both being equally verbally aggressive (Tremblay, Hartup, & Archer, 2005).

Physical aggression for girls tends to peak around three or four years old, while boys tend to peak in frequency of aggressive acts around six years old (Nagin & Tremblay, 1999;

Nagin & Tremblay, 2001). The fact that physical aggression peaks in early childhood when children's limbs are weak and their brains are at peak flexibility for learning alternatives indicates the extreme importance of teaching young children how to be assertive. Verbal aggression is found as early as social interactions and language development permit, and remains throughout childhood and into adulthood. Social aggression is present at eight years, but is mostly seen in children eleven years and older (Underwood, 2003).

Children of various ages and developmental stages will require different types and degrees of coaching to handle the aggression of their peers. Adults need to take action when they hear, see or have aggressive acts reported to them. (The most common way aggressive acts are reported is through tattling.)

The Time Machine will help you teach children how to assertively handle interpersonal conflicts with each other. Such things as name calling, teasing, pushing, poking and distracting others from learning are all wonderful opportunities to teach children assertiveness skills. The difficulty is that many of us were never taught these skills, nor did we see them modeled by the adults around us as we grew up.

Recently at the office, I was having an issue with one of my workers. She was not writing down things when I spoke with her. In my mind, she was never going to remember all the things I was asking of her. The more I talked, the more irritated I allowed myself to become. My inner speech was busier than my outer speech, saying, "She is not going to remember this. I am going to have a mess on my hands when this doesn't get done. I never should have hired her. What was I thinking? It's just one more thing I have to take care of, like everything else." Instead of assertively telling her what I wanted her to do, I went out to lunch with two other people and complained about her behavior.

Sound familiar? We often turn to our spouses, co-workers, family members, friends and others, instead of approaching the "offending" person directly. Children who lack assertiveness skills do the same thing, but generally the person they turn to is the teacher. Yet when we see this same behavior from others, it drives us nuts! We demand children use their words to speak directly to the person involved rather than running to us or talking behind someone's back. How often do you hear one of the following?

> "She called me a name. I hate her!"
> "She butted in line."
> "He wrote on my paper."
> "She didn't clean up."
> "He's talking."
> "She's looking at me."
> "He's not doing his part on our group project."
> "They wouldn't let me play with them."

For all the acts of hurtfulness we hear in the classroom, many more occur beyond our sight. Teaching assertiveness minimizes the number of acts that are brought to our attention (and irritate us). It also minimizes the acts we never see or hear about because it empowers the children who feel encroached upon to speak for themselves. The first step to assertiveness training is to retrain our focus to be on the positive.

The Power of Attention

In Conscious Discipline, the skill of assertiveness develops as we rely increasingly on the Power of Attention. The Power of Attention states that what we focus on, we get more of. Simply put, if you focus on strategies to help children "stop hitting," your focus is on "hitting," and you will get more "hitting." If you focus on strategies to help children set limits and ask for what they want, you will get more healthy communication. Our choice of where we put our attention teaches children what we value. If we focus on what children have done wrong, we will teach them to value judgment, criticism and problems. If we focus on what we want to have happen, we will teach respectfulness and a focus on solutions. This shift in focus can be extremely difficult because most of us have spent our lives focusing on what's not good enough, what's wrong and what not to do! A teacher shared the following story that shows how this shift from focusing on the action you don't want (stop calling me names) to what you do want (call me Jackie) played out in her classroom:

> *William, Dante, Bradley and Jovanny were the best of friends. Despite repeatedly encouraging them to tell each other, "Stop, I don't like it when you ___," their interpersonal problems persisted. One day, the five of us sat down for a discussion. I said, "I know you are good friends, but your actions are not showing it right now. When you keep coming to me instead of attempting to use your words as we have practiced in class, it*

tells me you want to get your friends in trouble instead of solve the problem." All four boys wiggled in their seats. Finally, Dante spoke up:

"That's not it. Bradley and Jovanny don't listen when I say stop." William and Bradley then jumped into the conversation saying the others didn't listen to them either. Finger pointing ran rampant, but the problem was finally clear. They were using their words, but failing to listen to each other. To find out more, I set up a role-play that was typical of their day-to-day interactions.

I instructed Bradley to snatch the book Dante was reading. Dante immediately said, "I don't like it when you take my book. Stop it!" Then they both froze and looked at me. "Oh, I get it," I thought to myself. "They aren't following through with what they want the other person to do differently." I turned to Dante and said, "Tell Bradley what you want him to do with the book." Dante's face lit up with comprehension, he looked directly at Bradley and said, "Give me my book back so I can finish reading." Bradley handed it over and the problem was solved. All four boys seemed to simultaneously "get" the essence of using their words. Up until this point, they thought it was something they were supposed to say. Now they realized it was a way of communicating their wants. As they walked away, Jovanny looked over his shoulder and said, "You're pretty smart for a teacher."

Assertiveness coaching is not complete until you set a limit in a way that offers a positive "do this" action instead of just a "stop it" approach. This is no small task, as most of us have spent years focused on the action we want to stop rather than the one we want to see happen.

Power of attention: What you focus on, you get more of.
Skill: Assertiveness
Structure: I Solve: Conflict Resolution Time Machine
Value: Respect. Healthy boundaries are essential to healthy relationships.

The most valuable teaching moment in the classroom is tattling. Almost every time I give a workshop, I am asked, "How do I stop children from tattling?" I think a more helpful and positively focused question is, "How can I use tattling to teach life skills?" This issue of tattling is addressed extensively in the *Conscious Discipline* book (Bailey, 2000). The five Conscious Discipline principles below are necessary when children experience physical, verbal or social aggression. These basic principles are the cornerstone of teaching assertive language and are the foundation for the Time Machine.

- Speak to the victim first.
- Describe what you see.
- Ask, "Did you like it?"
- Provide children intent, tone and words to use to set a limit on the aggressor's behavior. "Tell ____ , I don't like it when you ____. Please ____."
- Coach the victim in how to ask for a positive action in the future.

Research indicates that 400 aggressive acts occur in the average elementary school classroom on an average day (Tremblay, Hartup & Archer, 2005). Teachers intervene in about 25 percent of these acts. Early childhood classrooms have an even greater number of aggressive acts and have often been recognized as a breeding ground for aggression. We are missing some significant moments to teach children how to be assertive and to create classrooms where respect is practiced, not just preached.

The following stories will help you understand the process of creating teaching moments by using the language of assertiveness throughout your day.

Preschool: *At circle time, Elijah wanted to sit next to Aaron. In his attempts to get close, he sat on Aaron's leg. Aaron was about to elbow Elijah in the head when the teacher intervened. "Aaron, Elijah wanted to sit next to you in circle. He was too close and sat on your leg. Did you like it?" "No," Aaron said as he made a mean face at Elijah. "Tell Elijah, 'I don't like it when you sit on my leg. It hurts,'" responded the teacher. The teacher gave this sentence to Elijah with the words to say, a helpful intent and a positive tone. After Aaron delivered his words to Elijah, the teacher coached him further by saying, "What do you want him to do when he wants to sit next to you at circle?" Aaron thought for a moment and said, "Give me some room." The teacher coached Aaron to tell Elijah to "give him some room." She then concluded the process by coaching Elijah to commit to change by saying, "Okay, I can do that."*

School Age: *During a math lesson in whole group instruction, four students at a table were listening intently to the teacher. Two students at the table were talking and giggling in a low, but disturbing manner. The teacher approached the table and addressed those who were listening, "Is it hard to focus on the lesson when Destiny and Grace are talking?" The four nodded in agreement. The teacher continued her coaching process, "Then tell them, 'Please be quiet, it's hard to hear the teacher.'"*

The most important thing to remember is to give the victims the words to use, and also the intent and tone of voice. If the intent is helpful and the tone is respectful, the intrusive person's willingness to embrace the positive behavior change is drastically increased. Any hint of sarcasm, aggression or resentfulness in the request will sabotage the behavior change and possibly escalate the conflict.

E = Environmental Structure: Time Machine

The Time Machine is the environmental structure designed to help teachers and children with specific skills to transform aggressive acts into life lessons through the use of respectful, assertive communication. It is the hub of your bully-prevention program.

Purpose: The Time Machine provides a designated space with specifically coached steps for children to "go back in time" to change a hurtful event to a helpful one. As they re-enact the situation, children strengthen their ability to choose cooperative outcomes, which builds confidence in their communication skills. The Time Machine accomplishes the following objectives in your classroom:

1. Provides constructive practice that helps change the inner state of the children from upset to calm, in order to access higher-level thinking skills.
2. Provides children with specific steps that teach how to assertively handle all forms of classroom bullying.
3. Utilizes children themselves as teaching tools by modeling how to be helpful instead of hurtful for others.
4. Teaches the active verbiage needed for both parties to agree on a change in behavior instead of just saying, "I'm sorry."
5. Assists teachers in learning the process of assertiveness so they, in turn, can teach and inspire the children in their care.

The Time Machine integrates many components into teaching the language of respect. Children physically take steps, they emotionally calm themselves through self-regulation, they socially experience willingness and the joy of reconnecting with others after a hurtful interchange, they spiritually experience group support for valuing each other, and they are academically required to think, read and communicate effectively. The Time Machine is a helpful structure for children ages four and up. Children younger than three years of age would benefit more by using a simplified version of daily teaching moments.

The teacher's role in the use of the Time Machine is that of a coach. How and what needs to be coached depends on the developmental and chronological age of the children. The following examples will help you know the coaching progression of skills to teach.

Four-year-olds: Coach the child who has been intruded on to say, "I don't like it when you push me." Then generate a positive action statement for the child. For example, you might say, "Devon, Mark wants you to walk around him and watch where you are going. Pushing him is hurtful. Are you willing to walk around him?" Then coach the aggressive child to say, "Okay, I can do that."

Five-year-olds: Coach the child who has been intruded on to say, "I don't like it when you push me." Then help the child think up the positive action he or she wants the other child to take: "Please ____." You might assist the child by saying, "What would you like Devon to do instead of push you?" If the child responds, "Walk around me," then you would repeat the child's statement to build awareness: "So, you want him to walk around you instead of pushing." Then coach him by saying, "Tell him, 'Please walk around me next time.'"

Six through 12-year-olds: Older children will be able to conduct much of the Time Machine process themselves, but will still need coaching about what positive action they would like the aggressive child to take. We are conditioned to think in terms of the behaviors we don't want instead of the positive behaviors we actually desire. Shifting the focus to a positive action is a difficult skill that requires a shift from being stuck in

the pain of the problem to being emotionally free enough to move toward a solution. It is a difficult shift, but one that is necessary for successful communication.

Bilingual children: Write sentence starters in the bilingual students' native language and place them on top of the English words on the mat. This is also a great way to help monolingual teachers begin learning helpful phrases in other languages.

How to Set Up the Time Machine: There are three components to a successful Time Machine. The first is a physical item that symbolizes participants' willingness to go back in time to redo an interaction. Homemade items I have seen in classrooms include an eraser indicating a willingness to erase the old way and learn a new way, a remote control to rewind the situation, or a carpet square indicating we are stepping back in time. The most effective Time Machine is a mat that steps children through the process with specific actions and verbiage, like the I Solve: Conflict Resolution Time Machine offered by Loving Guidance.

The second component of a successful Time Machine is built-in steps for self-regulation. We must assist children in calming themselves enough to access the higher centers of their brains. Being a S.T.A.R. or using another deep breathing activity is absolutely necessary before attempting to solve the problem.

The third and final component is a series of language starter sentences to help children talk about difficult issues in healthy ways. These sentences offer a healthy alternative to hurtful, manipulative attempts to influence others. The starter sentences and procedures for talking can be written on the Time Machine, laminated as a handout or written on a poster. The starter sentences will vary depending on the age of the child. For young children, icons or pictures are needed along with the words.

The I Solve: Conflict Resolution Time Machine pictured on p. 248 is available from Loving Guidance. It clearly meets all components for a successful Time Machine, and comes with detailed instructions and responses for common intrusions. You can make a similar Time Machine by purchasing a tablecloth, cutting it in half length-wise and writing starter sentences on it.

How to Introduce the Time Machine: There are four ways to introduce the Time Machine: **1)** during whole group instruction, **2)** during small group instruction, **3)** as interest is shown or **4)** when it is needed. If you introduce the Time Machine during whole group instruction, small group instruction or when a child asks, "What's that?" you will role-play. Select a conflict you have seen or ask the children for a conflict they have experienced to use in the role-play.

If you introduce the Time Machine "when needed," you will simply wait until one child intrudes upon another and then begin the process. This method of introduction is especially effective when working with older children. Inevitably, one child will intrude on the space or dignity of another. You might overhear, "You stupid butthead, back off and get out of my face." At that moment, walk over to the situation and do the following:

1. Describe what you just saw and heard. "Jacob, Tamara called you a name and pushed you away, just like this (demonstrate the shove)."
2. Ask the victim, "Did you like it?"
3. Briefly introduce the Time Machine and ask if the children are willing to use this moment to redo the conflict and help everyone in their School Family learn a new way of handling the situation. "We have a conflict resolution mat in the classroom. It's called the Time Machine. It helps those who are willing to go back in time and change hurtful words into helpful communications. Jacob, are you willing to redo the conflict to help your School Family learn a new way? Tamara, are you willing?"
4. Frame the event as a brave and helpful gift that Tamara and Jacob are sharing with the class. You might say, "We call our class a School Family. In our class, my job is to keep you safe and your job is to help keep it safe. Tamara and Jacob found themselves in a hurtful situation and they are willing to help the whole class by teaching us another way. This could be hard for them. Let's wish them well as we all learn how to use the Time Machine."
5. Bring out the mat and begin the process, using the "How to use the Conflict Resolution Time Machine" section below.

Regardless of when you choose to introduce it, you will ultimately lead children in a discussion of the following:

1. We all make mistakes and say hurtful things to one another. Brainstorm hurtful and helpful ways to speak to one another. You might say, "If a friend

writes on my paper, I could say, 'Stop it, stupid,' or I could say, 'This is my paper. Write on your own paper.' Which one would be helpful and which one would be hurtful?" For younger children, you could act out two scenes. In one scene, a child grabs a toy from another. In another scene the child asks, "May I have a turn?" instead. After you act out the scenes, ask which one is helpful. If possible, help them discover that they are more likely to say hurtful things when they are feeling unsafe, afraid or angry.

2. When we feel angry and scared, it is hard to think of helpful words. Our helpful words are easier to remember when we are calm and willing to solve our problems. Show children how the Time Machine helps them calm down by breathing and wishing well. For older children, you can explain the Conscious Discipline Brain Model so they can understand the science behind each step.

3. Discuss what it feels like, looks like and sounds like to be willing to solve a problem. Have a child stand with her arms folded and an angry-looking face. Ask the class if they think she is willing or not willing. Then discuss what she could do to become willing. Ask the children to demonstrate nonverbally, "I am willing" and "I am not willing." Ask if they can feel the difference in the two. What are some words to describe the difference? This discussion could result in the following ideas for ways to change from unwilling to willing:

- Go to the Safe Place and calm down.
- Take a composure lap and give it some time.
- Use specific language like, "No, I'm not willing at this time." (Give children specific language to address this such as, "Okay. When would be a good time?")

Once you have introduced the Time Machine to the class, use it regularly so children can internalize the process. Some of the best times to do this are in the morning after your Brain Smart Start, immediately following recess and right before the close of day.

How to Use the Time Machine: When a hurtful interaction occurs between two students, ask the students, "Are you willing to go back in time to solve the problem so you and the School Family can learn a helpful new way to handle the situation?" If they agree, you are ready for the Time Machine. If they respond, "No," ask when would be a good time to solve the problem. Sometimes children will need time in the Safe Place to calm down before willingness is forthcoming.

Step 1: Roll back time.
Have entire class roll hands backward, signifying going back in time.

Step 2: Ask for willingness.
"_____, are you willing to go back and redo the conflict to help your School Family learn a helpful solution? _____, are you willing to help your School Family learn?"

Step 3: Be a S.T.A.R.
Have the entire class Smile, Take a deep breath And Relax.

Step 4: Wish each other well.
Have the entire class place their hands on their hearts and extend their love outward as they extend their arms toward the problem solvers.

Step 5: Focus on the goal.
Have the children chant, "1, 2, 3," and the problem solvers say, "Let's do it."

Step 6: Coach the children to use helpful words.
Have the child who perceives himself or herself as the victim speak first. Coach the child to finish the sentence on the mat: "I don't like it when you ____." Then help the child learn the difficult thought process of focusing on a positive form of action by saying, "Please _____." Most children will say, "Stop" or "Don't do it anymore." Your job as the coach is to help the child rephrase these negative statements into positive, assertive requests. "Please say, 'Move please,' instead of pushing me."

The response from the other child is "Okay, I can do that." If the other child feels he or she was also intruded on, they can flip sides on the mat and repeat the process with the other child using his or her assertive voice.

Step 7: Ask the children to show there are no hard feelings by sharing a symbolic gesture.

The gesture could be a handshake or hug. Encourage the children to come up with what they feel is most appropriate for them. Young children enjoy hugging each other while older children may choose to touch knuckles.

If a child says he is unwilling, or says he is willing but discovers in the middle of the process that he's still too upset to solve the problem, you would intervene. You might say, "Your face is going like this (demonstrate). Your body is telling me that you might need a little more time before you're willing to solve the problem. Would you like to go to the Safe Place or work on something at your table until you are willing?" Encourage the child to talk. Provide the

words to say such as, "I feel too angry to talk now," or, "I thought I was willing, but now I want to pass." Then instruct the other children by saying, "(Name) needs more time before he is willing to solve the problem. What could we do to help him?" Lead the class in wishing the child well. Check back in with the child at a later time (after recess, at the end of the day, etc.) to see if he is ready. When he feels able to participate, begin the Time Machine process again.

Often when I am visiting or working in classrooms, I will ask children, "What is your favorite part of Conscious Discipline?" The Time Machine, especially in the older grades, is one of the most common answers. One third-grade student said, "I like the Time Machine because it gives you a chance to go back and do things differently. It lets you really solve your problems and get back to being friends instead of pretending everything is fine and being mad for days." Below are some examples of actual classroom use of the Time Machine.

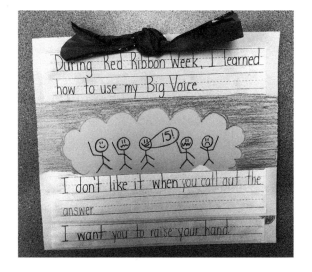

First grade: Each day after her Brain Smart Start, a brilliant first-grade teacher named Claire Duke asks her students, "Does anyone have anything they would like to handle in the Time Machine that might have occurred on the bus, at breakfast or on your way to class this morning?" She does this to clear the air and start the day off without lingering, unresolved problems. She shared the following story with me:

One morning Samuel immediately hopped up to the Time Machine. I asked, "Who would you like to join you in the Time Machine?" He named Dylan, so I asked, "Dylan, are you willing to enter the Time Machine with Samuel this morning to help your School Family learn a helpful way to solve problems?"

Dylan agreed and took his place on the mat. The rest of the class sat in a circle watching. I asked, "Are you both willing?" The boys nodded and stepped on the first set of footprints. I coached, "Be a S.T.A.R.," and the class joined in deep breathing to lend moral support. The boys took the next step and I helped, "Wish each other well," and the class wished well, too. I was pleased to see the boys make eye contact and smile gently at each other.

They took another step on the mat and I asked, "Samuel, did something happen this morning that was upsetting to you?" He responded, "Yeah," with head down and foot tapping. "Dylan was singing, 'Samuel and Boogie sitting in a tree. K-i-s-s-i-n-g.'"

When I asked "Did you like that," Samuel found his voice and remembered the process. He said clearly and loudly, "Dylan, I don't like it when you sing that song."

"What do you want him to do?" I asked.

"Stop singing," he replied, and before I could step in, Dylan said, "Okay, I'll stop." I knew the problem wasn't solved until the boys had found a positive goal. "Stopping" was not a positive goal, so I kept going,

"Dylan, you were wanting something from Samuel when you were singing the song. What did you want?" Dylan said, "Samuel usually comes to breakfast. He wasn't there."

I immediately understood the underlying problem and was able to help the boys. "Samuel, you missed breakfast this morning and Dylan was looking forward to seeing you. He didn't know how to let you know he missed you at breakfast, so he sang the song to get your attention instead. Samuel, you didn't like the song at all. You wanted Dylan to talk to you more directly." Both boys nodded in agreement and seemed to understand how the problem happened. I prompted Dylan to say, "Samuel, I missed seeing you at breakfast, let's play together at recess." I then assisted Samuel by saying, "Samuel, are you willing to play with Dylan at recess?" He nodded "yes." I wrapped it up by asking, "What could you two boys do right now to indicate you're still friends?" The boys gave each other a hug and we all learned a great lesson.

Fourth grade: A fourth-grade classroom I once visited referred to the Time Machine as the "Solution Station." The teacher, Mrs. Dye, informed me that generally the Solution Station was utilized after lunch and at the end of the day. Sometimes life happens, and the children request a special Solution Station session be added. Luckily for me, I arrived at one of these special sessions.

The class was calm and assured of the safety of the procedure; they had been doing this process for almost three months. Madeline walked over to Brianna's desk and said, "I have something I would like to work out with you. Is this a good time?" Brianna nodded her head and both headed to an area in the classroom that had lights strung on the wall and a sign marked "Solution Station." Two posters sat below the sign. One read, "My Perception: How I see the situation. Your Perception: How you see the situation. Each perception is real to that person. Neither perception is ultimately right, correct or the truth." The other poster contained sentence starters, an outline of the process, and coaching tips for both the speaker and the listener. The two girls methodically worked through the steps on the poster with loving, but assertive intent. Each girl aired her side of the grievance, came to a positive solution and made a commitment. The poster they used for a guide appears below. The girls' statements are in italics.

	Time Machine SPEAKER	Time Machine LISTENER
Step 1:	**Ask for willingness.** "I have something I would like to handle with you. Is this a good time? If not now, when would be a good time?"	**Respond to being asked.** "Yes or no"; if no, commit to a time when you would be willing.
Step 2:	**I don't like it when you _____.** *"I don't like it when you talk to your friends about me behind my back."*	**Mirror back the concern.** "What I heard you say is that you don't like it when _____. Did I get that right?" *"What I heard you say is that you don't like it when I talk about you to my friends behind your back. Did I get that right?"*
Step 3:	**What I want is _____.** *"What I want is for you to talk to me first if you have a problem with me."*	**Mirror back what is wanted.** "What you want is _____. Did I get that right?" *"What you want for me to do is come to you first and talk to you if I have a problem with you. Did I get that right?"*
Step 4:	**You can count on me to _____.** *"You can count on me to ask you if there is something you need to handle with me."*	**You can count on me to _____** *"You can count on me to come to you before talking to my friends."*
Step 5:	**End with a connection.** Hug, handshake, high five, all is well signal.	**End with a connection.** Hug, handshake, high five, all is well signal. The listener then has the right to become the speaker and the speaker has the responsibility to become the listener.

*Adapted from the writings of Harville Hendrix, Ph.D and Imago Relationship Therapy

Adult: Adults benefit from the Time Machine process, too. This story comes directly from a workshop participant.

> *I know from experience that having children do the Time Machine in front of a large group can be intimidating. Recently, I attended the Conscious Discipline Institute. I have been involved with Conscious Discipline for many years and thought that I was prepared for just about anything. At this workshop, I saw an old friend named Vicky. She came up and gave me a big hug as we talked. All I could think about was that she hugged me. I am not a touchy-feely person. I enjoy my personal space more than others. And she hugged me. During the progression of the workshop, she hugged me several more times, never meaning any harm or ill will. Vicky just loved to hug.*
>
> *As the workshop continued, Becky talked about how important and beneficial touch was to people. At that point, I was thinking, 'I must be broken, because I am not helped in any way by people touching me! When I can see touching coming, I brace myself. When it is a sneak attack, I cringe.' At a break, I spoke to Becky about the situation with Vicky. She asked if I had said anything to Vicky. Well, of course I hadn't! I wasn't going to hurt Vicky's feelings because I was broken. Becky quickly took us aside and asked if we were willing to do the Time Machine in front of the group so we all could learn helpful ways to resolve conflict. We both agreed. Vicky had no idea what this was about, and I could see fear in her face. I felt anxious, too.*
>
> *A good chunk of time passed before we had the opportunity to do the Time Machine. Finally, we went in front of the entire group and did it. Beforehand, I was feeling nervous, scared and guilty for hurting Vicky's feelings. But as soon as we went through the process, those feelings changed. Our positive solution was for Vicky to ask before hugging me. As soon as we finished, when Vicky asked if it was okay to hug me, I felt empowered. I knew I had the right to let people know how I want to be treated. It was one of the most frightening experiences ever, but it left me feeling 100 percent more powerful.*

But What About Consequences?

Often after explaining and demonstrating the Time Machine, teachers and child care professionals will ask, "But what about the consequences?" In essence, they are saying, "Shouldn't we be punishing the aggressive child?" Children who are able to accomplish a positive change in behavior through problem solving benefit more directly than those who are given artificial consequences. The interactions undertaken in the Time Machine are consequences. The consequence of hitting someone is usually to get hit back. In a Conscious Discipline classroom, the consequence of hitting is to learn a better way to get your needs met. Children gain confidence, self-control and an expanded skill set when they are able to see that mistakes are opportunities to learn a better way.

Positive Action Guide: Below are key phrases that illustrate how to help children express what they want rather than what they don't want. Instead of the common statement, "Please don't ____," reframe to what behavior is desirable.

> **I don't like it when you write on my paper. Please write on your own paper.**
> **I don't like it when you call me names. Please call me Elin. That is my name.**
> **I don't like it when you push me. Please say, "Move, please."**
> **I don't like it when you talk when the teacher is talking. Please be quiet so I can hear.**
> **I don't like it when you back up in line and step on me. Please walk forward so we'll both be safe.**
> **I don't like it when you thump my head. Please call out, "Hey, Omar" if you want my attention.**
> **I don't like it when you cut in line. Please go to your spot. This one is mine.**
> **I don't like it when you take my pencil. Please give it back and find your own.**

Children will begin to seek out, use and value the Time Machine once they believe it is important to them. This will occur when the process is authentic and safe. The goal is not just to teach words for children to use, but to help them understand the value of speaking up for injustices, setting healthy boundaries with other people and solving conflicts in a healthy, helpful way.

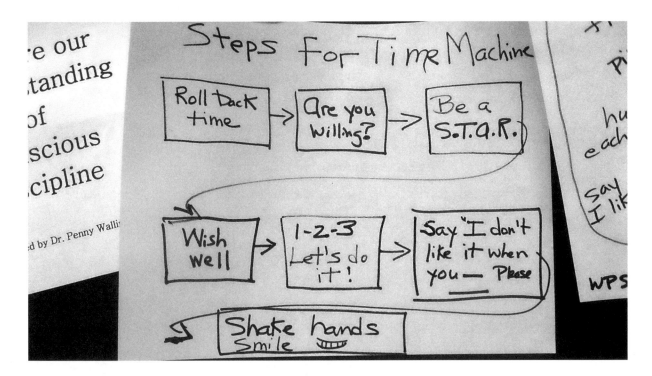

General Activities
All Ages

Shubert's BIG Voice

This book demonstrates using an assertive voice and is essential to teaching the Time Machine at all ages. In it, Shubert models the words to use when others intrude upon your property, space or dignity and helps children understand that their words have power. Read the story to the children. For younger children, you can paraphrase as needed to shorten the story. Role-play the conflict resolution sections of the book to help make Shubert and Benny's interaction "real." Use the Shubert worksheets provided at www.ConsciousDiscipline.com as a tool to deepen children's understanding. Present the following questions for discussion:

> **How do you think Shubert felt when Benny took his apple?**
> **Have you ever felt like Shubert did? Explain.**
> **How did you handle the situation?**

Chapter 12: Time Machine 265

Did you like how you handled the situation? Did it work?
What happened when Shubert used his BIG voice?
How do you think Shubert felt when Benny gave him back the apple?
What does "my words have power" mean to you?

Make Your Voice Match Mine

It's important for everyone, especially children, to use an assertive tone of voice when setting limits. A passive voice sounds uncertain, an aggressive voice is threatening and an assertive voice carries the calm but firm nonverbal message "just do it." Many children will need extensive practice to find their "big voice." Explain to the students that they are going to be a tape recorder. As a tape recorder, they are going to repeat back what they hear exactly as they hear it (loud, soft, etc.). Begin with some fun echoes:

HIPPOPOTAMUS (deep voice, big gestures)
Mouse (squeaky voice)
T u r t l e (slow, exaggerated voice)
I'm going to the circus! (excited voice)

Now, progress into assertive, aggressive and passive examples, and identify what kind of voice you are using:

"Can I have my marker back?" (whiny little passive voice)
"Stop!" (assertive voice)
"These are called chairs." (assertive voice)
"You can use this when I'm done." (assertive voice)
"This is mine. Get your own." (aggressive, screaming voice)
"Stop! I don't like it when you push me." (assertive voice)

Discuss how it feels to use each of the three voices. Ask which voice children think is most likely to be successful. Have younger children practice repeating all of the above phrases in an assertive voice. Have older students play "guess my tone" with similar phrases using passive, aggressive and assertive voices.

General Activities — Younger

Helpful or Hurtful Game

Role-play the following scenes and have the children decide which one is helpful or hurtful.

1. A child is pushed. The child begins to cry and hides under the table.
2. A child is pushed. The child says, "I don't like it when you push me. Please watch where you are going."

1. A child hits a friend. The friend hits back.
2. A child hits a friend. The friend says, "I don't like it when you hit me. Please talk to me."

1. A child calls a friend a name. The friend tells the teacher.
2. A child calls a friend a name. The child says, "I don't like it when you call me names. Please use my real name. It is _____."

Big Al

In this story, by Al Clemmens, all Big Al wants is to make friends, but the other fish hide or swim away when he approaches. After Al rescues the other fish from the fishing net, they are able to see him as a friend. Use this book to illustrate the importance of teaching others how you want to be treated by reading the story, stopping at the part when Big Al is being misunderstood and asking, "What could Big Al do to change the situation?" Record the children's responses on a story web.

Next, act out the story with one child playing the part of Big Al and several children playing the parts of the other fish. Point out that Big Al has no friends because he has not been able to teach the other fish how he wants to be treated. Ask children, "What might happen if Big Al had the Time Machine?" Have children role-play being Big Al or one of the other fish as they practice going through the Time Machine to show how the story could be changed.

Then revisit your story web and have children add new responses based on their Time Machine experience. Complete the activity by writing a new ending that incorporates the children's responses, including Big Al and the other fish going through the Time Machine.

That Bugs Me!

Purchase or create some kind of bug hat for children to use during this activity. Explain that sometimes people say, "That really bugs me!" when they feel angry, frustrated or bothered by something. Put on the hat and model by sharing something that really bugs you. You might say, "It really bugs me when my son Christian doesn't do his homework!" Pass the hat around the circle, giving each child a chance to share one thing. When you begin, some children will have a hard time identifying what bothers them. The more you play, the more conscious of their own feelings they become.

At some point, add a "solution" step to the activity. For example, if someone says, "It really bugs me when you get in front of me in line," ask students what they think they could do to change that bothersome behavior. Model by saying, "I can take the bug hat off by using my big voice. I can say, 'I don't like it when you cut in front of me in line. Please go to the end of the line.'"

"Give me back my apple!"

After reading *Shubert's Big Voice*, pass a real apple around the circle, role-playing the Shubert and Benny roles when Shubert asks for his apple. You can create hats or visors decorated like the characters in the book. Purchase a pair of butterfly wings and antennae to play Mrs. Bookbinder.

General Activities — Older

Conflict Fold Up

Ask your students to rank themselves from 1–10 for how they handle conflict.

1 – I avoid confrontation.
2 – I dislike confrontation.
3 – I feel uncomfortable with confrontation.
4 – I feel uncomfortable with confrontation, but if I must confront, I will.
5 – I don't care either way. I will fight some battles and walk away from others.
6 – I hope that I don't have to confront others, but I will if I have to.
7 – I am comfortable with confrontation but don't look for it.
8 – I am comfortable with confrontation.
9 – I think that confrontation is appropriate.
10 – I look for the fight. I want to prove I'm right!

Have students write their number on a large piece of paper. Instruct them to line up in order from 1–10 without talking. They can hold up their paper, but they may not talk while lining up. Once the class is lined up, count to the halfway point, and then fold the line in half. This should station the 10s across from the 1s. Then have both partners answer, discussing these points:

> **When something doesn't go my way, I normally ____.**
> **I feel ____ when I do this (or when this happens).**
> **If I could do anything when conflict happens, I would ____.**

As they share their answers, listen to the students. See what the reaction is as they each share their side of situations.

Jungle Bullies

Read *Jungle Bullies* by Steven Kroll. In this story, a monkey has a problem and he doesn't know what to do. He asks his mom for help and she seems to understand how she can teach him to solve problems using his big voice.

Ask the students to brainstorm the steps for solving problems. Guide the students to:
1. Breathe
2. Use your words
3. Tell what you want the person to do if this happens again. Include "ask for help, if needed" as a step, so that students know you are willing to help them if the problem seems too big.

Take pictures of the steps and post them near the Time Machine in your classroom. To reinforce the steps, have students break into groups and sequence the steps to problem solving.

Class-Made Books

Younger

What (School Family Name) Do When They Are Bugged

This book is created after students have done the "That Bugs Me!" activity (p. 268) several times. Before beginning this activity, photograph each child wearing a bug hat and making an angry face. Then take a photo after they take off the bug hat and solve the problem, usually a happy face.

On the first day of the activity, have the children write and illustrate what bugs them. If they can't write, take dictation to record their thoughts. On the next day, have them write and illustrate how they get the bug hat off (how they solve the problem). Glue the picture of each child in his bug hat on the "bugged" page and the happy face on their "solved" page. Bind the book together so the problem appears before the solution for each child.

How to Use the Time Machine

Create a routine book using photographs of children going through the steps on the Time Machine. Add the text that is on the mat to each page. Add extra pages that include helpful phrases for common problems, for example: "When someone gets in front of me in line" (take photo of someone getting in line in front of someone), "I can say, 'I don't like it when you get in front of me, please go to the end of the line'" (photo of same child standing at the end of the line), or "When someone calls me names, I can say, 'I don't like it when you call me names. Call me by my name.'" To generate these pages, have the children brainstorm intrusions or things they don't like on chart paper. Then brainstorm what they could ask the intruder to do instead. Use two different-colored markers to write the problem and the solution. Then have the children act out the scenes while you take the photographs.

Class-Made Books

Older

"Ask a Peer" Solution Book

Begin by role-playing a common conflict using the Time Machine and modeling, "I don't like it when you_____, please_____" language. Then give each student a piece of notebook paper. Have them write a short description of a conflict or intrusion at the top of the paper. Then have students rotate around the room, writing one different way to solve the problem on each paper. Rotate until you have three or four answers per paper. Make suggestions of your own on the pages as needed, and then bind them together to form a book titled "Ask a Peer." Keep the book in your Safe Place or reference area for students to look at when they need ideas for solving conflicts.

Music & Movement

All Ages

"BIG Voice"

Have the children sing the song "BIG Voice" on the *Kindness Counts* CD. Practice having the children act out the chorus with a partner or in a group. Have a discussion about the song and the book, *Shubert's BIG Voice*. What is similar in the song and in the book? What is different?

My Words Have Power

Use this song to help students remember their words have power.

Tune: "Twinkle Twinkle"
My words have power—yes, it's true.
When you listen to me and I listen to you,
We can solve problems every day.
When we work and when we play!
Words can solve problems between you and I,
Use your "BIG Voice"—just give it a try!

C = Commitment

I am willing to allow myself and others to make mistakes. These mistakes are not flaws or unforgivable moments that need punishment; they are demonstrations of a lack of skills. From this understanding, I open myself to more willingness to commit to change. When hurtful interactions occur with those I love, I will ask, "Are you willing to go back in time and do the interaction over?" From my willingness, I will open my heart and speak from a place of love instead of fear.

Signature _____ **Date** _____

I will start implementing the Time Machine in my life, school and classroom by:
- ___Starting with myself, my significant others and my children.
- ___Reading *Shubert's BIG Voice*.
- ___Purchasing or creating a Time Machine.
- ___Becoming more aware of the teaching moments in my classroom.
- ___Working toward empowering victims instead of punishing aggressors.
- ___Spending one week focusing on activities to introduce the Time Machine.

Signature _____ **Date** _____

H = Helpful Resources

Music — All Ages

Kindness Counts **by Dr. Becky Bailey and Mr. Al**
Songs: "Turn Back Time," "BIG Voice"

Come Join the Circle **by Paulette Meier**
Songs: "T.I.M.E. at the Peace Table," "Cool Cooperation"

Hello World **by Red Grammer**
Song: "We're All in This Together," "I Want You To Listen"

Literature — Younger

A Picture Book of Rosa Parks **by David Adler.** A biographical account of the long-time, committed civil-rights activist, whose role in initiating the Montgomery bus boycott in 1955 helped change history.

A Weekend with Wendell **by Kevin Henkes.** Sophie does not enjoy energetic, assertive Wendell's weekend visit until the very end, when she learns to assert herself and finds out Wendell can be fun to play with after all.

And to Think That We Thought That We'd Never Be Friends **by Mary Ann Hoberman.** This book takes on quarreling and its consequences, and shows how turning fighters into friends leads to greater peace.

Stand Tall Molly Lou Melon **by Patty Lovell and David Catrow.** Molly Lou is the smallest girl in first grade, but stands up for herself when bullied because she remembers what her grandmother told her.

Literature — Older

Mean Jean the Recess Queen **by Alexis O'Neill and Laura Huliska-Beith.** Jean is the class bully until a new little girl joins the class. The class figures out that Jean was mean because no one had ever asked her to play.

***Cinderella (As If You Didn't Already Know the Story)* by Barbara Ensor.** This version features Cinderella writing letters to her dead mother complaining about how hard life is even though she tries to be nice. Watch how Cinderella changes after the traditional "Cinderella story" ends, and she learns to become a talented diplomat, fully capable of improving her country and the world all around her.

Additional Aids

I Solve: Conflict Resolution Time Machine from www.ConsciousDiscipline.com

Bully Prevention Presenter's Series CDrom from www.ConsciousDiscipline.com

Conflict Resolution Audio Lecture CD by Dr. Becky Bailey

Shubert Puppet from www.ConsciousDiscipline.com

Teacher Tip:

It is essential that we help children reconnect after resolving a conflict. The connection signals the conflict is over and the friendship remains intact.

Chapter 13

Celebration Center

Fern Creek Elementary School, a Conscious Discipline S.T.A.R. School in Orlando, was having its monthly School Family Celebration assembly. It was an inspiring day for 500 children and 80 adults who joined together to celebrate and honor each other. I watched them dance together and sing welcome songs for new children, staff and faculty who had joined their School Family during the month. They sang "On the Day You Were Born" by Red Grammer for those celebrating birthdays. Principal Kim Whitney spoke about how each person is valuable, and the importance of using your BIG Voice in certain situations. Then came the time when children, staff and faculty were invited to state their names and tell the group something they were celebrating. One after another, students filed onto the stage. "My name is Anthony and I am celebrating doing my homework all week." "My name is Isabella and I am celebrating being in a play at my church." "My name is Carlos and I am celebrating my new baby brother." The auditorium erupted in cheers again and again.

Then came Alex, a kindergartner. He froze as he came to the microphone. A hush went over the crowd. Out of 500 children, not one was laughing or giggling at his dilemma. Principal Whitney bent down by his side, getting at eye level with the fearful child. She started taking deep breaths and rubbing his back. She said nothing, but was nonverbally encouraging him. As I looked around, I saw something I will never forget. The majority of the children and adults in the auditorium were taking deep, slow breaths. Many had put their hands over their hearts to silently wish him well. Finally, Alex spoke and said, "I'm Alex and I didn't hit anyone." He then stepped away from the microphone. The crowd went wild with cheers. Alex scooted back to the microphone and announced, "All day!" It was a beautiful moment. The assembly ended soon after, with everyone singing and signing the song "It's in Every One of Us" from the *Kindness Counts* CD.

As I left the assembly, I thought about what I had experienced: an assembly that truly operated on the School Family model. They came together to celebrate, commemorate and remember each other in an unconditionally loving way. They didn't put constraints on what was valuable to celebrate and what was not. Everyone counted. They didn't give awards for the best this or that. I thought back to other assemblies I had attended where only certain students who had met specific standards such as the honor roll or perfect attendance were celebrated and honored. The feeling at those assemblies was one of herd management. Most teachers were busy with crowd control, as bored or jealous students tried to stay focused in hopes of being good enough to have extra free time at recess. What a glorious difference I experienced at the School Family assembly at Fern Creek! Each child felt a stake in what was happening in the assembly and felt free to contribute to the celebration. The difference was the power of love, a universal resource that goes largely untapped in schools.

The Shift from Rewards to Celebration

For many teachers, one of the hardest parts of Conscious Discipline is letting go of giving rewards for good behavior. Shifting from rewards to celebrations is a slow process, but one that is necessary to create truly cooperative and compassionate School Families where healthy competition can emerge as children grow into middle school. After years of helping educators shift from rewards to celebrations, I have come to realize it's a difficult shift for the following reasons:

1. Teachers have been systematically taught to use rewards in their professional training.
2. Rewards seem, for most children, to work in the short term.
3. Rewards do not ask adults to change internally. Rewards require us to manage paperwork and give out stuff, but do not require us to manage ourselves.

A huge internal change in mindset occurs when we shift from rewards to celebrations. The intent behind rewards is to motivate children to repeat desired behaviors labeled "good" and/or to achieve a defined performance standard. Rewards work on a deficit model: You are deficient in these areas, so I will "motivate" you to strengthen these areas through offering the possibility of rewards. The intent behind celebrations, on the other hand, is to see the best in everyone and to deliberately look for each person's strengths. Celebrations are about honoring life, with all of its dilemmas, problems, difficulties, joys, successes and accomplishments.

The children in the School Family assembly I described above chose many different things to celebrate: academic achievement, moments of self-control and the birth of a new sibling. If adults had designed the content, the range of life experience that was acknowledged would most likely have focused on reading and math scores. There is so much more worth celebrating! Families have celebrations for diverse events, from losing a tooth to gaining a driver's license. Think for a moment about how we celebrate a child's first steps. We pick him up, squeeze him and laugh with glee. We take photos and email them to everyone we know. We call people to come over and witness the miracle. In school, celebrations (beyond outright reward-giving) have historically been limited to birthdays, some holidays and the last day of school. Conscious Discipline suggests that we extend the process of celebrating beyond what is written on the calendar, and begin celebrating the kaleidoscope of life with exuberance and joy.

Celebrations exist so we can see ourselves in each other, express our values about life and strengthen our emotional connections. We celebrate our own success when we celebrate another person's success. The roar in the auditorium as we celebrated Alex's ability to control his impulse to hit was a mirror for the whole assembly. We've all had moments when we were able to control an impulse to hit, overeat, say something hurtful and so on. When we celebrate Alex's personal restraint, we also celebrate and strengthen our own self-control.

Award assemblies display a school's values. Generally, schools place value on high grades and good attendance. Fern Creek's celebration demonstrated a value system that says, "We care about each of you as precious individuals." In this system, students feel a sense of community and self-worth that is integral to their success in life. Fern Creek serves a disproportionately large number of children who are considered high-risk and high-need. Principal Whitney brilliantly commented one day, "A lot of my children will join a gang. I would like it to be the Fern Creek gang." The celebrations she leads reinforce a value system and a sense of inclusion that helps to assure that Fern Creek is the children's support group of choice.

Cognitive Development and Awards

Some of you, especially those teaching in upper elementary grades, might wonder, "What's wrong with awards' assemblies and rewards? Don't we need to recognize those who work hard?" My answer: "Certainly!" However, it's important to understand the child development process to determine when and how to introduce awards. For children to understand why some children will receive an award and others will not, they must also understand the concept of hierarchical classification. Developmentally, children younger than eight years old have trouble grouping objects into hierarchies of classes and subclasses (for example, a system that includes a set called "animal" and subsets called "mammals" and "reptiles," each of which has specific attributes that differentiate them from others). In the case of awards, you might have a category called "Student of the Week." Under this category you would have a subset of specific attributes that are needed to earn the Student of the Week award. Since this system of thinking is not fully developed in young children, they cannot understand the classification involved, and the result is, "How come I didn't get an award?" "It's not fair!" "When will it be my turn to get one?" and "The teacher doesn't like me!"

Early elementary school experiences are also important in determining whether motivation for self-regulated learning is strengthened and internalized, or whether children begin to feel helpless (Bronson, 2000). Children between the ages of five and seven are beginning to judge the adequacy of the work they produce and develop their own ideas about personal adequacy. As they become increasingly self-aware, they begin to compare themselves and their skills with peers. At this age, teaching methods that compare children in ways that produce winners and losers may contribute to feeling inadequate and helpless (Deci & Ryan, 1987). During this vulnerable time when self-consciousness is just beginning, positive experiences are especially valuable for nourishing motivation. A few awards given to a small percentage of students can anchor a sense of inadequacy within the many children who go unrecognized.

For these reasons and more, the School Family uses celebrations instead of awards. We celebrate hard work and perseverance; however, we celebrate these traits whether they result in learning long division, standing up for yourself by using helpful words, mastering a skateboarding trick or, like Alex, using self-control.

But Don't Traditional Rewards Work?

"Reward" is defined as any consequence that is predictable and has market value to the learner. It's the stuff we use to entice students to behave. Recent research indicates that rewards reduce intrinsic motivation, impair higher-order thinking skills, reduce contextual memory and eliminate the love of learning (Jensen, 1997), yet use of reward systems continues!

I often hear teachers say they use rewards to "motivate" children. I have bad news for these teachers: It is impossible to motivate someone else. Motivation means you want to do something. It may be possible to make someone do something with a bribe or a threat, but that's not motivation—it's coercion. The best we can do to truly motivate children is to create the kind of classroom and offer the kinds of lessons that will tap into and nourish the children's own motivation. The good news, however, is that motivation is natural. I have yet to meet a young child who wasn't motivated to figure things out, explore and find answers to meaningful life events. Anyone who has been around young children knows it's hard to stop them from learning or to reduce their natural motivation. However, research has repeatedly found that the enthusiasm for learning declines sharply through the elementary school years (Harter & Jackson, 1992; Anderman & Young, 1994; Lepper, Sethi, Dialdin & Drake, 1997). Having read the studies, examined the brain research and spent countless hours with children and educators, the answer is clear to me: Our use of rewards has hijacked children's natural motivation system.

The brain operates differently, when it is externally coerced through reward systems, than it does when its natural internal motivation system is stimulated. The brain triggers the release of certain neurotransmitters when we rely on rewards to manage behavior. These neurotransmitters inhibit higher-order learning functions. Children become focused on receiving or not receiving the reward instead of engaging in learning. This is demonstrated in classrooms by children's own comments, concerns and conversations. "How come Marissa got a sticker and I didn't? I was good, too." "It's not fair." "Marcus is talking. He shouldn't get anything." The focus rests on the "haves" and "have-nots" rather than on the learning at hand. On the other hand, when internal motivation is activated and anticipation of success is mounting, the brain triggers the release of dopamine, which maximizes learning potential. Dopamine is vital for learning and is considered the most important biochemical we produce for motivation and curiosity (Hannaford, 2010).

Another deficiency of rewards is the stimulus-response pattern they are based on. If your reward and punishment system is consistent, a stimulus is presented (read four books this month), and when the correct response is given (you comply), then a reward is presented (visit to the treasure box, award lunch, etc.). This sounds logical and effective, but when we train children to be stimulus-oriented, we strengthen the subcortical regions of the brain. We skip the phase called "thinking." Here's a simplified example: I take my dogs for daily walks. When they see me pick up the leash, excitement reigns as they pair that stimulus with the walk response. One day I had just finished a shower and was dripping wet. The leashes were on the bathroom counter. I picked them up so I could reach my towel, and two large dogs went crazy believing they were going walking with their naked owner.

Stimulus-response creates habitual actions, not wise responses. It sets children up to be great consumers as they respond to the stimuli presented by television and other media, but it does not create a generation of thinkers. When we stimulate the higher centers of children's brains with thoughtful celebrations and other Conscious Discipline structures, we create a stimulus-pause-response paradigm. In the pause phase, called "impulse control," there is a space that allows us to reflect on long-term benefits over instant gratification.

The Power of Love

In Conscious Discipline, the power of love states, "See the best in each other." It is the power that allows us to create classrooms based on unconditional love, which inherently values diversity and promotes cooperation. Seeing the best in others is easy to do when those others look like you, act like you or think like you. It becomes much harder when we believe others are behaving inappropriately. In our culture, over the past several decades, there has been a self-growth movement encouraging people to love themselves and get beyond the pains of their childhood. Somewhere in this process of "turning inward," some of us forgot our interconnectedness—that we are united in the same energy. It is time for us to look outward again, using the power of love and the skill of positive intent. Love and positive intent require us to see the best in ourselves and each other. It allows us to transform conflict situations into teaching moments that broaden our minds and open our hearts to a new way of perceiving and being. Our willingness to look beyond the negative behavior displayed empowers us to see the child's true need, whether it's belonging, power, fun, freedom or survival, and to teach a new skill rather than seek to punish.

Power of love: See the best in each other
Skill: Positive intent
Structure: Celebration Center
Value: Diversity

We aren't raised to see the beauty in each moment. We are geared, at best, to celebrate that which we judge good and point out the hurtfulness in the bad. The key to retraining our minds to seek and celebrate beauty instead of find fault is the skill of positive intent. Positive intent allows us to see the best in every situation. It allows us to shed light on a child's behavior, transforming what appeared to be a negative moment into a learning opportunity worth celebrating.

Rarely do I spend time in middle schools, but one day, I was doing a friend a favor by visiting her school. As I was walking outside the building, searching for the office, I ran into a student spray-painting the back wall of the school. It was a shock for both of us that reminded me of coming unexpectedly upon an animal in the woods: You both freeze momentarily and stare. Consciously noticing my survival state, I took a deep breath. With that breath came my willingness to offer this boy positive intent. I said, "It seems like you want to let everyone know you're having a bad day, maybe a bad year." My statement seemed to lesson the grip of his fear of being caught. He nodded yes. I continued by asking, "Who in this building do you think cares about you and what happens to you?" He shrugged his shoulders and mumbled, "No one." My face softened as my heart opened to this boy. I smiled and said, "Well, no wonder you didn't know what else to do with your anger. Is there anyone in this building that other kids talk to or trust?" He responded, "Coach Carnes." We walked inside to see Coach Carnes, and the boy began to get the help he needed to feel more connected, express his anger appropriately and clean the paint off the wall. My willingness to offer positive intent was the key to the outcome of this situation. I didn't know this boy. If I had done anything differently, my guess is that he would have run off, verbally attacked me, or both. As he began turning his life around, many opportunities arose for him and others to celebrate. Having positive intent for this boy was the first step.

Begin offering positive intent to the negative behaviors in your classroom, and then stand back and decide for yourself if the change in your intent works miracles. The following language will get you started. The *Conscious Discipline* book provides much more information about how to offer positive intent.

Positive Intent:	"You wanted (desire), so you (hurtful action)."
Benefit:	"You didn't know what else to do."
Limit:	"You may not (hurtful action), (hurtful action) hurts."
Teach:	"When you want (desire), say (or do) (helpful action)."
Practice:	"Say it (do it) now for practice."

Example: Child pushes a friend in line.

"You wanted her to move, so you pushed her."
"You didn't know the words to say."
"You may not push, pushing hurts."
"When you want someone to move, say 'move please.'"
"Say it now for practice."

For very young children, you would simplify the process by saying, "You wanted her to move. You may not push. Say, 'Move, please.'"

E = Environmental Structure: Celebration Center

Purpose: The purpose of the Celebration Center is to celebrate life events, individual or group achievements and contributions to the School Family. Celebrations could include such things as losing a tooth, riding a bicycle, welcoming a new sibling into a family, great-grandmother's birthday, learning to read, earning 100 percent on a spelling test or helping friends through a difficult time. Be careful that you stay true to the purpose of celebrations. They are not a way for teachers to reinforce behaviors they would like to see again; they are a way to authentically see the best in children and celebrate their diverse talents. The Celebration Center for the whole school is called the School Family assembly.

How to set up a Celebration Center: In general, the Celebration Center is a specific place in the classroom. For young children it might be a colorful chair chosen just for this purpose. For older children it could be any chair brought to the front of the classroom or a page on the class website. You may decide that older students simply stand up at their tables to be celebrated. The School Family assemblies are set up on a specific timetable, and occur in whatever place will house your entire school population. The timetable for some schools may be the last Friday of each month or every six or nine weeks. Some schools have auditoriums and some schools will celebrate in the cafeteria.

How to introduce the Celebration Center: At any age, it is best to introduce the Celebration Center as the need arises in your classroom. For example, a child who announces, "I made my first soccer goal this weekend," might start the ball rolling. The most important

thing is to celebrate all aspects of your class, from making a rap song, to acing a math test, to learning how to tie shoelaces. Each child has a gift for your class; your job is to find it and celebrate it.

How you structure your celebrations is crucial. All celebrations will have a beginning, middle and end. Keep the beginning and ending the same so that the novelty of the middle part will be framed by predictability. For example, begin with a song or chant to signify the start of the celebration and unify the group, share the individual events to celebrate and then end with a closing that relates the celebration to every student. You will also need to establish and teach procedures for sharing.

Begin with a Song or Chant: Use a song to signal it is time to celebrate. The following can be sung to the tune of the "Mickey Mouse Club" song:

> **C-E-L-E-B-R-A-T-E**
> **Celebrate today!**
> **Because you did it!**
> **Because you did it!**
> **You worked real hard and now, Hooray! You did it!**
> **We do our best the brain-smart way,**
> **Today and everyday!**
> **I'm proud of myself,**
> **I'm proud of you, too.**
> **Celebrate today!**

Other songs teachers have used include "Let's Celebrate" from *It Starts in the Heart*, "Celebration" by Kool & the Gang, "I Just Want to Celebrate" by Rare Earth, and "The World's Greatest" by R. Kelly. Select about 30 seconds from the song and play it as a signal that the celebration is about to take place.

In the Middle: The age of the children and the type of celebration will determine how your celebration is structured. Events and achievements are the two basic types of celebrations. Event celebrations include losing a tooth, the arrival of a new sibling and birthdays. Achievement celebrations include academic improvement, better behavior management, learning a new skill or accomplishing a personal goal.

Event celebrations can be planned in advance if the day is known (a birthday), or they can be spontaneous (birth of a sibling). Your celebration procedure will be consistent from one event to the next. If a child comes into class with unexpected news of an exciting event, sharing may occur at your first meeting time or at that moment. It's likely that young children will want to share important events when they first arrive, while older children are better able to wait until the designated sharing time. Begin with your celebration song or chant to signal the group that someone's about to share. Give the child a celebration prop such as a hat or decorated celebration stick. Then invite the child to share, either from his or her seat or from a particular place (like the celebration chair). Close with a unity activity.

Achievement celebrations are more highly structured. These can be held daily or weekly. Select a way of recording the accomplishments, such as writing them on index cards and placing the cards in a celebration box so they can be saved for the designated sharing time. Young children will need help in recording their accomplishments, while older children can write their accomplishments themselves. When the scheduled time arrives, begin with your celebration song or chant. Use a toy microphone or other prop in younger classrooms to designate whose turn it is to share. In older classrooms, students often like to call it a "shout out," and manage taking turns without external aids. End with a unity activity.

End with a Unity Activity: As you celebrate individuals for their accomplishments, it is vital to end the process by showing how the celebration relates to every student. Red Grammer's "On the Day You Were Born" is a wonderful birthday celebration song. It begins with, "On the day that Becky was born, the angels sang and they blew on their horns." As the song proceeds, it extends the celebration by saying, "On the day (fill in your name) was born, the angels sang and they blew on their horns." The song ends by singing, "Right now somewhere someone's being born," bringing the celebration full circle to celebrate all birthdays. In this way, the celebration starts with individuality and ends with unity. If you celebrate someone learning to read, you might end by celebrating everyone who worked hard on something. If you celebrate a new baby in a family, you can end by extending that to celebrating all new things, from babies, to friends, to pets and experiences. The close of the celebration is a movement to celebrate all people.

> **The Three-Step Process for a Classroom Celebration:**
> Step 1: Start with 30-second song signal.
> Step 2: Have a procedure for sharing.
> Step 3: End with unity and a movement that honors all.

School Family Assemblies: School Family assemblies operate on a slightly modified Brain Smart Start procedure, and therefore consist of four parts: activity to unite, activity to disengage stress, activity to connect and activity to commit. Use this format because it creates an optimal integrated (organized) brain state, which is extremely helpful when you bring 300 to 1200 children together.

School Family assemblies are led by a group of three or four brave faculty members who will be on stage. They lead the songs and model the motions for the children. Quite often, these "masters of ceremonies" will be the principal and other administrators who feel comfortable in this role.

Start the assembly with a unifying activity. An entrance song with precise routines is ideal. Coach every child to walk into the building the same way, sit down and start singing immediately until every child is inside the auditorium. The song you select must have hand motions; following the hand movements keeps students organized and engaged in a unified manner. Once everyone is seated, the principal will welcome the students, and then play a second unifying song. "Get the Beat from Your Seat" by The Learning Station is one great choice. For expediency's sake, I suggest cutting the songs used during the assembly down to two minutes or less in length. After each high-energy activity, lead students in an activity to disengage stress (S.T.A.R., drain, balloon, pretzel). This gives you the opportunity to reaffirm these four skills and calm the energy in the room.

Next, conduct your connecting and celebrating activities. Below are the components and songs I recommend for this part of your assembly:

1. New arrivals: Welcome all new students, faculty, families and visitors. Ask the new arrivals to stand while the children sing the song "Welcome" from *It Starts in the Heart*. (Remember to cut the song down in length.)
2. Birthdays: Invite children with birthdays during the months since your last assembly to stand up and be celebrated. I suggest the song "On the Day That You Were Born" on Red Grammer's *Hello World*.
3. Individual celebrations: Teachers will preselect students from their classrooms to come to the microphone and state their name, grade and teacher, followed by the statement, "I am celebrating _____." Some may choose to celebrate their mom having a baby or getting a job. Others may choose to celebrate getting 100 percent on their spelling words. The major point is to let the children choose what they wish to celebrate for themselves. After each child shares, invite the rest of the assembled students to cheer. The cheer can be a silent cheer, hand clapping or saying, "Good for you, you did it" in unison.

The next part of your assembly will be a Conscious Discipline mini-lesson lasting three to five minutes. The lessons are based on each of the seven skills of Conscious Discipline. If you have one assembly a month, you will cover all seven skills. If you choose to have fewer assemblies, you will cover the skills you deem essential for your school. I recommend the following mini-lessons:

Assembly 1: Teach S.T.A.R. and the three other composure skills (draining, ballooning, and the pretzel). Also introduce the job descriptions, "My job is to keep you safe. Your job is to help keep the classroom safe."

Assembly 2: Wish well and look for kindness. Demonstrate how to wish well (take a deep breath, fill your heart with love by putting your hands on your heart and send it out to others). Demonstrate real-life situations where you and the children can wish each other well: Someone has a dog that died, feels down on the playground, is upset because of a bad grade, is angry and losing control, makes a mistake reading out loud in the classroom and so on. Challenge the children to wish each other well and have them commit to look for kindness. Start a school kindness tree and challenge students to fill it up by the next assembly.

Assembly 3: Use your BIG Voice. Teach children who are pushed, called names or have their property damaged how to speak up. Teach them to say, "I don't like it when you _____. Please _____." Emphasize the statement after the "please," and be certain it is a positive action ("Please say my name when you want my attention," not "Please stop hitting me."). Show children ways to teach others how to treat them. Role-play some situations, such as:

- Child pushes another. "I don't like it when you push me. Please walk around me."
- Child backs up in line. "I don't like it when you step on my feet. Please walk forward."
- Child calls name. "I don't like it when you call me names. My name is Becky. Please use it."

Challenge children to a month of respect where each person is going to teach another person how they want to be treated. Have them make a commitment by repeating an affirmation like, "I commit to using my BIG Voice this month."

Assembly 4: What are my choices? Teach children that they always have choices and they are always making choices. Often, we want to focus children on making "good" choices. I encourage you to have children think about all the choices they make in a given situation. Role-play a scenario, then blow a whistle to stop it mid-action. Ask, "What are some of the choices _____ has at this moment?" The stop-action scenes could include:

- Another student pushes me: Stop action. Two choices include, "I could push back or I could use my BIG Voice and teach him or her how to treat me."
- I didn't finish my homework: Stop action. Two choices include, "I could lie and say I left it at home or I could tell the truth and see if I can get it done today."
- A friend is teasing me: Stop action. Two choices include, "I could tell the teacher or I could say, 'I don't like it when you tease me. Please treat me with respect.'"

Challenge children to think about their choices. Provide a commitment by having them repeat, "I promise to think about my choices, asking myself, are they helpful or hurtful?"

Assembly 5: See the best in others. Teach children to frame misbehavior as a call for help instead of meanness or badness. Introduce a pair of heart-shaped glasses like the ones in *Shubert Sees the Best*. Demonstrate through stop-action role-playing that there are different ways to see the same event. The stop-action scenes could include:

- A child hits another child to get a pen: One way to see the aggressor is as a bully or mean person. Another way to see the aggressor is as a child who needs help in learning how to say, "May I borrow your pen, please?"
- A child has trouble reading out loud: One way is to see the child as stupid. Another way is to see the child as needing help from all of us by wishing well.

Challenge children to see the best in others. Give them a commitment by asking them to repeat the affirmation, "I commit to see the best in others."

Assembly 6: Show you care. Teach children there are many ways to show you care, and many gifts we can give that do not cost money. Talk about gifts like walking a hurt friend to the nurse, smiling at people and teaching others how to treat you.

Challenge children to show each other how much they care. Give them a commitment by asking them to repeat, "I commit to showing my School Family how much I care by being the best me I can."

Assembly 7: Oops! Teach children that mistakes are an opportunity to learn, rather than something to avoid or a sign that we've done something wrong. Mistakes give us a chance to do things differently. Role-play helpful things you could say to yourself when you make a mistake. "Oops, I made a mistake. Take a deep breath. I can handle this." "What are my choices?" "I'm going to _____."

Challenge children to think through their choices out loud until they learn the process. Children under nine years old do not have mature private speech, so you will need to help them develop healthy private speech by encouraging them to talk through their problem-solving out loud. Have students commit to the process by repeating, "I commit to saying, 'Oops,' and making a different choice when I make a mistake."

Each of the above skills is covered by a book in the Shubert series. Teachers can support the School Family assembly by reading the corresponding book before and after each assembly. The book list for each assembly is:

Assembly 1: *Shubert Is a S.T.A.R.*
Assembly 2: *Shubert's Helpful Day*
Assembly 3: *Shubert's BIG Voice*
Assembly 4: *Shubert's Choice*
Assembly 5: *Shubert Sees the Best*
Assembly 6: *Shubert Rants and Raves*
Assembly 7: *Shubert's New Friend*

After the Conscious Discipline mini-lesson, conduct a high-energy song with motions. Ideally, this song will support the lesson learned (for example, use the "Star Song" on *Kindness Counts* in the first assembly) and will be cut to about two minutes in length. Then lead the students in a deep breathing activity to calm the energy in the room, and make any necessary school announcements. At the end of the assembly, enjoy a final unifying song with your School Family.

The Process for a School Family Assembly:

Step 1: Organized activity entrance song
Step 2: Welcome and unity song
Step 3: Celebrate and connect (new arrivals, birthdays, individual celebrations)
Step 4: Mini Conscious Discipline lesson
Step 5: Lesson-related song and an active calming activity
Step 6: Announcements
Step 7: Final unifying activity and dismissal

A = Activities

General Activities — All Ages

Create a Celebration Chair

Children of all ages enjoy having a special place designated for celebrations. Find an old wooden chair and have the children decorate it with your assistance. Younger classes may want to use handprints so each child can contribute a piece of him- or herself to the chair. Older classrooms may want to bring in magazine pictures of celebrations to découpage the chair. The type of decoration can be as original and varied as the class itself. Paint the chair with primer at the beginning of each school year in preparation for your new School Family to personalize this classroom structure.

General Activities — Younger

Celebration Bag

Younger children delight in using props during their celebrations. Purchase a bright gift bag and label it "Celebration Bag." Fill the bag with symbolic objects that represent common things young children might celebrate, such as a tooth toy (representing losing a tooth), a pair of shoelaces (learning to tie your shoes), a baseball cap (winning a T-ball game), a baby rattle (birth of a new sibling), and a pompom, which could celebrate a variety of accomplishments. When

> **Teacher Tip:**
>
> Some teachers make up specific songs or chants for common celebrations. A child sharing how he lost his tooth might sit in the celebration chair wearing a tooth necklace while the class sings (to the tune of "The Farmer in the Dell"):
>
> You lost a tooth,
> You lost a tooth,
> You are growing day by day.
> You lost a tooth.
> New teeth will grow,
> New teeth will grow.
> You are growing everyday.
> So grow, grow and grow.

celebration time arrives, encourage children to choose a symbolic object from the bag to hold while the class celebrates.

Star of the Week

Star of the Week is an excellent way for your children to get to know one another at the beginning of the year. It helps create the connections between you and the children, and among the children as everyone shares their stars. Place each child's name in a basket labeled "Star of the Week!" Show the class that everyone's name is in the basket. (For some children, you may have to reassure them by showing them more than once.) Explain that everyone will get a turn and that it is hard to wait. Randomly select one star person to celebrate each week. Encourage children to manage their disappointment and truly celebrate the person chosen.

Cut out a large star. The center of the star states, "This is me," and has space for a photo or drawing of the child. Then print one of the following on each of the five points of the star: my favorite food, my favorite place to go, myself as a grownup, my family and my favorite thing to do. Send the star home with the star child Friday afternoon with instructions to fill in the spaces as a family over the weekend and return it to school on Monday. Build time into your morning circle so the star person can share. (If the star has not returned by Tuesday or the child says no one will help, work on the star together at school.) After sharing, place the stars on a classroom wall or bind them into a class book.

Celebrating Everyday

Utilize "Cheer Leader" as a job in your School Family. The Cheer Leader's job is to look for rea-

> **Teacher Tip:**
>
> Before you pull out a name, say, "When I pull out a name and it is not yours, you may feel disappointed." Show them a picture of a child whose face shows disappointment. "We have two choices when a name comes out. You can fold your arms, pout and think, 'That's not fair, I wanted my name to come out!' or you can be a S.T.A.R., wish well and say, 'Congratulations _____!'" With positive reinforcement and frequent reminders, you will hear a few faint congratulations at first, but after about a month with your School Family, you'll hear genuine heartfelt congratulations.

sons to cheer! Create a "Cheer Box" from an empty box of Cheer detergent, a box of Cheerios, or one of your own creation. Fill the box with printed-out cheers from various sources. (Dr. Jean Feldman has cheer cards you can download on her website at www.drjean.org.) The Cheer Leader then selects a cheer from the Cheer Box to use as he shares good news and accomplishments. A few reasons to celebrate everyday include:

We celebrate one another every day!

- Learning to tie shoes
- Finding something that was lost (from a shoe, to a library book)
- Sharing a child's celebration
- Scoring a basket or getting a hit at T-ball
- Receiving a class compliment from a lunch monitor or administrator
- Learning to write your name
- Reading a book
- Keeping your commitment
- Walking quietly in the hallway
- Being on time for lunch

General Activities
Older

Celebration Station

Create small postcard-style cards on the computer. Type a different statement on each, then print and cut out the cards and place them in a basket. Encourage students to take a card whenever they see something to celebrate with another student, write a short note on it, then give the card to him or her. Celebratory statements include:

You rock!
You rule!
I noticed _____.
I appreciate that you _____.
You did it!
You went above and beyond.

> **Teacher Tip:**
> Write and send a handful of these notes to the students each day. You may also wish to display them on a bulletin board to reinforce that your School Family values and celebrates each other. At the end of each week, return the celebration cards to their owners so you can start fresh the next week.

294 *Creating the School Family*

Class-Made Books

All Ages

Your Amazing Achievements

Read *Celebrate! Your Amazing Achievements* by Joanne Barkan, which celebrates all the great things children do in schools, and then create your own "Amazing Achievements" book. For about a month, document students' achievements using a camera. In younger classrooms, you will be in charge of all the photography. In older classrooms, assign a different student to take two or three photos of helpful acts and achievements each day. (After each child serves as the photographer once, it is your turn to take photographs. Use this time to ensure that every student is the subject of at least one photo.) At the end of the month, compile all the photographs into an "Amazing Achievements" album so children can celebrate each other's accomplishments over and over again.

Class-Made Books

Younger

_____ Is Important in Our School Family

This activity builds on the "Star of the Week" activity from the General Activities section. Each child draws a picture of him- or herself with the Star of the Week. Then they write why the Star of the Week is important in the School Family. (Take dictation and rewrite as needed.) Provide examples of things the children might say, like, "Steven helped me find my jacket when I lost it," or "Crystal shared her markers when I needed the green one." Bind the pages together with a cover that says, "_____ Is Important in Our School Family." Send the book home with the child on Friday as part of the Star of the Week activity with his or her family.

Classroom Birthday Book

Create a page for each month of the year. On the page, add a large die-cut birthday cake and the name of the month. Place students' photos on the cake that corresponds to their birthday month. Play Jack Hartmann's "Birthdays" from *Math All Around Me* and invite children to stand up when their birthday month is sung.

"Grandma's Feather Bed"

"Grandma's Feather Bed" is a song by John Denver that author Christopher Canyon made into a book; it celebrates the fun had at Grandma's. The book and CD combination make for a wonderful reading, music and movement activity.

C = Commitment

I am willing to consciously see the best in each moment. If I am not seeing the best, I will offer positive intent to the situation or person. As I reframe the situation from negative to positive, I will celebrate my life's successes.

Signature _____ **Date** _____

If I am currently using rewards as motivators in my classroom, I will begin to shift away from rewards by slowly replacing them with these celebrations (place a check by the ones you will implement):

	___Create a Celebration Center in my classroom for individual celebrations.
	___Select a beginning and ending procedure for celebrations.
	___Commit to ending celebrations with the focus on unity.
	___Allow myself and the students to be genuinely exuberant and authentic in their celebration of others and themselves.

If I am not using rewards, I will strengthen my classroom by (check all that apply):

	___Creating a Celebration Center.
	___Adding more individual celebration opportunities.
	___Selecting two activities from this chapter to implement.

Music — All Ages

It Starts in the Heart **by Dr. Becky Bailey and Jack Hartmann**
Songs: "That Was Helpful," "Caring Friends," "Friendship Chant," "Let's Celebrate"

Kindness Counts **by Dr. Becky Bailey and Mr. Al**
Songs: "In Every One of Us," "We All Count"

Brain Boogie Boosters **by The Learning Station and Dr. Becky Bailey**
Songs: "You Are Heart," "It's a Marvelous Day"

Hello World **by Red Grammer**
Song: "On the Day You Were Born"

Math All Around **by Jack Hartmann**
Song: "Birthdays"

Celebrate! **by Kool & the Gang**
Song: "Celebration"

Road Rock **by Rare Earth**
Song: "I Just Want to Celebrate"

The R. in R&B Collection, Volume 1 **by R. Kelly**
Song: "The World's Greatest"

Literature — Younger

I Can Do It Too! **by Karen Baicker.** With caring support from family and friends, an African-American toddler finds out she can do some "grown-up" things, too.

All By Myself **by Mercer Mayer.** In this picture book, Little Critter shows us all the things he can do by himself, from tying his shoes (almost) to pouring his own juice (and only spilling a little). The illustrations show that Little Critter doesn't do everything perfectly, but he makes an effort to do the best he can.

***Shubert Sees the Best* by Dr. Becky Bailey.** Shubert helps his class see situations from a different and more supportive perspective. Children see the benefits of shifting from hurtful name-calling to finding ways to be helpful as others learn new skills.

***Chrysanthemum* by Kevin Henkes.** Chrysanthemum loves her name until she starts school. She learns how to deal with the teasing and ends up celebrating her beautiful name.

Literature — Older

***The Blue Ribbon Day* by Katie Couric.** A grade-school girl learns everyone can shine when they discover what their own strengths are.

***Hooray for You! A Celebration of You-Ness* by Marianne Richmond.** This celebration of self-esteem highlights diverse cultures, physical traits and individual dreams.

***Listen to the Wind* by Greg Mortenson.** Greg wants to thank the Pakistani villagers who nursed him back to health after an accident. As he and the children work to create the school they have dreamed of, celebration pulls the village even closer together.

Additional Aids

www.drjean.org Downloadable "cheer cards"

Chapter 14

We Care Center

When my mother passed away, I received many cards from friends and family. I opened them, glanced at the senders and put them in a box until the funeral arrangements were made and I had figured out how to help my father. Just the act of opening them and tossing them into the box had a calming effect on my soul. The morning after the funeral, I remember saying to myself, "Wow, this is a pile of love. I have a pile of love in a box in my bedroom. I am not alone." At that moment, my emotions let loose. Holding the box of cards and sobbing on the floor, I allowed myself to be present with all my feelings– sadness for losing my mom, relief for her quick passing, fear of being alone and gratitude for being blessed with years of loving guidance from a woman I so adored. The box of cards, those simple symbols of love, empathy and compassion, held me together that morning when I thought I was falling apart.

This experience deepened my faith in human relationships. Looking back in my life, I can see many missed opportunities where a gentle word, helping hand or small note from me would have made a difference. Empathy understands the resilience of the human spirit. Empathy has the power to take us from despair to hope, from resentment to forgiveness, from fear of our weakness to faith in our potential. Each of us is evolving, and empathy is the inner force that allows us to adapt and change in response to our experiences. Without empathy, we fear our own emotions and become a prisoner of impulsive behavior and rigid control. The "We Care Center" provides children of all ages with a symbolic way to express their empathy for others. This classroom center encourages children to send a note or hand somebody a teddy bear to say, "I care, you are not alone and you can handle these feelings." Expressing empathy is the key to experiencing it. Empathy, like love, is something we "get" only when we are willing to give it to others first. For this reason, it is critical to provide opportunities that encourage children to express empathy to each other.

Empathy: Teaching Children to Care

Empathy is one of the most powerful skills we can develop in regard to discipline. Discipline starts with upset. Upset can be directed outward at others in the form of blame and attack or reflected inward upon one's self. Inward reflection allows our feelings to act as an internal barometer for the wisdom of our choices and leads to personal responsibility. Whether we direct our upset outward or inward is largely determined by the degree of empathy we received from the adults in our lives when we were young. You can determine how much empathy a person has received based on how much they blame others for their upset. Many teachers find themselves exasperated with children's constant blaming of one another: "She started it first!" "I didn't do it, he did." Instead, I invite you to use the amount of blame a child places on others as a diagnostic tool for the amount of empathy you need to offer that child.

My parents did not experience the skill of empathy from their parents as they grew up. As a result, they did not have this skill to share with me. Instead of empathy in upset situations, I was more likely to hear, "You want something to cry about? I'll give you something to cry about." When I would express my anger toward a friend with words like, "I hate Debbie! She's not my friend anymore," their response would be, "That's not a nice way to talk about people," or "You know you like Debbie, she's been your friend for a long time." I did, however, receive sympathy at times, with phrases like, "You poor thing," followed by, "You're okay," and a hug.

Watching how a child responds to other children in distress is one of the quickest ways to determine the type of empathy he or she experiences at home. The same is also true of adults. We can watch how teachers and parents respond to distressed children to gain insight about how they were emotionally treated during upset times while growing up.

Benjamin was three years old. He had trouble separating from his mother when he came to preschool. His screams of anger could be heard throughout the classroom. The teacher left him alone, justifying this by saying, "He's just trying to get attention." His classmates offered different things. Taylor attempted to comfort him by rubbing his back and Jorge brought him the gummy bears from his lunchbox. When Joseph arrived, he darted over, squeezed Benjamin's arm very tightly and said, "Stop it!" This scene reveals a lot about the upbringing of the children and the teacher, and the important role of empathy in healthy socialization. What insights can you gather about the teacher's, Taylor's, Jorge's and Joseph's emotional lives? We could guess that the teacher's intense feelings as a young child were ignored. Taylor's family probably comforts him physically. Jorge's family likely soothes him (and themselves) with food. And Joseph indicates that upset is not tolerated at his home.

Research suggests that empathy is the foundational skill for altruism, prosocial skills, compassion and morality (Salovey & Sluyter, 1997; Staub, 1995). Empathy literally wires and integrates the brain so we can take responsibility for our own behavior. Empathy is the link that integrates thoughts with feelings to create self-reflective understanding. This self-reflective stance allows you to move beyond reactive emotional outbursts that blame and judge others. It allows you to step back from emotional reactivity, see from another's perspective, gain insight into the interaction and respond to others in ways that are life enhancing. With the skill of empathy, you trust life to unfold without fearful attempts to control situations, events and other people. In essence, empathy signals acceptance of things as they are, not as you judge they should be.

The Myths About Empathy

Empathy is about "happying up" children or making them feel better. This notion of empathy is misguided and dangerous. Empathy is not about happiness. It is about brain integration and owning our feelings instead of projecting those feelings onto others. How we respond to children's emotional expressions teaches them how to relate to their emotional selves and to others' emotions. Happying up is another way of saying, "Don't feel what you are feeling, feel happy because if you feel happy, I can be happy. Your true feelings are dangerous and scary."

Empathy is a warm, fuzzy practice that takes precious time away from teaching the skills that foster academic success. This myth justifies our lack of emotional intelligence. It says empathy is a luxury in the classroom. If some teachers come by it naturally, so be it. This notion flies in the face of what we know to be true. Research has shown significant correlations between students' achievement in empathetic understanding and their grade-point averages (Bonner & Aspy, 1984). Program evaluation studies have also shown that schools where classrooms are designed to increase empathy and create caring communities have greater higher-order reading comprehension than comparison schools (Kohn, 1991). Gallo (1989), in a review of research on empathy, states, "The empirical evidence establishes that it is not just moral reasoning, but reasoning in general which benefits from empathetic understanding. Without access to your feelings you lose self-control, higher order thinking skills, and the ability to attend."

Empathy is about labeling feelings. Labeling feelings is one step in the empathy process but not the whole of it. A teacher might hold up two puppets, asking children which puppet is feeling sad and which is feeling angry. Hitler could pass this test, but his empathy skills were nonexistent. Teachers sometimes come to Conscious Discipline workshops saying, "I said to the child, 'You seem angry,' and the child displayed more anger instead of less." Empathy isn't just about labeling feelings, it's about being present with someone (or yourself) so they are able to experience their feelings and the guidance those feelings offer. Empathy also requires a cognitive component that allows us to see from another's point of view. Once you can see the situation from all sides, then and only then is true problem solving possible.

Power of Acceptance

All discipline encounters start with upset. Either the adult is upset with the child, or the child is upset with the adult, a sibling or a friend. Upset occurs when the world is not going our way—when we are resisting what is. From this resistant stance, empathy is impossible. We cannot simultaneously see from another person's point of view and attempt to make the world go our way. Empathy requires the power of acceptance, which states, "The moment is as it is." Without accepting what is, we become convinced our perception is the only one and the right one, and empathy dies. Acceptance requires us to surrender our self-centered view of the world in order to participate fully in another person's experience. It requires us to make a conscious choice to set aside biases, judgments and theories about how the moment should be. We must relinquish the need to judge an event as good or bad and accept that it "is." Without using the power of acceptance, we tend to do one of the following:

We listen to someone's explanation with our mind already made up about what really happened. You have a fight with your coworker and you're thinking, "He can talk all he wants. I know exactly what happened and what was said. It's no use for him to try to justify his way out of this one." We start rehearsing our defense or response in our head without completely listening to the situation. A friend begins talking about her son and you immediately think, "Here she goes, talking about Brett again. I've heard all this before," and prepare in your mind to share a story from your life. Without the power of acceptance, we basically leave the current moment and go into our heads. Our presence with the other person is halfhearted. We might look like we're listening—nodding and smiling or furrowing our brow at the appropriate times—but we've secretly let our minds wander. We are focused on our experience, not that of the person speaking. If we wish to offer empathy, we must consciously choose to be present, listen to the other person, grasp his or her experience and see from their point of view.

Empathy asks us to be willing to give up our thoughts and feelings temporarily in order to more accurately understand those of others. It asks us to quiet our own minds so we can listen from our hearts instead of our heads. It is the way we instill a soothing internal voice that says, "All is well, you can handle this," for our children. Most of us have a different internal voice. It says, "You stupid idiot, you screwed up again," or something equally critical. Is your inner voice an optimistic, supportive, positive voice or a censoring, scolding, humiliating one? By choosing empathy, we give the next generation the gift of a supportive inner voice to manage their inner world peacefully and external conflicts with grace.

The We Care Center is the structure in your classroom that represents your commitment to acceptance and creating an empathetic environment for children. It lets the moment be as it is, while offering children the opportunity to respond to the moment from their hearts. This center grows seeds of empathy for yourself and for the children in your care. When you choose to create an empathetic environment, you help optimize the neural plasticity in students' brains, allowing all children to learn more and heal from past hurts.

> Dear merceline
> we miss you and we are sorry you made the wrong choices we hope you make better ones and think before saying samthing once again we miss you come back, and please don't be suspended anymore we need you in our class family. It's not the same when you are not here. The class is falling apart. Come and help us build it up Again.
>
> Sincerly class

Mrs. Sandusky's kindergarten classroom has an extensive We Care Center. It consists of a mailbox for each child and a writing center. The children love writing and drawing notes of empathy, compassion and celebration. Mrs. Sandusky has been incorporating this center into her classroom for several years. One year, the children decided to make cards for School Family members and their home families whenever someone was sick. When Morgan's aunt was in the hospital for surgery, many of the students made cards for her. Morgan took the cards home and her mom delivered them to the hospital. Morgan's aunt sent a thank-you note to the class, impressed that the children were learning to care for others at such a young age. The aunt was a high school teacher, and after experiencing the healing power of empathy firsthand, she decided to create a We Care Center in her high school English classes. At the end of the year, she sent the following note to Mrs. Sandusky:

> *Thank you so much for opening my eyes to the power of a simple note. I implemented the idea into my English classes at high school. This year one of our students was killed in a car accident. The student driving the car felt so guilty that he was contemplating suicide. He shared this with us at the end of the year, and told how the notes of empathy kept him from following through on his plan. Amazing how something so simple is so powerful. My niece Morgan loved your class and loves school, so thank you.*

Power of acceptance: The moment is as it is
Skill: Empathy
Structure: We Care Center
Value: Compassion

Opportunities for using the We Care Center occur daily and unexpectedly. We need only to recognize them. To help children become conscious of each other's need for empathy, we must teach them the language of emotions. The language of emotions is nonverbal; our inner emotional states are reflected in our bodies. Until age six or seven, children wear their emotions on their sleeves. What you see is what you get. It's easy for adults to see that four-year-old Shane is feeling sad or that his friend Cameron is feeling angry. By noticing a child's nonverbal language with empathy, you teach all the children in the classroom to do the same. You might say, "Shane, your head is down, your shoulders are rounded and your face is going like this (demonstrate by mirroring). Your body is telling me you might be feeling sad this morning." Shane might respond, "I want my mommy." This moment helps Shane to become self-aware and teaches the class how to read body language. It teaches everyone that this type of body language likely means Shane is experiencing sadness and that this particular sadness is because he misses his mother.

> **Decoding the language of emotions**
>
> Describe a child's body language without judgment, physically mirror it to build body awareness, and then make an educated guess about the emotion the child is feeling. Use a tone that invites the child to correct or refine the label you've used for the emotion. Naming the emotion raises the whole classroom's emotional awareness and empowers them to offer empathy to each other.

Older children are more like us: They have become better at hiding their true feelings. We must be more observant to read their subtle nonverbal language. Older children are also increasingly verbal in expressing their feelings, which is often labeled as talking back, disrespect and sassiness. Our response to inappropriate verbal expressions like these creates a teaching moment. If Anthony says, "This is stupid. I hate math," your response will teach the whole class a skill. If you respond with empathy, "You seem frustrated—some of those math problems are tough," then you teach Anthony and others to decode the world of feelings. Everyone learns that name-calling and "hate" are code words for frustration. Eventually, Anthony and others will be able to recognize their own frustration, raise their hands and say, "Mr. Clark, can you help me? I don't understand this math and I feel so frustrated I can't think straight." On the other hand, if your response lacks empathy, it might sound like, "Don't sass me. Finish your math or you'll end up with another D." What lesson have you taught Anthony and the class? Are you scaffolding an inner voice of judgment or of emotional intelligence for your students? The We Care Center is the structure for the empathy process; a teacher capitalizing on teaching moments is the foundation for that structure.

As we use children's feeling states as positive teaching moments, we draw attention to the emotional world. We model ways to empathize with the feelings of others. Empathy is an innate skill that begins early in life, as one toddler brings another her special blanket when he cries. The We Care Center extends and supports this natural process. It encourages children to begin noticing the emotional states of others and provides them with a way of responding. While observing a preschool classroom, I saw a memorable scene. It was circle time, and the teacher was organized and ready. They were singing "Johnny Works with Hammers." One little girl was not participating, but her body language clearly said, "It's been a hard morning." A boy in the class noticed her and retrieved the We Care bag as the class continued to sing. The teacher nodded to him as if to say, "Yes, you know what to do." The bag contained a little blanket, a teddy bear, a box of bandages, a star necklace and a variety of stickers. While the class continued to sing, he carried the bag over to the forlorn girl, held it in front of her and said, "Would anything in here help?" The little girl reached in and took the teddy bear, hugging it to her chest. She held it tightly for the rest of circle time. At her worktable, she tucked it under her arm so she could color. Finally, around lunchtime, she placed it back in the We Care bag and continued her day.

I have seen similar actions in older classrooms. In these classrooms, children write cards and notes that say, "I see you, I hear you and you are not alone," in many creative ways. I have seen students use the We Care Center to write rap lyrics for a frightened classmate who was scheduled to have his tonsils removed or to make a collage in support of a child's sadness after losing her golden retriever, and I've read many notes written to encourage a friend struggling with a particular school subject. These expressions help students become conscious of each other, see through the eyes of acceptance and offer empathy for others' emotions.

E = Environmental Structure: We Care Center

The We Care Center is a creative center where children express their caring for others. It is a concrete way for children to offer empathy to one another in support of their natural inclination toward thoughtfulness.

Purpose: The We Care Center provides children with a symbolic way of expressing empathy for others. The symbolic form will vary depending on the age and literacy of the children. The We Care Center accomplishes the following objectives in your classroom:

1. It allows children to have empathetic personal interactions. Children learn empathy through their own experience with how it helps them and others transition from difficult emotions to feelings of acceptance and problem solving.

2. It gives children the opportunity to generate ideas and provides ways to carry out empathetic responses.
3. It strengthens connections for children, especially those who have difficulty managing emotions.

How to set up a We Care Center: How you decide to design your We Care Center depends on the developmental age of the children. As you create this center, think about your students' talents and abilities and provide them with tools to express themselves accordingly.

At any age level, you may wish to include the We Care Person or the We Care Committee in your School Family job list. This child (or group of children) is in charge of writing notes or deciding how to express empathy to School Family members. Even if you do use this job, keep the We Care Center open for all class members who would like to extend their caring to others. The We Care Person or Committee would simply be most directly in charge of it.

The youngest children will use a large decorative gift bag or basket labeled "We Care." Place bandages, a small blanket, a stuffed animal, a stuffed heart, heart-shaped or star-shaped glasses, heart-shaped stickers and tissues in the bag or basket. Young children will express care by offering these comforting items to each other in times of distress.

Children who are just beginning to write will use a We Care bag plus a way to create messages and a message delivery system. First, find ways to incorporate writing thoughtful messages into your existing writing center and lessons. Then create a We Care Center that contains the following items:

- **Paper, pencil, marker, crayons**
- **Commercial greeting cards (both blank and with preprinted messages)**
- **Prewritten sentence strips so beginning writers can copy the words onto their own cards**
- **Stickers, stamps and stamp pads**
- **Thank you notepaper and other stationery**
- **Tape, glue, scissors, stapler**
- **We Care Cards featuring Shubert and his friends, printed from the *We Care* CDrom from www.ConsciousDiscipline.com**

Finally, create individual mailboxes for each child and a common mail area or space on a bulletin board where children can pick up and deliver their We Care notes.

Older children will benefit from the types of We Care items described above, as well as computer-driven We Care projects. Mass retailers have a variety of inexpensive software that allows you to create and print your own cards. If you have a web connection, there are  also many free online card-making websites to print from and send e-cards through. Older children may also wish to express themselves through music, poetry, plays and in other ways, as shown in Coco's story:

Coco was a fifth grader in Mr. Garcia's class. A drunk driver killed her brother in an automobile accident. Mr. Garcia's School Family wanted to reach out to their classmate to let her know they care. During a class meeting, Mr. Garcia encouraged the students to brainstorm ways to express empathy for Coco's family. They came up with the following ideas:

- **Donate money for flowers**
- **Attend the funeral**
- **Raise money for Mothers Against Drunk Driving (MADD)**
- **Write notes and put them in a book for Coco**
- **Have someone keep track of the classwork and help her catch up**
- **Agree to set up two Safe Places in case Coco wanted to stay in the Safe Place for long periods of time**

The class voted and decided they wanted to raise money for MADD and attend the funeral. They worked with the school principal to make and sell lunch to the teachers on Friday to raise funds. They attended the funeral and sat together to send Coco the message, "We are with you and we care about you." This fifth-grade class showed their empathy and compassion in some very grown-up ways, and they did it *themselves*.

How to introduce the We Care Center:

You can introduce the We Care Center by teaching it as a lesson or by teaching it when an opportunity for empathy arises. The experiences and concepts for the We Care Center will evolve over the course of the year as children become more conscious and confident in their ability to offer empathy.

If you introduce the concept as a lesson, the book *Shubert's Helpful Day* is a wonderful beginning. In the book, Lucinda is upset and the ant triplets bring over the We Care bag to see what, if anything, would be helpful. After reading the book, brainstorm items the class would like include in their We Care Center. Next, role-play how the We Care Center can be utilized, using common situations that arise in your classroom. Examples include when someone is disappointed because he didn't get another turn or when something sad has happened, such as sickness or loss. Invite children to choose a scenario, then coach them to respond in helpful, empathetic ways.

If you introduce the center when a teaching moment naturally occurs, begin by offering empathy to the child who is experiencing a difficult emotion. Then offer the moment to the class as an opportunity to be helpful. You might say, "Class, Jada is having a tough morning. In our School Family, we have a way to show others that we care about them." Then introduce your We Care Center and its components.

Using the existing situation, provide children with the opportunity to respond to the child's difficult moment by having them draw a picture or write a note for the child right then and there. Broaden their understanding by offering additional examples of times when empathy is helpful and additional ways they can show they care. Encourage children to view empathy from different perspectives. For example, responding with genuine empathy may be more difficult when you are excited about winning and someone else is sad because she lost.

Conduct a brainstorming activity like drawing a heart on chart paper with the words "We Care" and asking for ways children might show each other they care. The list will help you create a set of prewritten sentence strips for early readers and writers. The following are some possible prewritten messages:

"We miss you!"	"Thank you for _____."
"Get well soon."	"I love you!"
"Happy Birthday!"	"I'm sorry."
"Congratulations!"	"Way to go!"
"We will miss you."	"Good luck!"

During group time, create class cards as a model for writing letters. As the weeks go by, incorporate the We Care Center into your current language arts lessons. If you are focusing on punctuation, adjectives or a certain spelling word list, design a We Care activity that practices those lessons.

As the year progresses, continue to notice children's inner states, offer empathy to them and extend this learning to the class. Say things like, "Class, Shane is having a hard time this afternoon. What do you think we could do to help him?" Statements like this will reaffirm the empathy skills you strive to teach.

A = Activities

General Activities — All Ages

Shubert's Helpful Day

Read *Shubert's Helpful Day*, by Dr. Becky Bailey, and complete the Shubert worksheet for your age group, available at www.ConsciousDiscipline.com

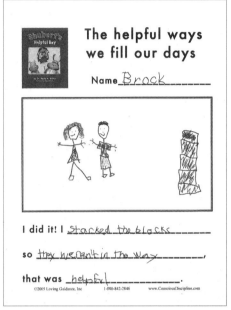

Wish Well Program

As part of your morning circle or meeting, provide time for children to request well wishes. After completing your absent student ritual, ask, "Would anyone like us to send well wishes to someone?" Listen as children share, and then send well wishes or sing the "Wish Well" song from *It Starts in the Heart*. Taking the time to listen to their concerns first thing in the morning helps students focus better throughout the day. The steps for wishing well are:

1. S.T.A.R.
2. Put your hands on your heart.
3. Close your eyes and picture something precious in your mind.
4. Open your arms and send that precious feeling to those around you.

General Activities — Younger

The Caring Quilt

Read *The Kindness Quilt* by Nancy Elizabeth Wallace. After reading the book, create a School Family caring quilt. Ask children to report ways they showed care for others. Record this list on chart paper for a week to give each child the opportunity to contribute. Then have the children illustrate

Chapter 14: We Care Center

and write (or take dictation) about their kind act on an eight-inch square of white construction paper. Mount the squares on 9" by 9" colored paper or wallpaper samples, then assemble them together to look like a quilt.

The Hating Book
In this story, by Charlotte Zolotow, two friends have a misunderstanding. Each girl has a different perspective. Read the story and then pass out cards that have either a one or a two on it. Ask all the "ones" to play the part of the first girl and the "twos" will play the second girl. Give each student three speech bubbles. Reread the first conflict that happens in the book. Have both the ones and the twos write how they feel in the situations. Then have the ones make a circle facing outward and the twos make a circle facing inward. Each discusses his/her point of view for the situation, then adds, "If it were me, I would want _____ to help me feel better."

Do You See What I See?
Do You See What I See is an exercise in perspective-taking. There are two sides to every story! Before school starts, place an unusual item in a box (this item should have different-looking sides). Tell children that every situation that occurs in the classroom will have at least two sides to it because each person sees the situation a little bit differently. Have children form a circle around the box. Stand in the center of the circle, open the box and display the item. Ask the students to describe what they see from wherever they stand. Each group/student will see something different. None of these is right or wrong, just different. Have the group discuss other situations where they may see things differently than someone else. Acknowledging another person's unique perspective is key to empathy.

Problem Box
Every day, students come to school with problems that are tough to handle, presenting numerous opportunities to use the We Care Center. It can also be helpful to establish a "problem box" next to your We Care Center. The problem box is where students keep their problems so they can continue with their classwork. They can take their problems from the box to think about them at various times during the day, or they can choose to leave them there all day. When a student enters the class upset, ask him to write or draw something representing the situation and his emotions. When the writing or drawing is done, it goes into the problem box.

I Wish You Well

Music & Movement — All Ages

Wishing well is one of the most powerful tools in your empathy tool kit. You will want your We Care Center to include an item (like a plush heart) that signifies wishing well. Explain that wishing well is something you can do at any time, from any place, in order to show someone you care. Play the song, "I Wish You Well" on *It Starts in the Heart* and practice wishing well. Many teachers also incorporate a clip of this song in their morning absent-child and wish-well rituals daily.

Guess What That Face Is Saying

Class-Made Books — Younger

This book helps young children decode the world of emotions, a key factor to offering empathy. To prepare to make this book, have the children pair up with two students per mirror. One child will hold the mirror while the other practices making different feeling faces. Then they will switch so each child has a turn. This is difficult for young children so it is helpful to play "Make Your Face Match Mine," and have the children try to match their faces to yours for different emotions. Happy, sad, excited, scared, frustrated, disappointed and mad are the core emotions to practice.

Next, have each child make a feeling face, take several pictures of each child, print them out and attach them to pages that say, "See (child's name)'s face. Her face is saying, 'I feel (emotion).' " You will have duplicate feeling photos, but try to show as many emotions as possible.

Finally, help children identify ways others can show they care by filling in the blanks, "When I feel (emotion), the (item) from the We Care bag lets me know you care."

Sometimes I Feel Angry

Class-Made Books — Older

Ask children to draw a picture of how their face looks when they feel angry or sad. On a separate page, have them write a paragraph about a time they felt this way. Then have them write a paragraph about "When I feel that way, I want _____." Coach them to include items that are in the We Care Center. Bind the pages together so each child's paragraph faces his/her picture. Put the book in the We Care Center to use as a resource for what each child wants when feeling upset.

C = Commitment

I am willing to consciously focus on offering empathy in my classroom, with my colleagues and at home with my family. I will do this by choosing to be present, reducing judgments, quieting "should be" messages and honoring the other person's unique experiences. I will begin this process by doing the following (check the tasks you commit to):

___I will implement a We Care Center in my classroom that consists of diverse, age-appropriate ways for children to express caring.

___I will read *Shubert's Helpful Day* to my students.

___I will lead a conversation about empathy by sharing a time when I was upset or anxious and how loved ones empathy.

___I will ask others to share as well.

___I will build awareness by noticing at least one child's nonverbal language daily by saying things like, "Jada, your arms are like this (mirroring) and your eyes are like this (mirroring). You seem sad?"

___I will incorporate academic lessons into the creation of We Care cards (or other activities) once a week.

Signature _____   *Date* _____

H = Helpful Resources

Music — All Ages

It Starts in the Heart by Jack Hartmann and Dr. Becky Bailey
Songs: "I Wish You Well," "Caring Friends"

Kindness Counts by Dr. Becky Bailey and Mr. Al
Songs: "Looking for Kindness," "Love Is a Circle"

Brain Boogie Boosters by Dr. Becky Bailey and The Learning Station
Songs: "You Are Heart," "Friends Connect"

I Will Be Your Friend: Songs and Activities for Young Peacemakers by Teaching Tolerance
Songs: "Courage," "What Do I Do?"

Hello World by Red Grammer
Songs: "I Want You to Listen," "When I Get a Feeling"

Getting to Know Myself by Hap Palmer
Songs: "Feelings," "What Do People Do?," "Be My Friend"

Literature — All Ages

Shubert's Helpful Day by **Dr. Becky Bailey.** Lucinda is having a difficult day. Shubert's class shows they care by offering her items from the We Care bag. Once Lucinda feels calm, they are then able to help solve the problem together.

Shubert's New Friend by **Dr. Becky Bailey.** Spencer is a new student, and he's not what the classroom was expecting! Watch as Shubert's School Family learns to see from another's perspective.

Feelings by **Aliki** provides delightful images and musings about a variety of feelings.

On Monday When It Rained by **Cherryl Kachenmeister.** Emphatic photos and a simple story help children identify and relate to feelings such as proud, scared, lonely and excited.

***Say Something* by Peggy Moss** follows a school-age girl who silently watches bullying in her school until she becomes one of those being teased. A great story of a young person learning to empathize with others.

Literature — Younger

***Dear Daisy, Get Well Soon* by Maggie Smith.** Peter offers Daisy his stuffed animals to help her feel better. Daisy is delighted as the animals come to life!

***Alexander and the Terrible, Horrible, No Good, Very Bad Day* by Judith Viorst.** Everything goes wrong for Alexander in this book. A perfect jumping-off point for a class discussion about how to show you care when someone's having a very bad day.

***Because of You* by B. G. Hennessy** showcases the helpful and caring things children do and relates how "small and precious" acts at home relate to a more peaceful world.

Literature — Older

***The Hating Book* by Charlotte Zolotow.** Two friends are at odds when one ignores the other in this book about friendship and different perspectives.

Additional Aids

We Care CDrom from www.ConsciousDiscipline.com
Shubert Worksheets. Free download at www.ConsciousDiscipline.com

If someone has a sick mommy or daddy, brother or sister, friend or relative they tell us. We listen and do what we can to help. We can wish them well or make them a card in the "We Care" center.

Teacher Tip:

Tie your literacy lessons into the making of we care cards. This adds emotional meaning to the writing process.

Chapter 15

Class Meetings

Years ago, I was visiting a kindergarten classroom. The teacher was beside herself from the constant chaos whenever the class left their room. Mrs. Lutman's class had a strange location in the school. In order to get from her room to the lunchroom, media center or art room, they had to walk through the auditorium. This created impulse challenges for a number of children who preferred to walk up the stairs and across the stage instead of walking in front of the stage as Mrs. Lutman had instructed. When I arrived, she told me, "I've tried everything with these children and nothing has worked." Since this was a chronic problem, I suggested a Class Meeting. She agreed, saying, "At this point, I will try anything."

We conducted the Class Meeting together so I could assist in coaching the critical pieces of the process. We started the meeting by learning a new song, "It's time to solve some problems, some problems, some problems. It's time to solve some problems, let's do it right now" (sung to the tune of "Have You Ever Seen a Lassie?"). I then proceeded with the Class Meeting process described in this chapter. When we got to the point of brainstorming solutions, one boy leapt to his feet, as if he were Einstein discovering the theory of relativity, and announced we could put a pillow from the Safe Place on the auditorium steps to remind everyone to walk in front of the stage. The teacher looked at me and rolled her eyes as if to say, "This is the biggest waste of time I've every witnessed." I must admit I thought the solution was a bit strange, but I decided to trust the process and the children. We decided as a class to go with the idea. We created a new job called the "Pillow Carrier" and placed it on the Job Board. It worked like a charm. The teacher was dumbfounded at first, but quickly became an advocate for all the wonderful things that can be achieved when power is shared in the classroom.

Consequences

For many educators, the term *consequences* has a unique and somewhat distorted meaning. A consequence is traditionally something a teacher devises and delivers to students for rule infractions. Picking up on this distorted definition, several authors have used clarifying terms and definitions such as logical consequences, which was conceived to help teachers and parents pull away from our tendency to punish. With logical consequences, the "something" we devise is related to the infraction and reasonable in terms of the actions taken and discomfort felt. Logical consequences are basically "make the time fit the crime" thinking.

Conscious Discipline asks you to go back to a more basic concept of consequences as it relates to the world of cause and effect. All thoughts, feelings and actions have an inherent consequence. We do not have to come up with "something" as a consequence; we just need to become conscious of the impact of our choices. On the most basic level, cause and consequence are inseparable. Consequences are not invented by teachers but are part of the simple, universal principle of cause and effect. Conscious Discipline utilizes consequences in just this manner. The key is simply to open our eyes (and the children's) to the consequences already occurring naturally.

Everyone reading this book has experienced the consequences of his or her actions. We have too much to drink or eat, too much shopping or too much exertion, and feel the consequences of our over-indulgence. In fact, most of us have experienced the same over-indulgence and its consequence more than once. However, there are also times when we have learned from the consequences of our actions. Take a moment and reflect on those times. What was different? What helped you learn from the consequences of your actions instead of repeating them? In my life, I have noticed the following: If I judge and therefore punish others or myself for my choices, I tend to repeat the mistake. If I reflect on the impact of my actions, I tend to learn. If I blame my actions on circumstances, situations

> There are no consequences without consciousness.

or people, I tend to repeat them. If I take ownership of my actions, regardless of the cir-

Reflection	Judgment
Ownership of choices = learn from mistakes and change	Blame choices on others = punish and repeat same choices again

cumstances or people involved, I learn from my mistakes. The simple conclusion I've come to is that for consequences to be effective, we need to help children learn to take ownership of their thoughts, feelings and actions and teach them to reflect on their choices instead of blaming others. Both of these are higher-level thinking skills that are culturally and socially determined. We can teach children to blame and project or to take ownership and reflect. The choice is ours.

In Middle School Family: LOTS of counseling!

In Conscious Discipline, we think in terms of three types of consequences. These three types, which are discussed in depth in the *Conscious Discipline* book, are natural consequences, imposed consequences and problem solving (Bailey, 2000).

Most people do not think of problem solving as a consequence to a life experience. Yet it is the most powerful consequence. To help you understand, imagine you find yourself with a flat tire on the side of the road. The consequence of this event is problem solving. You must discern the extent of the problem, explore options, make a plan, carry it out and reflect on its outcome for further revisions or actions. Without this type of consequence, we would be left with the natural consequence of being stuck on the side of the road. Or we would find ourselves at the mercy of consequences imposed by those who pass by. (If the imposed consequences were like the ones used in many classrooms, you might hear, "I'm going to turn your green card to red for lack of preparation.")

A successfully lived life, for the most part, is a series of problem-solving adventures. Every conscious moment asks us to reflect on our actions. Are our choices moving us closer to our desired goals or distancing us from them? If we are moving away from our goals, what can we do to get back on track? This requires us to set goals, prioritize and work toward them. Class Meetings are designed on this same pattern. They help a class set goals together, meet and evaluate those goals and stand by their commitment to those goals despite distractions and temptations. Therefore, students utilize and develop their prefrontal lobes during Class Meetings.

Meta-cognition!

Class Meetings:

1. Facilitate children's prefrontal lobe development, which is essential for goal achievement for the rest of their lives
2. Replicate the democratic process that's essential for active participation in a democratic society
3. Help us reflect on our intention, the most powerful of all energies

The Development of the Prefrontal Lobes

The prefrontal lobes are the best-connected system of the brain and are the system responsible for high-level functions, often called "executive skills." These executive skills are essential for reflecting on our choices and taking ownership of them. If children are to learn from the consequence of their actions, their prefrontal lobes must be activated. The prefrontal lobes are directly interconnected with every other functional system in the brain and, as such, can directly manage our lower-thinking systems (Goldberg, 2001). The prefrontal lobes are often called the CEO of the brain for this reason. Think of a large company like Coca-Cola or Microsoft. Its CEO must have a certain set of skills to manage the organization for success. He or she must be able to communicate effectively with all departments, be organized, set goals, make plans, prioritize, manage time effectively, maintain focused attention despite distraction, be flexible enough to shift attention when required, problem solve, empathically understand employees' needs, and possess the impulse and emotional control to weather economic challenges as well as the ability to reflect and change course if needed. All these skills can be boiled down to one core statement: the CEO must be able to make goals and achieve them. Think about how many times you've set a goal to lose weight, exercise more or maintain greater emotional control in challenging situations. How often have you been distracted from these goals by holiday parties, time restrictions, challenging teenagers at home or difficult children at school?

We need a strong set of executive skills to live a successful life. Such skills can liberate us from past conditioned habits, help us hold strongly to our goals in the face of temptation and empower us to make mindful choices. These skills allow us to move beyond the "do what I say, not what I do" syndrome that plagues our homes and schools. In my case, it allows me to be "Becky"—not a set of preprogrammed, conditioned habits and reactions from my upbringing, but the Becky I choose to be in this moment.

324 *Creating the School Family*

In school, we give students a problem and they must find the correct answer. Usually, the question is as clear-cut as two plus two and only one correct answer exists. Most real-life situations, however, are inherently ambiguous. The answer is indefinite and so is the question, such as, "What does 'the pursuit of happiness' mean?" The pursuit could be different for each individual, and it could mean different things to each individual at different times in his life. My own definition of happiness and how to achieve it has changed a million times in the course of my life. (Currently, I perceive happiness to be a state of mind I choose rather than something I achieve through relationships or status.) Most decisions we make and problems we solve do not contain one inherently correct answer. A child might be asking herself, "How to get a turn on a swing if Juliana refuses to leave?" or "Why do those boys keep calling me 'poop head' and what can I do so they'll leave me alone?" Our decisions at life moments like these are a complex interplay between the situation, our fears, our history with similar events, the intensity of our desires and our unique developmental level. The prefrontal lobes are essential to this complex problem-solving process. Development depends on the following:

- Children conducting problem solving in a social setting
- Adults lending their prefrontal lobes to children instead of punishing them for a lack of executive skills
- Adults scaffolding the executive skills for children until their emerging skills are internalized
- Adults understanding the importance of and developmental trends of prefrontal lobe development
- Children having the opportunity for adequate amounts of rich play

The current trends of removing art, music and play, advancing the curriculum (so we now teach first-grade skills in kindergarten), and narrowing the scope of learning to match what will be tested are creating a crisis in our educational system. This situation, coupled with a culture that's moving from face-to-face connection to digital tracking of each other's activities, from playful social interactions to team competition, and from playing together to playing video games is forcing this crisis toward a boiling point. Add to the mix more failed marriages than successful ones, increasingly busy parents and 12 million children under the age of five spending 40 hours a week in child care (when research clearly states that anything over 30 hours is counterproductive to development), we can clearly see why an increasing number of children enter school less able to self-regulate (NICHD, 2003, 2006). We

> ### A TOP WIFE Makes Good Tea
>
> **Researchers and theorists have attempted to define prefrontal lobe skills, and there are many variations of the exact list of skills considered "executive." I choose to use the skills represented by the acronym phrase, "A TOP WIFE Makes Good Tea."**
>
> **A** = _A_ttention: *The ability to sustain attention in spite of distractibility, boredom or fatigue.*
>
> **T** = _T_ime Management: *The capacity to estimate how much time one has, how to allocate it, and how to stay within time limits and deadlines.*
>
> **O** = _O_rganization: *The ability to create and maintain systems to keep track of information or materials.*
>
> **P** = _P_rioritization: *The ability to see what is most important and make a plan to accomplish it.*
>
> **W** = _W_orking Memory: *The ability to hold information in memory while performing complex tasks. The ability to draw on past experiences and learning, apply it to the situation at hand, and use it to project into the future.*
>
> **I** = _I_mpulse Control: *The capacity to think before you act, allowing you to evaluate a situation and how your behavior might impact it.*
>
> **F** = _F_lexibility: *The ability to revise plans in the face of obstacles, setbacks, new information or mistakes, and to adapt to changing conditions.*
>
> **E** = _E_mpathy and Emotional Control: *The ability to manage emotions to achieve goals, complete tasks, direct behavior and see from another's point of view.*
>
> **M** = _M_etacognition: *The ability to step back and take a bird's eye view of yourself in a situation, to observe yourself (reflect), self-monitor and self-evaluate.*
>
> **G** = _G_oal Achievement: *The capacity to have a goal and follow through to completion.*
>
> **T** = _T_ask Initiation: *The ability to begin projects without undue procrastination in an efficient and timely fashion.* (Dawson & Guare, 2009; Goldberg, 2001; Meltzer, 2007)

are systematically sabotaging the development of our children's prefrontal lobes, which will lead to the inability to regulate their own thoughts, feelings and behaviors, to set and achieve goals and to problem solve.

A culture, whether in schools, homes or communities, holds people accountable to certain rules. We are held responsible for certain actions and not for others. For example, vomiting in public from being drunk is a no-no, while vomiting following a heat stroke is understood. A traffic accident caused by cell phone texting is punished, while a traffic accident caused by a heart attack is excused. We are expected to be able to control ourselves under most situations, but impulse control requires more than just being conscious of right and wrong. It involves the ability to anticipate the consequences of our actions, to decide if the action is appropriate and to choose between action and non-action. For most of us, this requires us to squelch a conditioned response like yelling at children who fail to clean up in favor of a wiser choice, like offering them the option to start cleaning with the trucks or the blocks. This ability to control oneself cognitively (choosing thoughts that are helpful), emotionally (changing one's internal state from upset to calm) and physically (choosing helpful actions) is the cornerstone of a well-developed prefrontal lobe. Babies do not enter the world with these skills. It takes 24 years for the prefrontal lobes to mature, and this maturity largely depends on the quality of our social interactions.

This wonderful ability to respond consciously instead of react unconsciously to what life offers makes us different from all other animals. The tools to wisely handle any situation we encounter are ours to claim, we just need to develop them in ourselves and in our children. Class Meetings are one of many activities and structures in Conscious Discipline that foster the development of children's executive skills.

There is a clear connection between the executive skills and what is typically referred to as "discipline problems." Think of all the time you spend helping children focus their attention: *"Tylor, put down the markers and focus on your math. Gianna, it's Brandon's turn to answer the problem, give him your full attention. Tylor, it's time to clean up. Stop drawing and put those markers away. Tylor! What did I tell you? Do you want to use the markers tomorrow? Then put them away NOW!"*

Think of all the time you spend helping children manage their time: *"Boys and girls, you have five more minutes before clean-up time. I am not going to tell you again. It's time for recess, you need to have finished cleaning up and be sitting on the carpet. If the class is not ready by the time I count to three, then we will just have to miss recess! 1-2-"*

Think of all the time you help children organize themselves and their environment: *"Leo, the toy cars go in the tub marked 'Cars.' Pick them up out of the dollhouse and put them in the toy car tub. Gianna, write your homework into your planner. Did you write it down? No, you did not. Now, what books do you need to take home to complete the assignment? Where are they? Are they in your backpack? No, they are not."*

Think of all the time you help children with working memory: *"It is time to line up for lunch. If you brought lunch, remember to carry it. Ready? Push in your chairs, and table one, line up. Brandon, you are table two, not table one. Jocelyn, where is your lunch box?"*

Think of the all the time you help children with impulse control: *"Maylie, no hitting! Jackson is trying to help you put away the cars. Jon, is name calling helpful or hurtful? I have had it with you two; just leave the cars and go down to Mr. Mcintyre's office. Move it, boys!"*

Missing or emerging executive skills are at the root of what we call "discipline problems." Historically and sadly, children are punished for not having these skills at certain ages. I have seen teachers of four-year-olds lose their composure over children who lack the executive skill of flexibility. Four-year-olds who lack flexibility (a prefrontal lobe skill) may fixate on the one red marker another child has and refuse to use an identical red marker sitting unused in the bin. We can choose to see this as a misbehaving child or as a child who needs help to learn the executive skill of flexibility.

> **Teacher Tip:**
>
> For classroom management to be effective, teachers must lend their prefrontal lobes to children. Look again at the list of executive skills. Some of the skills on the list will be your strong suits, and some will be weak ones. We cannot lend skills we do not possess. For this reason, every structure in this book scaffolds the child's developing and emerging prefrontal lobes. The structures aid us in providing the "external" prefrontal lobes children require for optimal development. This scaffolding is especially important for Class Meetings. The Class Meeting creates a specific process and tone that empowers children to share power, successfully solve a problem and learn the executive skills needed for healthy problem solving throughout life.

I have seen fifth-grade teachers assign homework without scaffolding the executive skills needed to complete the endeavor. Homework requires almost all executive skills. Children must focus their attention on the goal, be able to initiate the task at night, organize their work into a system, remember the steps needed for the work required, prioritize and stick with it despite obstacles and frustrations. We are asking pre-teens to use every executive skill in the arsenal, yet these skills don't mature until age 24! This means that homework success is largely dependent on parents lending their prefrontal lobes to their children. Parents and teachers must assist children with study skills in order for them to be successful in the short term and in order for them to develop healthy prefrontal lobes for future success.

Teachers must lend their prefrontal lobes to children every minute of every day in order to scaffold the development of the child's executive skills. Moving students' clips, changing the color of their cards from green to red or giving out referrals does nothing to promote the development of executive skills; it solidifies lower-level unconscious skills that will be habitually repeated. Conscious Discipline asks teachers to shift from a traditional, unspoken task of making children behave to a new enlightened vision of helping children be successful. Instead of asking ourselves, "What will get/make this child do _____?" we must ask a new question: "What will help this child more likely be successful at _____?" We can look at the list of executive skills and see where the child needs scaffolding. By approaching classroom management in this fashion, we are constantly supporting the encouraging culture of our School Family and creating a culture that focuses on the expectation, scaffolds success in reaching the expectation and celebrates its accomplishment.

Class Meetings and Democracy

Conscious Discipline re-creates the experience of a democracy within the classroom. The cornerstone of democracy and a healthy family is shared power. The beginning process of governance begins with the Safekeeper job description: My job is to keep you safe and your job is to help keep it safe (Chapter 5). By doing such, the classroom remains based on equality for all. This job description begins a discussion about what safety and helpfulness look like, sound like and feel like. It leads into a general list of ways you want your class to be (Chapter 7). From that list of desires, you can generate the class agreements that will be the general guiding principles to govern the class. These guiding principles foster the daily commitments the children will make during the Brain Smart Start each morning (Chapter 8).

In a School Family classroom culture as I've described it, rules and consequences emerge as needed. A similar process was conducted by the founding fathers of the United States. The Declaration of Independence and the Constitution of the United States are the two most important documents in our nation's history. It has been said that the Declaration was the promise and the Constitution was the fulfillment. It's similar in a Conscious Discipline classroom. The Safekeeper job is the promise and the agreements generated during Class Meetings are the fulfillment of that promise.

Our nation's core documents empower us to create new state and federal laws as the need arises. Our laws change as the culture changes. For example, Jessica's Law is the informal name given to a Florida law that punishes sex offenders and reduces their opportunity to re-offend. This law was not on the books back in 1792 because it was not needed. It became a rule with consequences in 2005 in Florida, and later in 42 additional states, in order to meet a growing need to address the problem of sex offenders. Our governing documents' ability to change is considered one of their greatest strengths.

5th Rule

Most schools generally start off each year with a set of written rules and consequences, rather than inviting children to participate in the democratic process. The School Family culture, on the other hand, creates a spiral of perpetual growth and prepares children to live in a democracy. Democracy, after all, means to self-govern. It requires we contribute to and are responsible for our own decision making. Most children experience school as an autocratic system of governance, with power based on the roles of the members, a "dominant power" culture (Chapter 1) that is consistent with the outdated factory model of education. Freedom is sacrificed for conformity. Freedom is honored in a democratic system, yet freedom alone can lead to chaos, tyranny and entitlement. Freedom must be balanced by responsibility, guidance and compassion so each person can adapt to the optimal requirements of each situation. The School Family culture gives freedom a context of connection, guidance and responsibility to create a complete and successful system of governance and classroom management. The School Family's democratic process happens at Class Meetings.

The Power of Intention

Have you ever started humming or singing a tune and the person you're with says, "I was just singing that same song in my head"? As a mother, have you ever woken up just before your baby started to cry? Have you ever wondered how a flock of birds or school of fish could simultaneously shift directions at exactly the same time? Obviously, something is going on that we can't see. Fritz-Albert Popp, assistant director of the International Institute of Biophysics, was the first to discover that every living thing emits a current of light. He discovered what I learned as a young child holding onto the television antenna to make a clearer picture: We all are receivers and transmitters of energy. In our interconnected universe of energy, our thoughts and emotions impact one another. A sizable body of research carried out over the last 30 years in prestigious scientific institutions around the world shows that thoughts and intentions are capable of affecting everything from the simplest machines to the most complex living beings (McTaggart, 2007).

We now know that our intention in any situation affects its outcome. As astonishing as this may seem, it is something we all have experienced. If you walk into a situation with the intention of getting even with someone, the person senses this and becomes defensive. If you walk into the same situation with the intent to open your heart through compassionate communication, the outcome of the discussion is drastically different. What does this have to do with discipline, children and the School Family? A great deal. Conscious Discipline asks that we consciously become aware of our intentions. An unconscious intention to assign blame and dole out punishment will sabotage our efforts to problem solve. A conscious intention to seek solutions will help children take ownership and reflect on life choices. I classify three core intents in Conscious Discipline: the intent to punish (get even, find fault), the intent to rescue (save from emotional distress) and the intent to teach (reflect, seek solutions and move forward with a plan). When we set our conscious intention to teach, mistakes truly become opportunities for deep learning. For more information about effective consequences, read the *Conscious Discipline* book (Bailey, 2000).

Power of Intention: Mistakes are opportunities to learn
Skill: Consequences
Structure: Class Meetings
Value: Citizenship

A key component of Conscious Discipline is the conscious awareness of one's own thoughts, feelings and actions, and their outcomes. Teachers must become conscious of children's constant projections of their feelings, thoughts and blame. To do this, Conscious Discipline asks teachers to use the many forms of pivoting. Pivot is a military term similar to an "about face." One form of pivoting takes the child's external focus and turns it inward. If a child starts talking for everyone in the class by saying, "Everyone thinks the homework is too hard," we would help the child pivot by saying, "So you think the homework is too hard for you?" This shifts the ownership from "everyone" to the child.

Another form of pivoting helps children refocus from what they don't want to what they do want. One of the founding principles of Conscious Discipline is "what you focus on, you get more of." This law of attraction, like gravity, is at work whether or not we agree with or understand it. If you focus on problems, you see and get more problems. If you focus on solutions, you see and get more solutions. When children share problems, they generally name the behavior they find irritating. This behavior is what they don't want to see happen. It is the adult's responsibility to pivot the child's complaint from what they don't want to what they do want. Use a questioning tone to state what you think the child desires, leaving space for them to correct your assessment if needed.

Child: "Matthew was bossing everyone!"
Teacher (in a questioning tone): "So, you want Matthew to listen to what you have to say and take it seriously?"

Child: "Everyone is pushing and shoving in line."
Teacher (questioning tone): "So, you want the class to be careful of each other in line?"

Child: "I don't want to go to lunch."
Teacher (questioning tone): "So, you want to stay here and continue with the art project?"

By using the "so, you want" pivot strategy, you accomplish three things:

1. You pivot the mental energy into what one wants to accomplish.
2. You give the person speaking ownership of his thoughts.
3. You set up the situation for problem solving in a way that fosters encouragement.

These three accomplishments allow the children to take responsibility, reflect on what they want to happen and enjoy successes along the way. This sets up the situation for learning from one's mistakes, increases the motivation to succeed and stimulates the prefrontal lobe of the brain.

E = Environmental Structure: Class Meetings

Purpose: Creating the School Family involves all the structures within this book, with the Class Meeting at the hub. Class Meetings provide a forum and create a climate where children feel safe enough to celebrate, connect, solve problems, contribute to a system of self-governance, become mindful, and develop a conscious awareness of self and others. The list of what can be accomplished and discussed in your Class Meetings is unlimited. You will establish the class jobs, discuss what helpfulness looks like, sounds like and feels like, choose your School Family name and create your School Family song or chant in Class Meetings. Once you have established your School Family (which usually takes the first six weeks of school), Class Meetings become the governing body where problems can be brought to light and solved.

How to set up Class Meetings: Class Meetings happen in a circle. Young children are accustomed to sitting in a circle during circle time. After kindergarten, due to room size, desk arrangements and philosophical changes in how and what children learn, the circle disappears from the classroom. This, I believe, is a loss for both children and teachers. Even at my office, we sit around a large, square conference table. Each person is able to see the faces and eyes of the others so we can share, celebrate, create and problem solve together.

The circle carries great symbolic meaning from ancient times and from many cultures. Pythagoras represented the circle as pure potentiality, as in the case of the zero, from which all other numbers spring forth. It has been symbolically associated with the seed, womb or egg from which all life emerges. Almost all religions use the symbolism of the circle to represent something divine or sacred, like a halo. In many cultures the circle represents eternity and infinity.

It is important to arrange your Class Meetings in a circle or oval configuration so everyone can see and be seen by everyone else. In the circle everyone is equal, everyone is respected and the sacredness of the School Family is created and maintained. For children in older grades, this may require moving some furniture; if so, add "Furniture Assistant" as a job on the Job Board to ease the transition.

In the circle/Class Meeting area you will need the following supplies:

- CD player, MP3 player or some other way to play music
- Supplies for writing down ideas (whiteboard, chart paper, blackboard, markers)
- Boundary markers (such as carpet squares) for young children and those who need help keeping their bodies in their own space
- Safe Place Pass (a small card with the active calming icons described in Chapter 9, available on the Conscious Discipline *Make-N-Take* CDrom)

- Toy microphone or talking stick to designate the speaker
- Posted agreements for the Class Meetings (once they've been created at a Class Meeting)
- The PEACE process visual (available on the Conscious Discipline *Make-n-Take* CDRom or by creating your own from the PEACE process graphic)

Select a song to signal that your Class Meeting is about to start. Choose a song like "Come to the Circle" by Paulette Meier, and cut the length so it is just long enough for the children to assemble in a circle for the Class Meeting. Begin your Class Meeting with a modified Brain Smart Start. As you recall from Chapter 8, the Brain Smart Start includes activities to unite, disengage stress, connect and commit. In order to ensure the children's brains are prepped for optimal learning and participation, begin with an activity that will unite, disengage stress and connect. Review your class agreements and whatever method you have devised to recognize the speaker (toy microphone, talking stick), and ask for a verbal commitment to observe these guidelines during the meeting. Conduct the PEACE process for problem solving, and attend to any other business deemed necessary. The PEACE process is outlined below.

P = State the Problem as you see it and its impact on you.

"I've noticed ___. This is a problem for me because ___." State what you have seen occurring in the classroom without bias or judgment. You might say, "I've noticed some children are talking while I am reading a story. This is a problem for me because I can't hear myself read and I lose my place in the story."

E = Encourage the children to own the problem.

"Have any of you noticed children talking while I am reading a story? Is it a problem for anyone else?" This step allows the children the opportunity to own part of the problem. Children will help solve a problem and follow through with the plan if they believe there is a problem. Some children will not have noticed others talking, for example, but it has been my experience that some children will speak up to verify most problems.

A = Affirm the problem with positive intent and positive actions.

"So, our School Family problem is ___." Instead of summarizing with a focus on the problem—"So, our School Family problem is children talking during story time, distracting others"—it is important to pivot our thinking to focus on the positive action: "So, our School Family problem is that some children are having a hard time being quiet during story time." The pivot is essential. You cannot solve a problem by focusing on what you don't want.

C = Collect helpful solutions of how to solve the problem.

"What could we do to help all children be quiet during story time?" If the children persist in focusing on what they don't want, help them pivot. "Stop talking" becomes "So, you want everyone to be quiet and start listening?"

E = Evaluate to see if it is working.

"How will we know if it is working?" Set up a way for children to measure whether the solution is working and to celebrate their success. If the gauge shows the solution is not working, that sets the stage for a Class Meeting to find new solutions.

You will use the PEACE process to guide problem solving in every Class Meeting. Other business to conduct in a Class Meeting includes introducing new classroom structures, making your School Family Agreements, reviewing Conscious Discipline skills, making important announcements, and so on. Many teachers also use Class Meetings as a time to conduct Celebrations and other activities that build the School Family. End your meeting with a review, a verbal commitment to the problem-solving strategies your School Family devised and a music and movement activity.

 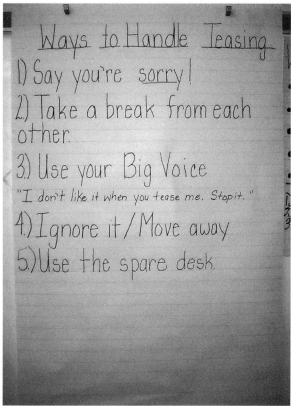

How to introduce Class Meetings: Hold your first Class Meeting a few weeks into the school year when you are well on your way to creating a School Family. A connected classroom is key to a successful Class Meeting. Your first Class Meeting will follow the steps outlined above and will be used to establish your School Family Agreements (Chapter 6). Explain that Class Meetings are the students' forum for governing their classroom. Give age-appropriate examples of problems you might solve and activities you might do in a Class Meeting. In this first meeting, invite students to describe the type of classroom they want to be part of, brainstorm how to accomplish that goal and then agree on a set of guidelines together. Ask if there are any agreements they would like to set specifically for the Class Meetings, like using a talking stick to designate whose turn it is to speak. In later meetings, you will introduce the PEACE process and use it to solve classroom problems. Younger children will need significantly more guidance than older children, but the process, the scaffolding of executive skills, modeling democratic values, promoting healthy power-sharing and fostering ownership in the School Family are the same at any age.

General Activities — All Ages

Pass a Touch

While sitting in your Class Meeting circle, "pass a touch" by touching the person next to you in some way. That person then passes your touch to his neighbor and adds to it. The touch is a cumulative process that continues all the way around the circle. For example, you might pass a high five. The next person passes a high five and adds a fist bump. The person after that passes a high five, a fist bump and a shoulder pat. In younger classrooms, you can all chant the type of touch together to help build attention and aid in children's success. In older classrooms, the challenge is to go all the way around the circle. In younger classrooms, you create a pattern of a five-touch sequence. The class then chants the sequence as the action is performed.

General Activities — Younger

The "I Notice" Exercise

Young children can have difficulty identifying why certain things are a problem. For example, the problem you are seeking to solve could be, "I noticed we are having trouble getting the room cleaned up in time to go to lunch. Is this a problem for anyone else?" Young children may not make the connection that being late for lunch means they must wait a long time in the lunch line. The "I noticed" game can help children bridge the gap between action and consequence. Before you ask, "Is this a problem for anyone else," ask, "What do you notice happens when we're late for lunch?" Write down a few responses and then summarize: "We noticed that when we are late cleaning up before lunch, we have to wait in a long line and hurry to eat before class starts again."

> **Teacher Tip:**
>
> For any solution to be successful, you must practice it. Practice your solutions at the Class Meeting so everyone knows what the solution looks like, sounds like and feels like.

Once you have made the connection from action to consequence, then ask, "Is cleaning up the room so we can get to lunch on time a problem for anyone else?" Clarify further by writing on chart paper, "Our School Family problem is _____. Possible solutions are _____," and then list their ideas. Choose a solution as a School Family, then practice the solution. If possible, take photos while they practice and post them as reminders of their idea for a solution. After a week, meet again to evaluate if the solution is working. If not, start the process over again.

General Activities — Older

Ambassador Problem Solving

Sometimes it's fun for older classrooms to shake up the PEACE problem-solving process. Once in a while, give students the opportunity to break into smaller groups to brainstorm solutions. After a designated amount of time, invite one person from each group to serve as an ambassador who will rotate into a different group to learn what that group discovered. The ambassador then returns to his or her original group to share the other group's solutions. Each group then can revise their thoughts. Ask the groups to rejoin each other as a School Family and have each ambassador share his/her group's solution. The class then chooses the solution they believe will work best.

Music & Movement — Older

Crocodiles!

Crocodiles is high-energy fun that teaches teamwork and problem solving. It works well as a Class Meeting activity; just be sure to follow it with deep breathing exercises to help return a sense of calm to the room. You will need to clear a large space in the classroom. You will also need a musical cue and one or two pieces of poster board or bulletin paper. It's fun to use a themed song like "The Lion Sleeps Tonight" by The Tokens or "Crocodile Rock" by Elton John. The paper should be barely large enough for the whole group to stand on all at once.

The goal is for the students to get from one side of the crocodile-infested classroom to the other, using the paper as their "raft." Begin the game with the students standing on the paper and the music playing. When you stop playing the music, it's safe for them to pick up their raft and walk on the ground toward their end point. When you start up the music again, the students have to get back on their raft within three to five seconds, depending on the size of the group. If they don't make it, they must all go back to the start area. Explain that the children must work together to move quickly from one side to the other. They must problem-solve together to determine how to move as a group, organize themselves and make sure that everyone from the strongest to the weakest link is included in the team effort.

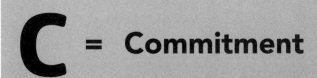

C = Commitment

I am willing to see problem solving as a form of consequences and use problem-solving Class Meetings for chronic problems or situations that impact the whole class.

Signature _____   Date _____

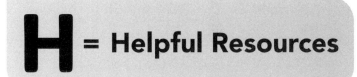

H = Helpful Resources

Music — All Ages

I Love You Rituals, Vol. 2 **by Dr. Becky Bailey and Mar Harman**
Song: "I'm a Helpful Person"

It Starts in the Heart **by Dr. Becky Bailey and Jack Hartmann**
Song: "That Was Helpful"

Come to the Circle **by Paulette Meier**
Song: "Come to the Circle"

Literature — All Ages

***Shubert's New Friend* by Dr. Becky Bailey.** When a new student arrives looking different, Mrs. Bookbinder models the skill of empathy to help the class accept and embrace diversity.

***Shubert's Helpful Day* by Dr. Becky Bailey.** Shubert arrives to class where an angry Lucinda lashes out. Everyone discovers ways to view misbehavior as a "call for help," not just acting out.

Literature — Younger

***Enemy Pie* by Derek Munson.** A little boy finds a recipe for turning your best enemy into your best friend.

***King of the Playground* by Phyllis Reynolds Naylor.** This book teaches children problem solving strategies as one little boy acts like the king of the playground.

***I Want It* by Elizabeth Crary.** Children learn how to take turns and share in this problem-solving book.

***Finklehopper Frog* by Irene Livingston.** Finklehopper wants to join a jogging group, but things don't work out the way he plans. Ultimately, he discovers the importance of coming together with friends while still being himself.

Literature — Older

***What a Wonderful World* by George Weiss and Bob Thiele.** Based on the song, "What a Wonderful World," you can use this book to notice the wonderful way the group comes together during class meetings.

***Flying Solo* by Ralph Fletcher.** This chapter book tells the story of a class that must fly solo without the teacher. It tells how the group had to be responsible without the adults present, and how wonderful it is to be together as group.

> Lindsey #22
>
> # Proud
>
> This is about our class rules. We made our own class rules. Our golden rule is treat people like you want to be treated. We alwayes folow our class rules. This is about everyons Job. evry one taks Proud in ther Jod. My tow favrit Jods are tv tuner, and teacher assistant. Our Jobs help us cepa our classroom Nice. This is about respecting each other. My class respests each other. We care about each other. And most in portinley we get along.

Teacher Tip:

Children's contributions to establishing class rules are only as successful as the teacher's ability to create a safe, connected, problem-solving School Family.

Epilogue

On the dedication page at the beginning of this book, I set out my intention that through the process of creating a School Family, we would all grow in awareness of the deep interconnectedness that links us in unity. It is harder to hit and hate when we understand we are all single cells in one body of humanity. Bully-proofing, like peace on earth, is a lofty goal, but one we must not lose sight of.

As you worked through this book, hopefully something touched your heart and resonated with your teaching philosophy enough for you to choose to implement it in your school or classroom. Implementing a School Family is a three-year process. The structures themselves may be instituted more rapidly, but it is my experience that truly changing our relationship with power takes at least three years.

Most classroom management systems are based on a dominant power model with a system of external controls. You may be using some form of external controls and rewards today. Children may be receiving trips to the treasure box for being good or cards that change color representing poor choices. If that is the case, keep this book, and keep your treasure boxes or current system. Start adding the structures that speak to you one at a time. At some point, you will feel safe enough to turn your treasure box into a Safekeeper Box. Eventually, you will replace your system for measuring poor behavior with a system for noticing kind acts. Your referrals for pushing and name-calling will decline in favor of a Safe Place to self-regulate and a Time Machine for conflict resolution. Over time, the exhaustion you feel from the false dictate that you must control children's behavior will be replaced by the deep calm of knowing you must only manage yourself.

Do not give up on the journey! It may be slower than you would like. You may get sidetracked along the way. Yet, the journey from correction to connection, from defiance to alliance, from external control to internal self-control is one we will all ultimately make if we are to thrive as a society. Why wait to change our schools and classrooms out of a sense of desperation and frustration? Why not begin your journey now, and continue with baby steps until you become the educator and person you know you are deep down. Begin creating a school climate that provides the soil needed for academic, social, emotional and moral growth right now. If we are ever to meet the academic challenges and standards demanded, we must first prepare the way. The School Family will help you do just that—guaranteed!

Wishing us all well,
Becky A. Bailey

References

Anderman, E.M. & Young, A.J. (1994) Motivation and strategy use in science: Individual differences and classroom effects. *Journal of Research in Science Teaching* 31–811–831.

Arnsten, A.F.T. (1998) The biology of being frazzled. Science 280(5370): 1711 – 12.

Bailey, B.A. (2000) Conscious Discipline: 7 basic skills for brain smart classroom management. Oviedo, FL: Loving Guidance, Inc.

Balfanz, R. & Legters, N. (2004) Locating the dropout crisis. Which high schools produce the nation's dropouts? Where are they located? Who attends them? Baltimore, MD: Johns Hopkins University.

Barkley, R.A. (2005) ADHD and the nature of self-control. New York: Guilford Press.

Barkley, R.A. (2005) Taking charge of ADHD: The complete, authoritative guide for parents. Rev. ed. New York: Guilford Press.

Bonner, T. D., and Aspy, D.N. (1984) A study of the relationship between student empathy and GPA. *Humanistic Education and Development* 22(4): 149 – 154.

Brendtro, L., Ness, A. & Mitchell, M. (2001) No disposable kids. Longmont, CO: Sopris West.

Bronfenbrenner, U. (1979) The ecology of human development. Cambridge, MA: Harvard University Press.

Bronson, M. B. (2000) Self-regulation in early childhood: Nature and Nurture. New York: The Guilford Press.

Broughton, D.D. & Allen, E.A. (1991) How to keep your child safer: A message to every parent and guardian. Alexandria, VA: National Center for Missing and Exploited Children®.

Cacioppo, J. T., Visser, P. S. & Pickett, C. L. (2005) Social neuroscience: People thinking about thinking people. Cambridge, MA: MIT Press.

Carter, G. (2008) Beyond high school reform. Is it good for the kids? ASCD.org

Cokerton, T., Moore, S. & Norman, D. (1997) Cognitive test performance and background music. *Perceptual and Motor Skills*, 85: 1435–8.

Dawson, P., and Guare, R. (2009) Smart but Scattered. New York: Guilford Press.

Dawson, P., and Guare, R. (2004) Executive skills in children and adolescents: A practical guide to assessment and intervention. New York: Guilford Press.

Deci, E.L., & Ryan, R.M. (1987) The support of autonomy and the control of behavior. *Journal of Personality and Social Psychology* 53: 1024–1037.

Elias, M. J., Zins, J. E., Weissberg, R.P., Frey, K.S., Greenberg, M. T., Haynes, N.M., Kessler, R., Schwab-Stone, M. E. & Shriver, T. P. (1997) Promoting social and emotional learning: Guidelines for educators. Alexandria, VA: Association for Supervision and Curriculum.

Espelage, D.L., & Swearer, S. (2004) Bullying in American schools. Mahwah, NJ: Lawrence Erlbaum Associates, Inc.

Foster, R. (2000) Face to face with our future. *Reclaiming children and youth* 8(4): 200 – 202.

Fox, M. (1990) A spirituality named compassion. New York: HarperCollins.

Gallo, D. (1989) Educating for empathy, reason and imagination. *Journal of Creative Behavior* 23(2): 98 – 115.

Gilliam, W. S. (2005) Prekindergarteners left behind: Expulsion rates in state prekindergarten systems. New Haven, CT: Yale University Child Study Center.

Glasser, W. (1998) Choice Theory: A New Psychology of Personal Freedom. New York: HarperCollins.

Goldberg, E. (2002) The executive brain: Frontal lobes and the civilized mind. New York: Oxford University Press.

Gredler, M.E. & Shields, C.C. (2008) Vygotsky's legacy: A foundation for research and practice. New York: Guilford Press.

Hannaford, C. (2010) Playing in the unified field: Raising and becoming conscious, creative human beings. Salt Lake City: Great River Books.

Hannaford, C. (2005) Smart moves: Why learning is not all in the head. 2nd ed. Salt Lake City: Great River Books.

Harter, S. & Jackson, B. (1992) Trait vs. non-trait conceptualizations of intrinsic/extrinsic motivational orientations. Motivation and Emotion, 16, 209 – 300

Hoffman, L.L., Hutchinson, C.J. & Reiss, E. (2009) On improving schools: Reducing reliance on rewards and punishments. *International Journal of Whole Schooling* 5(1): 13 – 24.

Imber-Black, E., and Roberts, J. (1992) Rituals for our times: Celebrating, healing, and changing our lives. New York: HarperCollins.

Imber-Black, E., Roberts, J. & Whiting, R.A. (2003) Rituals in families and family therapy. New York: W.W. Norton

Jensen, E. (2005) Teaching with the brain in mind. 2nd ed. Alexandria, VA: Association for Supervision and Curriculum Development.

Jensen, E. (2000) Brain–based learning: The new science of teaching & learning. San Diego, CA: The Brain Store.

Jensen, E. (1997) Brain compatible strategies. Del Mar, CA: Turning Point Publishers.

Kohn, A. (1991) Caring kids: The role of the schools. *Phi Delta Kkappan* 72(7): 496 – 506.

Lepper, M., Sethi, S., Dialdin, D. & Drake, M. (1997) Intrinsic and extrinsic motivation: A developmental perspective. In *Developmental psychopathalogy: Perspectives on adjustment, risk, and disorder*, edited by S.S. Luthar, J.A. Burack, D. Dicchetti and J.R. Weisz. Cambridge, UK: Cambridge University Press.

Macklem, G. (2003) Bullying and teasing: Social power in children's groups. New York: Plenum Publishers.

Malyarenko, T.N., Kuraev, G.A., Malyarenko, E., Khvatova, M.V., Romanova, N.G. & Gurina, V.I. (1996) The development of brain electric activity in 4-year-old children by long term sensory stimulation of music. *Human Physiology* 22(1): 76 – 81.

McBride, N.A. (2005) Child safety is more than a slogan: "Stranger-danger" warnings not effective at keeping kids safe. Retrieved from www.missingkids.com

McTaggart, L. (2007) The intention experiment: Using your thoughts to change your life and the world. New York: Free Press.

Meltzer, L. (2007) Executive function in education: From theory to practice. New York: Guilford Press.

Merrell, K.W., Gueldner, B. A., Ross, S.W. & Isava, D. M. (2008) How effective are school bullying intervention programs? A meta-analysis of intervention research. *School Psychology Quarterly* 23: 26 – 42.

Nagin, D.S., & Tremblay, R.E. (2001) Parental and early childhood predictors of persistent physical aggression in boys from kindergarten to high school. *Archives of General Psychiatry*, 58(4): 389 – 394.

Nagin, D., & Tremblay, R. E. (1999) Trajectories of boys' physical aggression, oppositional, and hyperactivity on the path to physically violent and non-violent juvenile delinquency. Child Development, 70(5), 1181 – 1196.

NICHD Early Child Care Research Network. (2006) Child care effect sizes for the NICHD study of early child care and youth development. *American Psychologist* 61(2): 99 – 116.

NICHD Early Child Care Research Network. (2003) Does amount of time spent in child care predict socioemotional adjustment during the transition to kindergarten?. *Child Development* 74: 976 – 1005.

Osterman, K.E. (2000) Students' need for belonging in the school community. *Review of Educational Research* 70: 323 – 367.

Payton, J., Weissberg, R. P., Durlak, J.A., Dymnicki, A.B., Taylor, R.D., Schellinger, K.B. & Pachan, M. (2008) The positive impact of social and emotional learning for kindergarten to eighth-grade students: Findings from three scientific reviews. Chicago, IL: Collaborative for Academic, Social, and Emotional Learning.

Perry, B.D. (1996) Maltreated children: Experience, brain development, and the next generation. New York: W.W. Norton.

Salovey, P., & Sluyter, D. (1997) Emotional development and emotional intelligence: educational implications. New York: Basic Books.

Schneier, B. (2003) Beyond fear. New York: Copernicus Books.

Schwartz, J.M., & Begley, S. (2002) The mind & the brain: Neuroplasticity and the power of mental force. New York: ReganBooks.

Seita, J.R., & Brendtro, L.K. (2002) Kids who outwit adults? Longmont, CO: Sopris West.

Smith, P.K., Pepler, D. and Rigby, K. (2004) Bullying in schools: How successful can interventions be? Cambridge, UK: Cambridge University Press.

Staub, E. (1995) The roots of prosocial and antisocial behavior in persons and groups: Environmental influence, personality, culture, and socialization. In *Moral Development*, edited by W. Kurtines & J. Gewirtz.. Boston: Allyn and Bacon.

Tremblay R.E., Hartup W.W., Archer J. (2005) Developmental origins of aggression. New York: Guilford Press.

Tutu, D. (2002) Foreword in L. Brentro, M. Brokenleg & S. Van Bockern, *Reclaiming youth at risk; Our hope for the future*. Bloomington, IN: Solution Tree.

Underwood, M.K. (2003) Social aggression among girls. New York: Guilford Press. United States Department of Agriculture. (2008) Household food security in the United States. Washington, DC: US Government Printing Office.

Van Duijvenvoorde, A., Zanolie, K., Rombouts, S.A.R.B., Raijmakers, M. & Crone, E.A. (2008) Valuing the positive or adjusting the negative? A neurocognitive analysis of feedback-based learning. *Journal of Neuroscience* 28: 9495 – 9503.

Vygotsky, L. (1978) Mind in society. Cambridge, MA: Harvard University Press.

Walker, M. (2004) How connections heal: Stories from relational-cultural therapy. New York: Guilford Press.

Wentzel, K.R., & Watkings, D.E. (2002) Peer relationships and collaborative learning as contexts for academic enablers. *School Psychology Review* 31: 366 – 377.

World Bank. (2008) World Bank updates poverty estimates for the developing world. http://econ.worldbank.org/WBSITE/EXTERNAL/EXTDEC/EXTRESEARCH/0,,contentMDK:21882162~pagePK:64165401~piPK:64165026~theSitePK:469382,00.html

Zins, J.E. & Elias, M.J. (2006) Social and emotional learning. In *Children's needs III: Development, prevention, and intervention*, edited by G.G. Bear & K.M. Minke (pp.1-13). Bethesda, MD: National Association of School Psychologists.

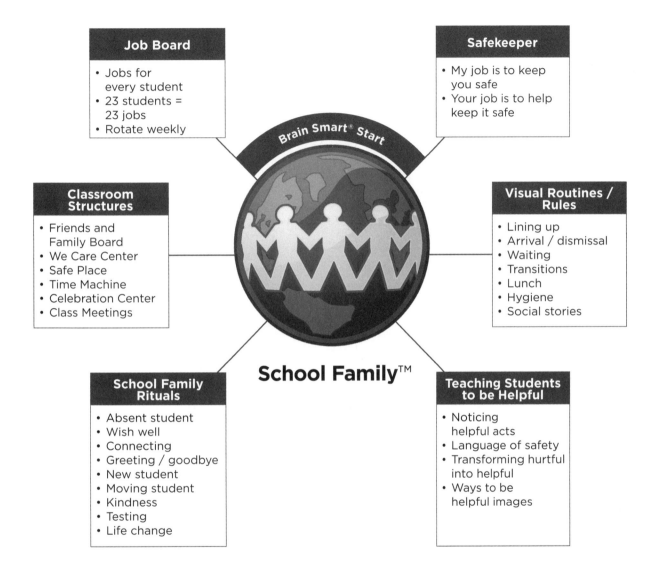

Becky A. Bailey, Ph.D., is an award-winning author, renowned teacher and internationally recognized expert in childhood education and developmental psychology. Her workshops touch thousands of lives each year, and her top-selling books have over 200,000 copies in circulation.

Dr. Bailey is the founder of Loving Guidance, Inc., a company dedicated to creating positive environments for children, families, schools and businesses. She is also the originator of Conscious Discipline (www.ConsciousDiscipline.com). Her core publication for parents, *Easy to Love, Difficult to Discipline*, has received national acclaim and is published in eight languages. Dr. Bailey lives in Oviedo, FL.